W9-AFU-086

the Unofficial Guide™ to Starting a Business Online

Jason R. Rich

IDG Books Worldwide, Inc.

IDG Books Worldwide, Inc.
An International Data Group Company
919 E. Hillsdale Boulevard
Suite 400
Foster City, CA 94404

Copyright © 2000 by Jason R. Rich

All rights reserved, including the right of reproduction in whole or in part in any form.

This publication contains the opinions and ideas of its author and is designed to provide useful advice to the reader on the subject matter covered. Any references to any products or services do not constitute or imply an endorsement or recommendation. The publisher and the author specifically disclaim any responsibility for any liability, loss or risk (financial, personal or otherwise) which may be claimed or incurred as a consequence, directly or indirectly, of the use and/or application of any of the contents of this publication.

Certain terms mentioned in this book which are known or claimed to be trademarks or service marks have been capitalized.

IDG Books Worldwide, Inc. does not attest to the validity, accuracy or completeness of this information. Use of a term in this book should not be regarded as affecting the validity of any trademark or service mark.

Unofficial Guides are a [registered] trademark of Macmillan General Reference USA, Inc., a wholly owned subsidiary of IDG Books Worldwide, Inc.

For general information on IDG Books Worldwide's books in the U.S., please call our Consumer Customer Service department at 800-762-2974. For reseller information, including discounts and previous sales, please call our Reseller Customer Service department at 800-434-3422.

ISBN: 0-02-863340-7

Manufactured in the United States of America

10 9 8 7 6 5 4 3 2 1

First edition

This book is dedicated to my two closest and dearest friends, Mark and Ellen, who constantly challenge and motivate me to achieve success in whatever it is I set out to do. It's also dedicated to my newer friends, including Sandy, who also played a role directly or indirectly in the creation of this book. Finally, it's dedicated to my family for providing me with the advantages growing up that eventually allowed me to pursue and achieve my own career goals and dreams.

Acknowledgments

I'd like to thank Randy Ladenheim-Gil, Jennifer Perillo, and John Jones for making this book possible and for offering me guidance as the manuscript was created. Thanks also to Jeff Herman, my agent, for making this deal happen, which led to my writing this book.

I'd also like to thank all of the people who agreed to be interviewed in this book and who provided me with valuable information to pass on to you. Finally, thanks to you, the reader, for picking up this book. It's my greatest hope that the information you're about to read will be useful in pursuing your own goals and objectives for launching an online-based business venture or e-commerce Web site.

If you'd like to share your thoughts or experiences, please drop by my Web site (www.jasonrich.com) or e-mail me at jr7777@aol.com. See you in cyberspace!

The *Unofficial Guide* Reader's Bill of Rights

We Give You More Than the Official Line

Welcome to the *Unofficial Guide* series of Lifestyles titles—books that deliver critical, unbiased information that other books can't or won't reveal—*the inside scoop*. Our goal is to provide you with the *most accessible, useful* information and advice possible. The recommendations we offer in these pages are not influenced by the corporate line of any organization or industry; we give you the hard facts, whether those institutions like them or not. If something is ill-advised or will cause a loss of time and/or money, we'll give you ample warning. And if it is a worthwhile option, we'll let you know that, too.

Armed and Ready

Our hand-picked authors confidently and critically report on a wide range of topics that matter to smart readers like you. Our authors are passionate about their subjects, but have distanced themselves enough from them to help you be armed and protected, and help you make educated decisions as you go through your process. It is our intent that, from having read this book, you will avoid the pitfalls everyone else falls into and get it right the first time.

Don't be fooled by cheap imitations; this is the *genuine article Unofficial Guide* series from IDG Books. You may be familiar with our proven track record of the travel *Unofficial Guides*, which have more than two million copies in print. Each year thousands of travelers—new and old—are armed with a brand new, fully updated edition of the flagship *Unofficial Guide to Walt Disney World*, by Bob Sehlinger. It is our intention here to provide you with the same level of objective authority that Mr. Sehlinger does in his brainchild.

The Unofficial Panel of Experts

Every work in the Lifestyle *Unofficial Guides* is intensively inspected by a team of three top professionals in their fields. These experts review the manuscript for factual accuracy, comprehensiveness, and an insider's determination as to whether the manuscript fulfills the credo in this Reader's Bill of Rights. In other words, our Panel ensures that you are, in fact, getting "the inside scoop."

Our Pledge

The authors, the editorial staff, and the Unofficial Panel of Experts assembled for *Unofficial Guides* are determined to lay out the most valuable alternatives available for our readers. This dictum means that our writers must be explicit, prescriptive, and above all, direct. We strive to be thorough and complete, but our goal is not necessarily to have the "most" or "all" of the information on a topic; this is not, after all, an encyclopedia. Our objective is to help you narrow down your options to the best of what is available, unbiased by affiliation with any industry or organization.

In each *Unofficial Guide* we give you:

- Comprehensive coverage of necessary and vital information
- Authoritative, rigidly fact-checked data
- The most up-to-date insights into trends
- Savvy, sophisticated writing that's also readable
- Sensible, applicable facts and secrets that only an insider knows

Special Features

Every book in our series offers the following six special sidebars in the margins that were devised to help you get things done cheaply, efficiently, and smartly.

1. **Timesaver**—tips and shortcuts that save you time

2. **Moneysaver**—tips and shortcuts that save you money

3. **Watch Out!**—more serious cautions and warnings

4. **Bright Idea**—general tips and shortcuts to help you find an easier or smarter way to do something

5. **Quote**—statements from real people that are intended to be prescriptive and valuable to you

6. **Unofficially ...**—an insider's fact or anecdote

We also recognize your need to have quick information at your fingertips, and have thus provided the following comprehensive sections at the back of the book:

1. **Glossary**—definitions of complicated terminology and jargon

2. **Resource Guide**—lists of relevant agencies, associations, institutions, Web sites, etc.

3. **Recommended Reading List**—suggested titles that can help you get more in-depth information on related topics

4. **Important Documents**—"official" pieces of information you need to refer to, such as government forms

5. **Important Statistics**—facts and numbers presented at-a-glance for easy reference

6. **Index**

Letters, Comments, and Questions from Readers

We strive to continually improve the Unofficial series, and input from our readers is a valuable way for us to do that. Many of those who have used the *Unofficial Guide* travel books write to the authors to ask questions, make comments, or share their own discoveries and lessons. For lifestyle *Unofficial Guides,* we would also appreciate all such correspondence, both positive and critical, and we will make best efforts to incorporate appropriate readers' feedback and comments in revised editions of this work.

How to write to us:

Unofficial Guides
Lifestyle Guides
IDG Books
1633 Broadway
New York, NY 10019

Attention: Reader's Comments

About the Author

Jason R. Rich (jr7777@aol.com/www.jasonrich.com), 32, is a freelance writer, author, and newspaper/magazine columnist. Rich has written a number of books on business-related issues, including the *Unofficial Guide to Earning What You Deserve* (Macmillan, 1999), *Job Hunting For the Utterly Confused* (McGraw-Hill), and *First Job, Great Job: America's Hottest Business Leaders Share Their Secrets* (Macmillan). For the Sunday *Boston Herald*, Rich writes a weekly column covering all aspects of the job search process. He also contributes career-related feature articles to *National Business Employment Weekly*, *The Wall Street Journal's Managing Your Career*, *Careers & Colleges*, and *Enter*.

Rich is also president of Teen Talk Communications and one of the country's leading experts on video games, computer games, and interactive entertainment, having authored or contributed to over two dozen best-selling computer and video game strategy guides. His writings have also appeared in *Disney Adventures*, *The Chicago Tribune*, *ESPN Magazine*, and *Parents' Choice*. In 1988, Rich created and was the columnist for the *Celebrity Teen*

Talk nationally syndicated newspaper column. Rich was a contributing producer and feature host for the weekly, Peabody Award-winning *Kid Company* radio show (WBZ-AM 1030), and is currently associate producer for *Kids Talk Sports*, a four-time Emmy Award winning interactive TV show.

The *Unofficial Guide* Panel of Experts

The *Unofficial* editorial team recognizes that you've purchased this book with the expectation of getting the most authoritative, carefully inspected information currently available. Toward that end, on each and every title in this series, we have selected "official" experts comprising the "Unofficial Panel" who painstakingly review the manuscripts to ensure: factual accuracy of all data; inclusion of the most up-to-date and relevant information; and that, from an insider's perspective, the authors have armed you with all the necessary facts you need—but the institutions don't want you to know.

For *The Unofficial Guide to Starting a Business Online,* we are proud to introduce the following panel of experts:

Jerry Osborne   Jerry Osborne, who was instrumental in the planning of this book, learned about commercial Web sites while planning his own site, www.jerryosborne.com/, a popular site introducing Web surfers to dozens of his commercial ventures. Osborne is a pioneer in the field of record collecting. He has published over 70 books in the field, including several definitive volumes on the life and music of Elvis Presley. Since 1986, Osborne has also written the weekly "Mr. Music," the well-known newspaper column answering readers' questions about music and records. He has been written about in countless magazines and newspapers, from *Reader's Digest* and the *Wall Street Journal* to *People Magazine* and *Rolling Stone*, and can be seen on T.V. as a guest on such shows as "Good Morning America" and the "Today Show." He also continues to lend his pop music expertise to networks such as HBO and ABC (including the Peter Jennings special "The Century"), while writing new books every year and updating the bestselling *Official Price Guide to Records*, the industry standard for record guides (now in its thirteenth edition).

Sara Unrue Koulen   Sara Unrue Koulen is a consultant and software developer at New Haven, Conn.-based Willow Solutions. Working with a variety of technology-based businesses to create and expand their Internet presence, she has developed online ordering systems, customer support systems, sales literature delivery, and company-focused intranets. A cum laude graduate of Yale University, Koulen can be contacted at SUnrue@willowsolutions.com.

Introduction

According to *Internet Computing*, "Consumer shopping over the Web will be a $6 to $8 billion dollar business by the year 2000." Forrester Research (www.forrester.com) reports, "Service industries will be shaken up by the Internet, as $220 billion in sales moves on-line by 2003. Providers will have to master Internet technology to thrive as 'eServices'—services designed for the Net—emerge."

By the end of 1999, over 38.8 percent of all U.S. households will have a personal computer. "Media hype and positive word of mouth propelled online penetration to 33% of North American households in 1998. We predict that the Internet will reach 38% of households by the end of 1999. On-line penetration will slow by 2001 but will still reach 56% of households by 2003."

The news from other Internet research firms and industry publications, including EC Review (www.ecreview.com), concur. "In 1997 and early 1998, experts were predicting levels of e-commerce trade by consumers to be in the $200–300 billion (US) range within the next 3–5 years. A year later, we're hearing trillion dollar estimates being circulated. The adoption rate of the Internet by the world's population continues to skyrocket as the Internet becomes more important and computer technology becomes faster and less expensive."

In February 1999, Intel Corporation outlined its vision of a billion Internet-connected PCs and millions of servers generating one trillion dollars of annual e-commerce revenues within the next few years. By the year 2002, Intel estimated that annual e-commerce industry revenues will top one trillion dollars.

If you're impressed by these statistics and you're someone with an entrepreneurial spirit looking to capitalize on this fast-growing marketplace, you're reading the right book!

As a Web surfer, your e-mail in-box probably gets bombarded by a constant inflow of offers from companies doing business on the Web. Aside from the countless invitations to visit the newest porno Web site, you've probably also received dozens of business opportunity offers via e-mail, explaining how you, too, can become rich using your computer to sell products or services on the Internet.

Yes, there are many business opportunity scams being hyped in cyberspace. The truth is, however, that if you're careful and make well-educated decisions, the World Wide Web offers an incredible chance for virtually anyone to establish a successful online business. For a far lower investment than starting most other types of companies, such as a retail store or traditional mail-order business, you can establish an online business (or e-commerce Web site) and begin selling products or services on the Internet.

The Unofficial Guide to Starting a Business Online was written for the average computer owner who is interested in setting up a small business or e-commerce site on the Internet. This book will guide you through the entire process of planning your online-based business venture, creating your Web site, promoting and marketing your business, and then managing the day-to-day operations of your business. If you already operate an established traditional business, this book will help you expand into cyberspace by helping you create an online presence.

If you're interested in starting an online-based business or e-commerce site (which involves actually selling goods and/or services online), there are many choices you'll need to make when it comes to actually planning and building your Web site. This book explores a handful of the options available to you in terms of using off-the-shelf software and online-based turnkey solutions for creating and managing your online business venture. Keep in mind, the focus of this book is to help small start-up companies or small, established businesses create a presence on the Web.

You've probably heard a lot of hype about the incredible moneymaking opportunities available to anyone selling virtually anything online. If done correctly, it's true that almost anything can be sold successfully on the Web; however, it's also important to remember that many of the online business success stories we're all familiar with (Amazon.com, eToys.com, Yahoo.com, eBay.com, etc.) were all backed by millions of dollars in initial investment capital. These businesses weren't created in someone's home as a part-time project.

Even if you have an incredible and totally original idea for an online business venture, it's vitally important to have realistic expectations once you go online. It's extremely rare for an online business of any type to be created and for people to immediately begin flocking to the site and place orders, especially if the online-based business isn't a spin-off of an already successful traditional business with a strong reputation in the offline business world.

This book will help someone with an idea for creating an online business transform that idea into what will hopefully become a viable, moneymaking business venture. When you hear reports about people from all walks of life launching their own online businesses, what exactly does this mean? Can someone like you actually create and operate a successful online business?

As many major corporations, large retail store chains, and established medium- to large-size companies have already discovered, having an online presence is becoming more and more important as we begin the new millennium. The buying habits of consumers are changing quickly. It's no longer just highly computer literate, well-educated, high-income people who shop online. Home computers have gotten cheaper, and millions upon millions of people, from all income levels, are gaining access to the Web. Many of these people are willing to make purchases online. As a result, many individuals, just like you, have found success establishing online-based businesses catering to niche markets that larger companies aren't reaching—online *or* offline.

People interested in working on a part-time basis from home in order to supplement their income are among the fast-growing group of online entrepreneurs. Homemakers, senior citizens, people with physical disabilities, and those with an entrepreneurial spirit are also among the people launching new online business ventures every day. In addition, people looking for a career change and those who want to become their own bosses and set their own work schedules have found success launching online businesses. In reality, there is no stereotypical success story for online-based business operators. Even people with minimal computer skills but an excellent business idea have achieved success.

So, could you be successful launching and managing an online-based business? The answer is yes, as long as you're willing to work hard and invest a significant amount of time (as well as money) into your venture, and your underlying idea for a business is sound. How well you market your online-based business will also be a major factor in whether or not it becomes successful. This book will help you gather the resources and knowledge you need, whether you're hoping to launch an online business on a shoestring budget or you have significant investment capital available.

Launching an online business requires an underlying understanding of how traditional businesses operate. You also need to understand basic marketing, have some basic computer skills (even though programming isn't actually required to start an online-based business), and be willing to spend a considerable amount of time doing research and managing your business once it's operational.

Launching an online-based business isn't a get-rich-quick scheme, so before you get started, it's important to establish realistic expectations, which this book will help you develop. If you're hoping to discover a way to strike it rich overnight by reading this book, you're going to be disappointed, because it's not going to happen! This book takes a realistic approach to learning about e-commerce and how to operate a successful online business venture.

In addition to walking you through the entire process of planning, creating, launching, marketing, and then operating your online business, this book offers a selection of interviews with experts from the e-commerce and Web site design fields. The final chapter of this book includes interviews with people who have already achieved success operating their own online-based businesses. These people offer extremely valuable advice that can help you follow in their footsteps and achieve success, while avoiding the many potential pitfalls online entrepreneurs experience as they set up their business ventures.

Obviously, the opinions expressed in these interviews are based upon each person's own experiences. Since there are no sure bets in this industry, you may choose to follow or totally ignore the advice offered by these people, as there are many different options and opportunities available to you. If nothing else, however, these interviews will give you some of the options and opportunities you, too, can take advantage of.

Likewise, throughout this book, many different software packages, online services, and companies are listed as resources. With new products and services designed to help online business operators being released almost daily, it is literally impossible to list all the available products, software packages, and services you could use in the planning, creation, and operation of your online business venture. The goal of this book is simply to provide a general overview of what's available and to help you locate the exact tools and resources you need.

You'll find that *The Unofficial Guide to Starting a Business Online* offers many answers and solutions; however, this is an industry that's changing extremely quickly. In the period of time that this book was being written, online auctions evolved into an online shopping phenomenon that allows people to earn profits online with even greater ease and without having to create a Web site at all. The focus of this book isn't to teach you how to profit from online-based auctions (using e-Bay, Amazon.com Auctions, Yahoo! Auctions, and so on), but if you're planning on selling some sort of product, using one of these services is one way to do some test marketing.

The e-commerce industry is new and constantly evolving, and there are no set rules or guaranteed methods for achieving success. As a result, use this book as a starting point, but be prepared to do your own research based on the type of business venture you hope to pursue. As you read this book, you'll be provided with hundreds of Web site addresses (URLs) that will lead you to valuable resources, services, and tools designed to help you plan, create, and manage your online business venture. Take full advantage of these resources and make an effort to benefit from the experiences and knowledge of others who already operate a business in cyberspace. Even if you've been successful operating a business in the offline world, you'll find that what works in cyberspace is often different.

As you'll soon learn from reading this book, the business idea you have is important and will have some impact on how successful your online business ultimately is; however, marketing your site and managing it properly are equally important. Just as if you were to operate a traditional business, retail store, or mail-order business, there are laws in place that you must adhere to as an online business operator.

For example, the Mail and Telephone Order Merchandise Rule spells out the ground rules for making promises about shipments, notifying consumers about unexpected delays, and refunding consumers' money. Enforced by the Federal Trade Commission (FTC), the Mail and Telephone Order Rule applies to orders placed by phone, fax, or entirely on the Internet, as long as the telephone is used to transmit voice, computer data, or other electronic signals.

The FTC ruling states,

> *You must have a reasonable basis for stating or implying that a product can be shipped within a certain time. If your advertising doesn't include a shipping statement, you must have a reasonable basis for believing that you can ship within 30 days. If you can't ship when you promised, you must send the customer a notice advising him about the delay and his right to cancel. For definite delays of up to 30 days, you may treat the customer's silence as agreeing to the delay. But for longer or indefinite delays—and second and subsequent delays—you must get the customer's consent. If the customer doesn't give you his okay, you must promptly refund all the money the customer paid you without being asked.*

Likewise, the use of testimonials and endorsements is also policed by the FTC. The agency reports,

> *Testimonials and endorsements must reflect the typical experiences of consumers, unless the ad clearly and conspicuously states otherwise. A statement that not all consumers will get the same results is not enough to qualify a claim. Testimonials and endorsements can't be used to make a claim that the advertiser itself cannot substantiate. Connections between an endorser and the company that are unclear or unexpected to a customer also must be disclosed, whether they have to do with a financial arrangement for a favorable endorsement, a position with the company, or stock ownership. Expert endorsements must be based on appropriate tests or evaluations performed by people that have mastered the subject matter.*

As you surf the Internet, visiting many e-commerce Web sites as you do research in preparation for launching your own online business venture, you'll see phrases like "satisfaction guaranteed" or "money-back guarantee." These statements are typically made as part of an overall sales pitch; however, they do have legal ramifications. "If your ad uses phrases like 'satisfaction guaranteed' or 'money-back guarantee,' you must be willing to give full refunds for any reason," according to the FTC. "You also must tell the consumer the terms of the offer."

These are just a few of the legal issues you'll need to consider before actually opening your online-based business. For many people who proceed with caution and make educated decisions, however, operating an online business is extremely emotionally and financially rewarding. After all, very few types of businesses require a relatively low initial financial investment and allow you to be your own boss, set your own hours, and work from virtually anywhere.

As you hop on the e-commerce bandwagon, if you'd like to share your experiences with the readers of future editions of this book, or if you have comments about this book, please e-mail me directly at jr7777@aol.com or visit my Web site at www.jasonrich.com.

Welcome to the exciting and fast-paced world of e-commerce and operating a virtual business. As you turn the page, your introduction to this industry and the opportunities available to you will begin!

Jason R. Rich
www.jasonrich.com

In Business, Preparation Is Everything

GET THE SCOOP ON...
Is an online-based business right for you?
- How to invest your time and money
- Do all businesses work on the Web?
- Defining your business idea

PART I

Making the Right Business Choices

So, you've heard all of the hype about the Internet's World Wide Web and the profit potential of starting a business on the Information Superhighway. Perhaps you've heard the opportunities available to small business operators on the Internet equated to the Gold Rush, or you've seen statistics that depict online businesses as being the best money-making opportunities for the twenty-first century.

The prices of computers are dropping rapidly, while with each new generation of microprocessor chips, their technological capabilities improve dramatically. Now more and more people are becoming computer literate and are beginning to explore the Internet on their own. People of all ages, from all walks of life, and from almost all income levels are finding their way into cyberspace in record numbers, thanks in part to the popularity of America Online and the tremendous marketing efforts of Internet Service Providers (ISPs).

Unofficially...
One survey suggests that the number of people over 16 years old in the United States and Canada using the Internet has climbed to 92 million.

It's true, thousands of new people are making their way into cyberspace every week.

These people, just like you, are consumers and most have major credit cards (not to mention a PC or Apple computer and at least some level of computer literacy). The Internet's fast-growing popularity has made it an attractive and viable marketing tool for companies looking to reach a broad audience of computer users, or niche markets made up of people with very specific interests and needs.

What's involved with starting an online business?

Just a few years ago, establishing a business online (or an "e-commerce Web site") was something that only large, well-funded companies were able to do; this is no longer the case. These days, virtually anyone with an idea for an online business, a computer, access to the World Wide Web, and software for creating a Web site can launch his own business venture in cyberspace, with relative ease and with a minimal financial investment. This book will show you how!

Every seller is welcome

The e-commerce industry is truly open to everyone; however, just because it's available doesn't guarantee your online business venture will make you rich, no matter what the statistics show or how good your idea is. Out of the hundreds (or even thousands) of online businesses launched each month, only a handful will ever become profitable. An even smaller number will make their founders wealthy.

To be sure, starting an online business typically involves far less risk than opening a retail store or traditional mail-order business. But launching an online business venture that has the potential for success will require a substantial investment of time on your part, not to mention what could turn into a significant financial investment.

Anyone who has explored cyberspace or studied the stock market has heard about all of the online businesses that have launched, gone public, and made their investors a fortune. But most online businesses haven't yet become profitable. Those that have generated profits have done so only after being in business for several years. Sizable financial investments (in the millions of dollars) were also put into marketing, advertising, and promotions.

Online businesses like America Online, Yahoo!, Amazon.com, Excite.com, eBay.com, Priceline.com, and others weren't launched as small start-up businesses. They were created by already successful business entrepreneurs who raised millions of dollars in investment capital and invested that money in the formations and marketing of their online business ventures.

Still, don't let this discourage you. As someone interested in starting your own online business, whether you're contemplating this as a full-time career move or a part-time way of generating additional income, you certainly have many opportunities available to you in cyberspace for launching a business on a smaller scale and making money. A number of small business operators have been successful establishing and profiting from e-commerce sites. The majority of them have avoided competing head-on with large companies. Instead, they've found a niche market and have sold their unique, customized, or narrowly focused products or services to a well-defined audience.

The e-commerce industry is relatively new. There are no hard and fast rules about what works or why. *Any* product or service you're looking to sell on the Web can be viable if you design your Web site correctly, target the right audience, and do extensive marketing, advertising, and promotions.

Every product is welcome

Just about everyone has seen the television commercial for Saturn automobiles where a college student orders his new Saturn on the Web, while his roommates order a pizza. This is not just advertising hype. If you explore cyberspace, you will find individual car dealerships successfully selling autos on the Web, not to mention promotional Web sites operated by all the automobile manufacturers. You'll also see real estate (houses, apartments, condos, timeshares, and land) being sold on the Internet, as well as yachts, jewelry, artwork, insurance, financial services, collectibles, and furniture.

These are only the high-ticket items. Companies have also found success selling all sorts of mass-market products and services to the general Web-surfing public:

- Airline tickets
- Books
- CDs
- Videos
- DVDs
- Movie/theater/concert tickets
- Clothing
- Vitamins and other healthcare products
- Make-up and cosmetics
- Toys
- Collectibles like trading cards, Beanie Babies, and dolls

Bright Idea
Although you should never believe everything you see on TV, it's a good idea to follow advertising. The Web is the one area where ads may be informative. So much changes every day that ads can be a good source of exposure to new technologies.

Chances are, if it can be sold via mail order, at a retail store, or at a flea market, someone has tried to sell it on the Web, too. If the idea of operating your own business is appealing, you have at least some level of computer literacy (programming knowledge isn't necessarily required), and you have a good idea for an online-based business, you have most of what it takes to get started. You'll also need a computer with access to the Internet, some type of Web site development tools, and a product or service to offer.

This book is designed to take you step by step through the process of launching an online business, from the initial concept stages to the actual development of your Web site, its ongoing maintenance, and the promotion of the site once it goes online.

It won't be easy

No matter what you've heard about the ease of starting a business online—how quickly it can be done, how much profit you can make, how little time is required, and how it can be done for little or no money—don't believe it! Establishing a successful online business will require much of the same efforts and resources as starting a traditional business, only the risks are somewhat lower. You'll need to develop a well-thought-out business plan, invest a significant amount of time, make some type of financial commitment, and do an incredible amount of research.

There are a lot of mistakes you can make when trying to establish an online business and create an online presence for that business. There are also many scams out there targeting would-be entrepreneurs looking to go online in pursuit of riches. This

Watch Out!
Beware of "get-rich-quick" schemes or Internet business opportunities that seem too good to be true. Many scam artists targeting would-be entrepreneurs focus on the glamor and ease of operating a home-based Internet business.

book will help you avoid many of these common mistakes, scams, and pitfalls. This book will also point you directly to hundreds of useful resources available to online business operators.

As you read this book, try to formulate in your mind (and write down on paper) ideas about what type of online-based business you'd be interested in creating, what resources you already have at your disposal, and what useful skills and knowledge you possess. Also, consider what information, skills, knowledge, and resources (financial and otherwise) you know you're lacking.

Once you come up with what you consider to be a brilliant online-based business idea, test it, do research, become an expert regarding who your potential competition will be, and learn everything there is to know about your product or service. Most importantly, you need to understand your target audience and what needs or desires your online business will be fulfilling (or what problems your product/service will solve).

For the purposes of this book, an *online business* refers to any type of business venture being launched on the Internet (typically on the World Wide Web). An *e-commerce site* refers to a Web site designed to accept orders for products or services. E-commerce sites typically accept credit card payments from customers and allow visitors to shop directly online, without having to call a toll-free phone number, send a fax, or mail an order form to place an order. Keep in mind, however, that there are countless other terms tossed around this industry to describe online businesses or e-commerce sites:

- Virtual businesses
- Virtual stores

- E-stores
- Electronic malls
- E-businesses

No matter what type of online business you're hoping to launch, the level of planning, the steps you'll need to take, and the amount of effort required will basically be the same, although, as you'll learn from reading this book, there are many options available to you. As an entrepreneur, you have taken the first step in identifying the Web as offering boundless opportunity. The next step is discovering how to focus on one aspect of the e-commerce industry in order to find a specific business opportunity that's viable—and of interest to you.

Is an online-based business right for you?

Just as there are many types of traditional businesses, there are many types of online-based businesses and e-commerce sites you can create. Actually planning and establishing an online-based business requires a lot of time and effort. Once the business is operational, the time and money you must invest to keep your business running on a day-to-day basis will vary greatly, depending on the focus of your business—what you'll be selling or what services you'll be offering.

As you investigate the online business opportunities available to you, you'll need to determine if operating the type of business you have in mind fits your lifestyle. Just a few of the questions you'll need to ask yourself include the following:

- If you're already juggling a full-time job and a personal life, will you have the necessary time to dedicate to the operation of an online business?

Timesaver
Don't exercise a false economy by scrimping on the time you invest when you are first setting up your business. The time you put into research and planning will repay itself many times over with saved time and money later.

- Are you prepared to operate your business for several months (or perhaps several years) before generating a profit?

- Do you have the computer technology necessary to access the Web and maintain your online presence?

- If you'll be operating your business from home, at least initially, do you have the available space to create a home office that will provide a conducive work environment?

- If your business will require you to maintain an inventory of products, do you have room in your home to store that inventory and enough money to maintain it?

Launching your online business venture will take time, money, and plenty of preparation. In this business, knowledge is power. Enter into your business venture fully understanding the basics of online commerce, your target audience, and your products. It's also important to choose a business opportunity that you're excited about and truly believe in.

How best to invest your time and money

There's an age-old saying: "Keep it simple." This is especially true if you'll be launching a start-up business on the Web and have limited business or e-commerce experience. There's no need for you to invest a fortune in creating a Web site that is cutting-edge (from a technological standpoint) in order to test the viability of your business idea. Using an off-the-shelf Web page development and management software package, such as ecBuilder Pro, Microsoft FrontPage, or Symantec's Visual Page, or an inexpensive e-commerce turnkey solution (such as

Moneysaver
Remember that more is not necessarily better. Turnkey solutions are inexpensive and offer all the features most start-up e-businesses need.

Yahoo! Store), you can get your business online inexpensively and relatively easily. These and other options are all explored later in this book.

After you've developed an idea for an online business—but before investing time and money to get online immediately—invest time researching and creating a comprehensive business plan. Then consider how the day-to-day operations of your business will work once you launch it. Preparation is truly one of the key ingredients for success, especially in an industry that is changing so rapidly as new technological innovations become available. Thus, investing your time in advance is as important as investing your money later.

As you'll soon learn, simply having a great business idea and a professional-looking online presence isn't enough. To make your online-based business profitable, you'll need to generate traffic to your site, and this can be one of the biggest challenges you'll face. Once people are at your site, they need to be motivated to make a purchase, which often means helping potential customers overcome their concern for security and privacy issues related to participating in online transactions.

Absolutely nothing will replace the need to get to know your target audience thoroughly. You need to understand their needs, desires, buying/spending habits, demographics (age, gender, income level, education level, and so forth), the problems they face, and how your products or services address these issues. The online presence you ultimately create for your business needs to cater specifically to your target audience, look professional, and be easy to navigate, even for novice Web surfers.

By spending the necessary time doing research, you should be able to pinpoint:

- What products and services have good market potential for sale online.

- Who your target audience will be for the products and services.

- What type of content your Web site will need in order to cater to your target audience.

- How what you're offering online addresses the needs, wants, or interests of your potential customers.

- What the best layout/design for your Web site will be in order to communicate your marketing message.

- What are the best ways to promote your Web site in order to reach your target audience.

Once you have the necessary knowledge about your product or service, determine how you plan to use the Web as a marketing and sales tool, and determine how you'd like to promote your Web site to your target audience. Then you'll be in a better position to decide how best to spend whatever business start-up capital you have available to launch your venture. Educating yourself about all of the options available to you in terms of creating, managing, and promoting your online presence will ultimately save you money and can make the difference between a successful or failed venture.

Which business ideas are best suited to the Web?

Obviously, the business idea you come up with helps determine if your online-based business will be successful, but it's only one ingredient. As you explore the Web, you'll find many successful businesses that, to judge only from the product or service they offer, might seem likely to fail, and vice versa. This is because in addition to the idea itself, a lot depends on how the idea is executed and marketed.

Unless you have a huge budget (say, millions of dollars) to execute your business idea, it's bad business practice to attempt to compete head-on with well-established and very large online businesses (such as Amazon.com), which have spent millions changing the buying habits of online consumers. Instead, as an entrepreneur planning to launch a small online business, you should focus on some type of niche market that isn't cost effective for the larger, well-established companies to serve.

As you kick around ideas for your online business venture, don't rule out anything initially. From the list of ideas you generate, choose the ones you're most interested in, do research to determine their viability, and then take your top one or two ideas and develop detailed business plans around them.

Early on, even if an idea is outrageous, don't immediately dismiss it until you've closely examined its viability and have done the necessary research. Ideas that wouldn't necessarily work as traditional retail or mail-order businesses may have potential on the Web. Make sure, however, that the ideas making your final cut are manageable, based upon your available resources and budget.

Forget the fads, watch the trends

At any given time, one fad or another is sweeping across America. People will spend almost anything in order to participate in the fad and get their hands on whatever items relating to the fad are for sale. As this book is going to press, collectibles like Beanie Babies, Furbys, Star Wars-related items, and

Bright Idea
As you begin formulating plans to launch an online-based business, invest your time and energy first. Never invest your money before you've done the necessary research and have formulated a business plan you're confident will lead you to success.

Watch Out!
When evaluating your top business ideas, make sure the idea you decide to run with is manageable based on the resources and budget at your disposal. You may have a wonderful idea, but if it'll require millions of dollars in marketing alone and you are planning to launch a small business using your own financial resources, you're sunk.

Pokémon toys are all highly popular and selling on the secondary market for 10 times (or more) their suggested retail prices.

If you're looking to capitalize on a fad by operating an online business selling products or services relating to that fad, watch out. Just as quickly as a fad starts, it can (and will) end, causing the market for those products to dry up almost instantly. Don't invest a lot of time and money creating an e-commerce site that caters to a specific fad, unless you're looking to make a quick buck and get out fast.

The fast-in, fast-out approach goes against most of the rules for establishing an online-based business. Typically, if you don't have a huge budget, you have to invest lots of planning, then months or years of operation to build traffic to and sales from your site.

Instead of developing an entire e-commerce site or online-based business focused around the exploitation of a current fad (which will take time and money), consider selling these goods through one of the online auction sites, such as eBay (www.ebay.com), Yahoo Auctions (auctions.yahoo.com), or Amazon (www.amazon.com). These sites allow anyone to buy or sell items of any price and pay a small fee to the site operator. With the fast-growing popularity of these services, people have managed to supplement their income selling all sorts of new and used items via online auctions.

The growing competition in cyberspace

It's the American dream to become your own boss, pursue your own professional destiny, and strike it rich doing something you love to do. In an era when giant corporations and mass merchants are putting small businesses and mom-and-pop retail stores out

eBay.com (home page shown) is one of the world's most popular online auction sites and a major success story in the e-commerce industry. Due to its success, many other online auction sites have popped up, including Yahoo! Auctions and Amazon.Com Auctions.

of business in record numbers, the Internet provides small business operators the chance to reach a global audience of Web surfers relatively inexpensively.

Realizing that virtually anyone can launch a successful business in cyberspace, people from all walks of life as well as companies of all sizes are staking their turf on the information superhighway and establishing their own Internet presence. Almost every Fortune 500 company has some type of Web presence. Likewise, large retail store chains, such as The Gap, Abercrombie & Fitch, Radio Shack, Electronics Boutique, The Disney Store, The Sharper Image, Barnes and Noble, FAO Schwartz, and countless others are popping up online. These traditional retail store chains are branching out into cyberspace because they see it as a fast-growing trend in how consumers shop.

It's no secret that companies like Microsoft and America Online are planning to make inexpensive "set-top" Internet connections readily available to

Many major retail chains, including The Gap (www.gap.com), now have an Internet presence and allow customers to shop online.

the public in the near future. Soon, for a few hundred dollars (or less), anyone will be able to surf the Web. A set-top connection, like Web TV, is a small box that connects your television set to the telephone line and transforms any basic TV into a terminal for surfing the Internet. This is one of the least expensive ways of gaining access to the Web from your home. Using a set-top box, it's possible to surf the Web and send and receive e-mail.

There's no doubt that in the near future, for the average person in America, surfing the Internet will be as commonplace as watching television, playing a Nintendo video game, or using the telephone. As a result, entrepreneurs and businesspeople alike are seeing dollar signs and coming up with ideas for generating income by marketing their products or services to Web surfers. Thousands of new Web sites are popping up every day. While not all of these sites are designed to sell products or based on an e-commerce business model, the number of individuals, businesses, and corporations trying to exploit the

Internet to generate revenue is growing extremely rapidly.

No matter what type of business you ultimately launch on the Web, there's going to be competition. Thus, you'll need to do things better, faster, cheaper, or more aggressively than the many other businesses in cyberspace, or find innovative ways to differentiate your product. The problem is, if you do come up with an innovative idea that's a tremendous success, you can count on that idea being copied many times over by your competition, sometimes in a matter of days or even hours.

Despite the ever-increasing level of competition from companies and organizations of all sizes, people just like you continue to launch new online business ventures. Should you be intimidated by all of the competition? No! You should, however, be aware that it exists and that the competition in cyberspace will probably become even more fierce in the future. If you plan accordingly and have the resources available to conduct your business is a way that's better (but not necessarily bigger) than the competition, your chances of long-term success increase dramatically.

Part of doing business online better than your competition is having a Web site that people enjoy visiting, and creating an online shopping experience that's truly intuitive. Providing top-notch customer service also is critical, since repeat business and word-of-mouth are important methods of generating traffic to your Web site.

Defining your business idea

In the early chapters of this book, the concept of defining your business idea will be dealt with in

Unofficially...
The major video game companies (Nintendo, Sony, and Sega) are planning to incorporate modems into their next generation of home video game systems, allowing youngsters easy access to the Internet without needing an expensive computer.

Moneysaver
Don't increase your advertising budget at the expense of offering excellent customer service. Great advertising (and even low prices) is no substitute for superior service and communication online, via telephone, fax, U.S. mail, or in person. Remember: Word of mouth is free!

greater detail. Since you're probably not equipped to launch a business venture with the capital needed to compete with the major players, it's important to develop an idea that caters to a specific niche audience. You need to truly understand what your product or service offers and why your target or niche market wants, needs, or would have an interest in it.

You must clearly define your business's goals and objectives, who its audience is, and what exactly you're offering to the public. If you can't do this in your own mind, there's no possible way your potential customers will understand what you're trying to do, and chances are they won't support your efforts.

With so much competition in cyberspace, branding is becoming increasingly more important. Unlike traditional business, how you brand your business, product, or service has little or no relevance to the actual size of your company. This creates a more even playing field between you (the small online business operator) and the big businesses now establishing a presence on the Web. The playing field is far from being truly equal, of course, but in cyberspace, your chances of competing successfully with large companies or a handful of smaller companies is far greater than if you were operating a traditional retail, mail-order, telemarketing, or locally focused service-type business.

As a small online business operator, it's important to define, develop, and then stick to your business idea, yet be flexible enough to compete in this ever-changing and evolving e-commerce industry.

Should you give up your day job?

All it really takes is a good idea, time, a bit of money, and a computer with Internet access to launch an online business venture. So just about anyone with basic computer and business knowledge and an entrepreneurial spirit can start an online business. Entrepreneurial spirit is important here, because as a business operator, you'll need to dedicate a lot of time, energy, and perhaps money toward making your venture successful.

Unfortunately, while everyone who starts an online business aspires to success and wealth working part-time from home (or whatever location they choose), there is no substitute for hard work and dedication.

Businesspeople, homemakers, work-at-home mothers, students, retired people, existing traditional business operators, and anyone else looking to supplement their existing income are among the ever-growing group of people establishing some sort of business on the Web. Do such people achieve financial success operating their own online businesses? Some become rich, some earn a respectable second income, and, unfortunately, some people fail. The primary reasons people fail when they launch an online business venture include:

- Lack of planning.
- Trying to sell a product or service people have no interest in buying.
- Poor (unprofessional-looking) Web site design.
- Inferior customer service or technical support.
- Ineffective advertising, marketing, or promotion.
- Insufficient financial resources.
- Following a poorly written business plan.

One of the primary goals of this book is to offer you step-by-step directions for designing, creating, launching, and maintaining your online business,

Bright Idea
No matter how much time and effort you initially expect to invest in starting your business venture, in reality it'll take more. Unless you're prepared to make the necessary time investment, think twice about establishing your own online business. However much time you estimate you'll need, double it.

while at the same time helping you avoid common pitfalls people run into when they attempt to launch an online business.

If you have an incredible business idea, and after doing extensive research you're convinced it will be the basis for a hugely successful online business, you have several choices. You can make launching this business venture a part-time project that you work on after meeting the responsibilities of your full-time job, or you can dedicate your professional life to this business project full-time.

Choosing to leave your full-time job and pursue a somewhat risky start-up venture is a decision that will have a major impact on your life, because you'll be giving up the security of a regular paycheck and perhaps a full benefits package. It could take several months before your online business makes its first sale, so you need to have the financial resources available to support yourself without receiving a steady paycheck. In addition, you'll also need money to invest in your business, to get online, to pay for inventory (if applicable), and to cover the cost of marketing, advertising, and promotion.

Any money you invest in your online business should be funds you can afford to lose, because if your venture fails, the money you invested will most likely be lost. Before giving up your full-time job, consider launching your online business venture as a part-time project to test its viability. You may also want to solicit outside investors to ensure you'll have the financial resources available to keep your venture operational until it becomes profitable.

For homemakers, students, and retired individuals, starting an online business can be an ideal income generator, because it's possible (in most cases) to work from home, set your own hours, and

Watch Out!
Don't make rash decisions about quitting your job and starting an online business venture, thinking you're going to strike it rich. Test your idea first. If it seems viable, seriously consider the ramifications of quitting your job before doing so. It's important to develop realistic expectations regarding the profit potential of your business idea.

get started with minimal financial investment. While computer programming skills are no longer required to establish a business presence on the Web, basic computer literacy skills and a general working knowledge of business management and marketing will certainly be useful.

How much does it cost to get started? Putting a dollar sign on what it'll take to establish your online business depends on many factors, including what type of business you'll be operating, whether you hire a professional to design your Web site, what hosting service or ISP you use, what company you establish your merchant account with, your inventory costs, and the cost of hiring employees. As you create your business plan, you'll need to make a series of financial projections in order to develop your budget. Throughout this book, we'll explore the costs associated with various aspects of starting an online business venture and the steps required to create a business plan.

Establishing your existing business on the Web

Established businesses, of all sizes and in all industries, are venturing onto the Web for many reasons:

- to expand their customer base and reach a global market

- to improve the customer service they offer (and reduce related costs)

- to make it easier for customers to place orders anytime (day or night)

- to distribute information about the company (to customers, potential clients, and investors)

- to broaden brand awareness

Timesaver
One way to expand any traditional business is to cater to a national or worldwide market by creating a presence on the Web. This will allow you to offer your (potential) customers information about your products or services, provide better customer support, and reach people you wouldn't ordinarily reach.

- simply because it's perceived as an important strategic business move for the company's future.

Whether you operate a small retail store, a service-based business, or one of the few Fortune 500 companies that still hasn't created an Internet presence, there are many reasons why your business should create a Web site. An existing company that sells products or services should seriously consider taking advantage of e-commerce technology in order to allow customers to make purchases directly online.

If a traditional company already exists and is well established, expanding into cyberspace is in many ways much easier than launching an online-based business from scratch. While many of the steps to get online and create a Web site are the same for everyone, there are additional considerations and possible pitfalls for existing businesses looking to expand onto the Web. These considerations and pitfalls are explored later in this book.

Be careful what you get involved in

In case you've spent the past few years living in a totally non-digital world and haven't yet begun exploring the power, vast penetration, and incredible growth of the Internet, the World Wide Web offers people a great opportunity to market and sell virtually anything.

This amazing resource has attracted thousands of con artists developing all sorts of scams, quasi-illegal "business opportunities," and countless other misrepresented offers. These swindlers target the would-be entrepreneur who isn't yet computer savvy, and promise limitless riches for doing little or no work, simply by exploiting the power of the

Internet. There are franchise opportunities, multi-level marketing "opportunities," pyramid schemes, and get-rich-quick scams being offered.

Because thousands of online businesses and e-commerce sites are being launched every week, many services—promoted as time- and money-saving solutions—are offered to would-be entrepreneurs. Some of these are totally legitimate and extremely useful tools and services, while others are promoted by fly-by-night operations looking to capitalize on the ignorance of others.

Chapter 8, "Fine-Tuning Your Business Before Going Online," is dedicated to showing how to avoid the many online scams and rip-offs. As a general rule, as you begin to formulate plans for your online business venture, it's critical that you take it upon yourself to do your own research (don't rely on what others tell you), and to make well-thought-out and educated decisions about which directions you choose to go. Always proceed with caution, be suspicious if something sounds too good to be true, ask lots of questions, do research, and never make rash decisions about anything relating to your business.

E-commerce in the new millennium

We're living in an exciting time. The power, capabilities, and worldwide reach of the Internet are quickly changing the way the world does business, and by reading this book, you'll learn how to get into the world of e-commerce while this industry is still in its infancy. For people starting new online-based business ventures or existing companies looking to expand onto the Internet, there's never been a better time to go online. The Web site development tools and resources available right now have

Watch Out!
The only people who get rich from "get-rich" schemes are the dishonest people perpetuating the scams. Of course, there are, for example, some legitimate multi-level marketing opportunities, but it's important to be extremely careful about anything you choose to become involved in.

Timesaver
While programming knowledge is not required for launching and operating an online business, basic computer skills and a strong familiarity with how to surf the Web is required. If your computer skills aren't up to speed, consider taking classes at a local computer store, community colleges, or adult education program.

never been easier to use. They're powerful, and what's more, they're becoming extremely inexpensive and usable by people with little or no programming knowledge.

What the Internet can do for you is limited only by your imagination and the amount of time and resources you put into your venture. You've taken the right first step by purchasing this book.

Just the facts

- With the decreasing prices of computers and increased technological capabilities, more and more people are becoming computer literate and exploring the Internet.

- An e-commerce site is not just an electronic brochure or interactive marketing tool; it sells products or services.

- These days, anyone with an idea for an online business, a computer, access to the World Wide Web, and the right software can launch a cyberspace business venture.

- Small business operators are most likely to succeed when they sell their customized products or services to a well-defined niche audience.

- Before investing time and money to get online, spend time doing research, create a comprehensive business plan, and consider how the daily operations of your business will work.

- To beat the competition, you'll need to do things better, faster, cheaper, and more aggressively, or find innovative ways to differentiate your product from those of other cyberspace businesses.

GET THE SCOOP ON...
Developing a business infrastructure
▪ Creating a set-up checklist ▪ Generating a
business plan ▪ Seeking professional advice
▪ Setting up office supplies

Laying the Groundwork for Your Online Business (I)

A t the heart of every successful online business is a solid infrastructure and well-thought-out business plan. Without these two elements, you'll find it extremely difficult to operate your business day today and plan for the future. Developing a professional-looking Web site to sell or promote a product or service is extremely important, too. But before going online and opening for business, make sure everything else is in place in terms of planning and implementing day-to-day operating procedures.

Starting your business: some considerations

Operating your own online business is very different from working for someone else, because you're responsible for everything—you're the boss. Poor planning or lack of follow-through on your part can and will lead to failure, especially if you don't have a detailed business plan in place to help you stay on track.

Advantages of self-employment

Aside from the obvious perks of being able to control your professional destiny by operating your own online business, you'll have control over your income potential. Being your own boss certainly has its advantages:

- You won't have a boss constantly looking over your shoulder.

- If you'll be operating your online business from home, there's never a commute to and from work (and no traffic jams).

- You can work at your own pace and set your own work hours.

- There's no dress code. Many people who work from home report their typical business attire (at least until mid-morning or lunchtime) is a robe or just underwear.

- It's usually easier to juggle your personal and professional life.

Questions to ask yourself

If you've been stuck in an office job up until now, being your own boss might sound like paradise, which is why so many people are taking advantage of this type of opportunity. There are, however, a few things to consider before making this transition in your professional life:

Bright Idea
If you have young children and want to spend more time with them, switching from an office job to an at-home Internet business can be an attractive choice. Just be sure to think about how feasible it will be to set up a usable work space and get work done when the kids are around.

YES NO

☐ ☐   Do you have organizing ability, personal drive, and leadership qualities?

☐ ☐ Are you able to endure long hours—at least in the beginning—before your business is fully operational?

☐ ☐ Are you psychologically ready to take some risks?

☐ ☐ Are you prepared to wait several months before making a profit?

☐ ☐ Do you have specific expertise in the business you want to start?

☐ ☐ Do you know how to find your particular niche in the market and how to identify your customers?

☐ ☐ Do you know how to sell enough of what you have, at a price that will return an adequate profit for you?

☐ ☐ Can you obtain the money you will need to start and keep the business running without getting into cash flow problems?

☐ ☐ Do you like to think ahead and plan for your future, then work to make it happen?

☐ ☐ Are you motivated and focused enough to do all of your work, in a timely manner, when you could be watching television, listening to the radio, catching up on your housework or errands, or just enjoying the weather if it happens to be a nice day?

☐ ☐ If you'll be working from home, do you live in an environment that's conducive to working productively? Do you have a separate room in your home that can be transformed into an office? Can this area

Watch Out!
Be honest with yourself. In the evenings, at night, and on weekends, once your work day is complete and you have no pressing deadlines to meet, will you be able to focus on your personal life instead of spending extra time in your at-home office, catching up on paperwork or checking your e-mail? If not, working at home may not be for you.

☐ ☐ be shut off from the rest of the house, so that you can have your privacy and quiet when you're hard at work and need to concentrate?

☐ ☐ Are you extremely organized and detail-oriented? (There's nobody else to pick up the slack for you or cover for your mistakes.)

☐ ☐ Are you customer service–driven? Will you be willing to take extra steps to keep your customers happy and win over new customers?

66

[Small businesses] create two of every three new jobs, produce 39 percent of the (U.S.) gross national product (51 percent of the private gross national product), and invent more than half of the nation's technological innovations. Small businesses employ 53 percent of the private non-farm work force.
—U.S. Small Business Administration

99

Developing a business plan

The true backbone of America's economy is the over 20 million small businesses, which account for the majority of new jobs created. (A small business is defined as one with fewer than 500 employees.)

When you decide to start your own small business online, you'll need to take the following steps:

1. Come up with a brilliant business idea.

2. Develop a detailed business plan and marketing campaign.

3. Perform the necessary research.

4. Raise the required start-up capital.

5. Seek out free or low-cost guidance to make up for your lack of business experience and/or computer literacy.

Assuming you have the intelligence, personality type, motivation, and financial backing to launch your own online business, the first step is to determine what product your online business will offer. Ideally, you want to create a business opportunity for yourself that makes full use of your background, knowledge, and talents. Next, you want to determine what opportunities are available based on the resources at your disposal.

Before investing your time and money in your idea, create a detailed *business plan* that specifically defines your business, identifies the goals of the business, and includes a balance sheet and cash flow analysis.

Upon creating a business plan, doing extensive research, and analyzing the demand for the products to be offered by your business, you should be able to accurately project start-up costs, operating costs, revenues, and profits. Keep in mind, though, that e-commerce is still a relatively new concept, so accurately predicting initial traffic to your site and customer demand for your product may be a bit challenging.

If you don't have a financial background, consider hiring an accountant or someone with the expertise to help you create a financial model for your company (in advance) and help you set up the financial aspects of your business. Right from the start, be sure to have an adequate accounting and recordkeeping system in place. Whether you plan on doing the necessary recordkeeping and accounting by hand or using an off-the-shelf computer software program is up to you.

Maintaining a current balance sheet and income statement (a profit and loss statement) along with accurate banking records is important for keeping your business on track financially. This represents the bare minimum level of accounting work that'll need to be done on an ongoing basis.

Unless you're planning on getting a home equity loan to finance your business venture, you'll either need to find investors or take out business loans in

Timesaver
For small businesses, QuickBooks Pro '99 (Intuit Software/www. intuit.com/ quickbooks) is one of the top-selling accounting and book-keeping software packages on the market. This and other good programs can save you time managing your finances.

Watch Out!
Don't get caught with insufficient funds. Most experts recommend that you should have enough money up front to cover all start-up costs and operating expenses for a year. If you rely on profits from your first-year sales to create cash flow, you are setting yourself up for disappointment.

order to generate the start-up capital you require. No matter how you intend to raise your start-up capital, potential investors and financial institutions will look carefully at your business plan, projected financial statements, and how much of your own funds you're investing in the business.

Unfortunately, no matter how strong your business concept is, there are no guarantees that it will succeed. To greatly minimize your chances of failure, implement well-defined management practices, ensure that you have as much industry expertise as possible, and make sure you also have whatever technical support you'll need to properly manage and operate your business. Carefully planning every aspect of your business is also critical.

Creating a well-thought-out business plan is an important first step for any business owner. This document will help you determine whether or not your idea for a business is viable, and can later be used to attract potential investors or help you obtain loans from financial institutions. The more detail your business plan offers, the better your long-term chances for success will be.

Getting help—people and software

An accountant will be able to assist you with the financial aspects of a business plan, while someone who studied business in school (at the undergraduate or graduate level) should have the basic know-how to create a coherent business plan once the necessary research has been done. To help you format your business plan and compile the information you'll need, the Small Business Administration's Web site offers several free and downloadable shareware and public domain software programs designed to help you create a business plan. For a directory of these programs, point your Web browser to www.sba.gov/shareware/starfile.html.

There are also a variety of commercially available, off-the-shelf software packages designed to assist start-up companies in the creation of business plans. PLANMaker (POWERSolutions for Business / 314-421-0670 / www.planmaker.com) helps create professional, well-documented business plans. PLANMaker's tutorial system and on-screen resources make this a powerful program for both the beginner and the experienced businessperson. The software is self-supporting, so it doesn't require a spreadsheet or word processor to operate. Priced at $129, this program is available for PC CD-ROM and operates under Windows 3.1/95/98. A Macintosh version is also available.

Business Plan Pro 3.0 (Palo Alto Software Products / 888-PLAN-PRO / www.pasware.com) is another popular and easy-to-use business plan package featuring context-sensitive audio help, 20 sample plans, a large database of venture capitalists, customizable business charts, and professional-looking full-color printouts. A free demo version of this $89.95 program is available for downloading from the company's Web site.

Other developers of business plan creation software include:

BizPlanBuilder Interactive
JIAN Tools for Sales
1-800-346-5426 / 415-254-5600
www.jianusa.com
PC CD-ROM, Windows 95/98
Retail Price: $99

Bright Idea
When you're planning your business on a tight budget, keep an eye open for self-supporting software—that is, software that can be used without another program such as Microsoft Excel.

Business HeadStart
Planet Corp.
1-800-366-5111 / 508-757-6555
www.planet-corp.com
PC CD-ROM, Windows 3.x (or higher)
Retail Price: $49.99

PlanWrite
Business Resource Software
1-800-423-1228 / 512-251-7541
www.brs-inc.com
PC CD-ROM, Windows 3.x (or higher)
Retail Price: $129.95

Smart Business Plan
American Institute for Financial Research
1-800-578-9000 / 919-932-3600
www.smartonline.com
CD-ROM, Windows 3.1 (or higher)
Retail Price: $149

Using a specialized software package to develop a business plan is an excellent idea for someone who hasn't done this type of thing before. The majority of the available software packages will guide you through the process and help you determine what information needs to be incorporated into your business plan and how best to format this information. Basically, a business plan is a resume for your business idea. This is a professional-looking document that combines text and graphics (charts, graphics, pictures, and so forth), as well as a spreadsheet with projected financial information.

Elements of a business plan

Based on the type of business being created, a well-written business plan will probably include most, if not all, of the following sections:

The Company Name   The first line on the first page of any business plan.

Executive Summary   A text-based overview of the business that can be anywhere from a few sentences to several pages long.

Objectives   Using bulleted points or short paragraphs, this section describes the goals of the business.

Mission Statement   A one-paragraph description that explains the overall purpose of the company's existence.

Keys to Success   What will the company offer that will make it successful? What will the company do differently?

Risks   What risks, financial or otherwise, is the company facing?

Company Summary   More detail about the company, including information about its products or services, is described in this section.

Company Ownership   Who are the executives/founders involved with the company?

Start-Up Summary   What will be required to get this company launched? What costs are involved? Financial projections and a list of start-up costs and expenses should be included here.

Start-Up Assets Needed   This is a listing of the assets the company must acquire prior to its launch. Depending on the type of company, what's included in this list will vary, as will the listed costs of the assets.

Investment   Based on the total start-up costs, this section of the business plan should itemize and describe where the initial start-up capital

Watch Out!
When you are preparing a business report, don't sugarcoat the difficulties or exaggerate numbers in your favor. Potential financial backers will not be fooled. You're better off being completely honest and indicating how you plan to surmount the challenges.

is coming from (such as loans and private investors).

Company Locations and Facilities This section of the business plan describes where the company will be located and will operate. From a business standpoint, what are the benefits and drawbacks of these facilities and the company's location?

Detailed Product/Service Descriptions Use this section to explain in detail what the company will be offering.

Competitive Comparison Describe your company's key competitors. What will your company offer that sets it apart from the competition?

Sourcing Who will be your company's suppliers?

Technology How will technology be used as a tool within your company?

Future Products/Services What new or specific types of products or services will your company launch in the future?

Market Segmentation How does your company fit within its industry? Will your company cater to a specific (or niche) market?

Overall Industry Analysis Provide a brief description of the industry in which you will do business. Describe the state of the industry, who the key players are, and whether or not the industry is expected to expand in the future.

Market Analysis Describe the target customer/audience for your company's products. Break down this information geographically,

Unofficially...
Note that there will be overlap among some of these categories. For example, Competitive Comparison, Market Segmentation, and Keys to Success will all involve analyses of other companies in the field who offer what you hope to offer.

by demographics, or however you can best demonstrate to the reader who would be interested in your company's products. This is just one section of the business plan where charts and graphs can come in handy.

Marketing Strategy   How will your company promote its Web site, products, and services in order to capture the attention of its target audience? This section can be broken down into subsections that describe your company's marketing, promotions, advertising, and public relations plans.

Sales Strategy   How will your company sell and distribute its products? How will your company make use of the Internet?

Service and Support   What type of service and support will your company offer?

Strategic Alliances   How will your company benefit from developing and implementing strategic alliances with other companies in order to achieve its goals?

Organizational Structure of the Company   Using a chart or text, describe the hierarchy of the company from the founder/president/ CEO down to entry-level people. Include projected salary costs for at least the first three years of business.

Financial Plan   This section of the business plan should contain detailed financial statements and projections.

Once your business plan is complete, make sure that you have it reviewed and critiqued by your lawyer, accountant, and/or someone who is an expert in business before submitting it to potential investors or financial institutions (to apply for a loan).

Seeking expert business advice

Even if you've graduated with a degree in business administration, you're an expert in your particular field, and you have a great idea for a business, if you've never run a business before the one thing you lack is experience. To help make up for your own lack of experience in the business world, you can hire someone with experience as a partner or employee. You can also take advantage of the free resources available to small business owners from the SBA and the Service Corps of Retired Executives (SCORE).

The SBA was created by Congress in 1953 to help America's entrepreneurs form successful small enterprises. Currently, the SBA (www.sba.org) has established offices in every state and offers financing, training, and advocacy services to small firms. The organization offers its services to any small business that is independently owned and operated, that's not dominant within its field, and that falls within the size standards set by the SBA.

SCORE, a division of the SBA founded in 1964, is dedicated to aiding in the formation, growth, and success of small businesses nationwide. This is a non-profit association comprised of over 12,400 volunteer business counselors throughout the U.S. and its territories. SCORE volunteers are trained to serve as counselors, advisers, and mentors to aspiring entrepreneurs and business owners. The organization's services are all offered free of charge. To date, over 3.5 million Americans have used SCORE's services, which include offering general business advice and helping entrepreneurs create and write detailed business plans. To reach SCORE volunteers in your area, call 1-800-634-0245 or take advantage of the services offered on the SCORE Web site, http://www.score.org.

American Express also offers information and services to small business owners on the World Wide Web.

Learn more about American Express' Small Business Services at their Web site, www.americanexpress.com/smallbusiness. To apply for one of the American Express cards, such as the American Express Gold Corporate Card or the American Express Executive Corporate Card, point your Web browser to www.americanexpress.com/apply/smalbus.shtml or call 1-800-SUCCESS.

Visa has teamed up with *Entrepreneur* magazine to create Visa's SmallBiz Insider (www.entrepreneurmag.com/visa/visa_smartbiz.hts), a weekly presentation of timely tips and information designed to help you better manage and grow your business. Visa also offers its own Web site targeted to small businesses that can be accessed at http://www.visa.com/cgibin/vee/fb/smbiz/main.html?2+0.

Setting up an office

If you plan to launch your online business from home, hopefully you're motivated, focused, disciplined, and have what it takes to be your own boss. This is the personal investment you'll have to make. As you'll discover, operating from an office (located in your home, in an office building, or elsewhere) will also require an investment in supplies and equipment. Here are some of the basics you'll need to run your business from a small home office.

Moneysaver
Promote your business for free using the Business to Business Directory on American Express' Small Business Exchange (www.americanexpress.com/smallbusiness). The site provides business planning as well as answers from business experts to your questions.

Timesaver
QuickBooks Pro
'99 is compatible
with the elec-
tronic banking
services offered
by many banks
and financial
institutions.
Utilizing this
feature can save
you time and
money handling
the everyday
banking-related
tasks you'll be
responsible for.
Contact your
bank or financial
institution to
determine if its
electronic bank-
ing services
support this
software.

The computer

A core business tool needed in virtually any office is a powerful desktop or laptop computer equipped with at least a 56K modem, to be used for designing and maintaining your online business or e-commerce Web site, surfing the Internet, accessing online services, or sending and receiving e-mail. The computer should also have an assortment of core applications installed, including a word processor, spreadsheet, database, contact manager, scheduler, and any specialized programs (such as accounting, inventory control, credit card processing, and shipping software) your business needs to operate.

Software

Microsoft Office Professional Edition or Microsoft Office 2000 for Windows 95/98/2000 (www. microsoft.com) is a popular and relatively inexpensive suite of business-related applications on one CD-ROM. The software bundle includes Microsoft Word, Excel, Access, Outlook, and PowerPoint.

One good software package for handling your bookkeeping and accounting is QuickBooks Pro '99. Using the EasyStep Interview and QuickBooks Navigator, QuickBooks users can quickly set up their business on this software, creating custom invoices, entering sales, performing electronic banking and bill payment, tracking customer contacts, tracking time, performing job costing, managing inventory, handling payroll, and preparing for tax time.

QuickBooks Pro offers a full range of services and features. It is a Windows 95/98-based program. The single-user version has a suggested retail price of about $220. A five-user (network) version is available for around $600. For more information about this software, visit the company's Web site.

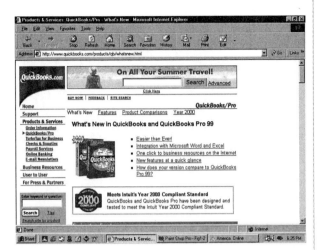

Intuit's QuickBooks Pro is a popular off-the-shelf bookkeeping and accounting software package for small businesses. The company's home page (shown here) is a good resource for small business operators.

Printers and back-up devices

Your office should also be equipped with a laser printer and a data backup device. Another important tool is a plain-paper fax machine. You may also need between two and four telephone lines to accommodate a personal phone number, a work/business phone number, a fax line, and a modem line.

The phone

Your telephone should be capable of handling two phone lines and should have a hold feature, along with an auto dialer that can store your most frequently dialed numbers. Depending on the size of your home office, consider connecting a 900 MHz digital cordless telephone to give you added convenience.

When ordering telephone service, consider adding call waiting, three-way calling, caller ID with name, call forwarding, and call answering to your plan. All are optional services offered for an additional monthly fee from your local phone company.

Moneysaver
To save money and space, consider investing in an all-in-one printer, such as the Hewlett Packard HP-1100A (www.hp.com/go/lj1100). This $499 unit is a laser printer, copier, and scanner in one. In some cases, the HP-1100A can also be used to print faxes your computer receives on standard 8.5" x 11" paper.

Moneysaver
SkyTel (1-800-480-4644 / www.skytel.com) is a leading provider of numeric and alphanumeric paging services. While you typically have to purchase your pager equipment (or lease it from SkyTel), the actual nationwide monthly service is cheaper than most local or regional paging services offered by the company's competitors.

Call answering will replace the need for an answering machine or voice-mail system. Having the ability to retrieve messages remotely from a touch-tone phone is a must.

Also, when ordering phone service, request a free copy of your city's Business-to-Business phone directory published by your phone company. You'll also want copies of your local phone directories (White and Yellow Pages).

For people who travel a lot or spend time on the road, a cellular telephone and pager is a critical tool for staying in touch with business associates and clients. Sprint PCS, Cellular One, Bell Atlantic Wireless, AT&T Wireless, NEXTEL, and OmniPoint are among the companies that offer nationwide digital cellular service, often at competitive rates.

Sprint PCS (1-800-480-4727 /www.sprintpcs.com) is one of the most economical nationwide digital cellular telephone services available. This service will soon offer full nationwide coverage. After purchasing your Sprint PCS phone (prices start at about $100), monthly service includes a low per-minute rate.

Other elements

If you have the money available, a desktop copy machine is also a valuable business tool in any home office. You'll also need basic supplies, such as business letterhead, envelopes, business cards, and everything from pads of paper to paper clips. (For basic office supplies, visit your local office supply superstore, such as OfficeMax or Staples).

If you have the space, set up two desks for yourself to help boost productivity and organization. One desk will be used for your computer and another for your paperwork. The desk used for your computer should have a built-in keyboard drawer or keyboard arm. This ensures that you'll have ample desk space and help you avoid clutter. Make sure the desk chair you select is comfortable and provides adequate back support.

Other furniture and home office equipment you should consider purchasing include:

- A desk set (desk pad, business card holder, letter tray, etc.).
- Bookshelves.
- Briefcase and pad/paper folio (for when you go out on appointments).
- Calculator.
- Cassette or microcassette recorder (for dictation or keeping track of ideas).
- Credit card processing software and equipment (if your business will be accepting credit cards as payment for your products or services).
- File cabinets.
- Floor laps and a desk lamp.
- Office supply storage cabinet.
- Postage machine and postage scale.
- Printer stand.
- Television and VCR.
- Telephone answering machine (if you don't have call answering from your telephone company).
- Wastepaper basket and paper shredder (if you deal with confidential documents).

As you set up your office, visit furniture showrooms and office supply superstores to help you choose the right office furniture to meet your

Unofficially...
A personal digital assistant (PDA) is a handheld computer that can store thousands of names, phone numbers, addresses, and appointments. These devices can easily transfer data to a desktop computer. Popular PDA manufactures include: 3M Corporation (manufacturer of the popular PalmPilot Professional and PalmPilot III), Casio, Sharp Electronics, Hewlett Packard, Philips Electronics, and Psion.

needs. Also, request the following mail order catalogs or visit the Web sites of the following companies that cater to small/home office operators:

- **BackSaver Products Company** (1-800-251-2225) An assortment of chairs, desks, and products designed to protect your back from pain and stress in a home office environment.

- **Day-Timer** (1-800-225-5005 / www.daytimer.com) Offers a catalog of time management and organizational products useful to business professionals and home office operators.

- **Hello Direct** (1-800-520-3311 / www.hellodirect.com) A complete catalog of telephone equipment, including traditional telephones, multi-line phones, cordless phones, cellular phones, and all sorts of telephone accessories.

- **Home Office Direct** (1-888-599-2112 / www.homeofficedirect.com) An online source of office furniture (including desks, chairs, computer carts, and cabinets) designed for a home office.

- **Home Office Furniture System** (www.hofs.com) An online home office furniture showroom.

- **Levenger** (1-800-544-0880 / www.levenger.com) A catalog of fancy pens, home office furniture, and other home office equipment.

- **Lizell** (1-800-718-8800) This catalog is filled with home office furniture, small business equipment, and other products useful to people who work from home.

- **Reliable Home Office** (1-800-869-6000) This catalog also is filled with home office furniture, small business equipment, telephone equipment, and other products.

Just the facts

- The advantage of operating your own online business is that you are your own boss; poor planning on your part, however, can lead to failure. Be sure to create a detailed business plan.

- Work with a financial planner or accountant to help you define your needs.

- There are many reasonably priced software programs on the market to help you manage your business's finances.

Moneysaver
Different mail-order companies have different specialties and prices. By spending a little time comparing prices, you can discover which stores have the best bargains. If your business will use a lot of supplies, however, consider approaching one company and bargaining for a volume discount.

GET THE SCOOP ON...
Getting your own insurance ▪ Choosing the
form of your business ▪ A planning checklist ▪ Handling credit cards through merchant accounts ▪ Obtaining financing

Laying the Groundwork for Your Online Business (II): Financial Issues

Don't be fooled by all of the e-commerce hype. Chances are, you've received junk e-mails explaining how you can start an online-based business for no money down, or for a very small investment. Even the promotional materials for Yahoo! Store state that the start-up costs are a mere few hundred dollars. If you're planning on launching a fully functional e-commerce site, there's going to be a financial investment of at least several thousand dollars (usually more) involved. A few hundred dollars might allow you to set up a very basic Web site and have an online presence, but there's still an investment in technology, marketing, advertising, inventory, office supplies, labor, and so forth, that will be required. We'll look at these issues in this chapter.

Benefits plans and compensation packages

Perhaps the biggest drawback of working for yourself is that you'll be giving up all of the benefits and perks an employer would typically provide. This means that in addition to your homeowner's or renter's insurance and auto insurance—insurance everyone typically has to pay for—you'll now have to acquire and pay for your own additional insurance. This can include:

- Health insurance (along with dental and vision care insurance).

- Life insurance.

- Long-term disability insurance.

- Umbrella insurance.

- Various types of business-related insurance (including fire, workers compensation, and business interruption policies).

- Malpractice insurance.

- Liability insurance.

As a self-employed person who is adequately insured against various types of disaster, you may have monthly premiums anywhere from $1,000 to $3,000, depending on your level of coverage and the types of insurance you acquire for yourself, your business, and your family.

In addition to having to pay for your insurance, you also have to personally deal with insurance agents, shop around for the best available policies, and then maintain all of the paperwork associated with having each type of policy. No longer will your contribution to your insurance premiums simply be automatically deducted from your paycheck, while

Watch Out!
Since insurance agents are typically paid on commission, what they offer you might not always be the best policy to meet your personal needs. Knowing what you want and need in advance, and then shopping around by speaking with several insurance agents, is an excellent strategy.

someone in your employer's benefits office administers the various types of policies and works with the insurance agents on your behalf.

Since paying for your own benefits (insurance in particular) will be expensive, it's an excellent idea to sit down with a personal financial planner, accountant, or some other impartial person who can help you define your needs.

Try to find an insurance agent you can trust, someone you feel comfortable developing a long-term relationship with. Make sure that the agent (or agents) you choose represents only the top insurance providers, and that he's familiar with the types of insurance policies you're looking to purchase. The best way to find a reliable insurance agent is through a referral from someone you know, someone who already has a positive business relationship with his insurance agent. At the same time, you can also research what the best (or highest-rated) insurance companies are for the types of insurance you want to receive, and then call those insurance companies directly for the names of their authorized agents.

As you review all of the different types of insurance policies that are available, try to avoid too much overlap, or you could easily wind up paying multiple times for the same coverage. Likewise, pay careful attention to the premiums, deductibles, and benefits offered by each policy.

When it comes to life insurance, for example, the lower the benefit you desire, the lower the premiums will be. (What you'll actual pay for life insurance will also depend on several factors, including your age and current health.)

Moneysaver
You can often save money on monthly premiums by choosing a policy with a higher deductible. The drawback to this is obvious. With a $1,000 deductible, for example, the first $1,000 of a claim comes out of your pocket before the insurance benefits kick in.

A few words about hiring employees

One of the biggest expenses associated with operating a small business involves hiring full-time or part-time employees. Once your business reaches a certain size, you'll need to expand, which means finding, hiring, and managing honest, hard-working, and dedicated people. While you may be hiring additional people to help reduce your personal workload, the extra responsibilities of hiring those people could easily require an even bigger time commitment on your part.

If the business you launch grows large enough that you need to hire additional employees on a full-time (or permanent part-time) basis, you'll probably have to offer these employees benefits, plus obtain the appropriate workers compensation insurance to protect yourself if they're working from your home (or your office). You'll also have to begin withholding federal income tax payments and Social Security taxes from their paychecks, and establish employee policies and procedures. These should be offered in writing to the people you hire.

Your level of responsibility also increases, because you'll now have people looking to you for ongoing guidance and relying on the success of your company for their paycheck. If you don't already have excellent managerial skills, you'll need to develop them if you plan on running a business with employees.

Hiring freelance consultants or workers such as Web programmers, graphic artists, writers, photographers, or marketing people can become costly, even if you don't have to offer them benefits. These costs should be factored into your operating budget and monitored carefully.

Should you incorporate?

For tax and legal reasons, you'll need to decide what form your business will take. Generally, all businesses fall into one of these broad categories: sole proprietorship, partnership, corporation, S corporation, and limited liability corporation. Your choice of business form will affect your exposure to personal liability, how you draw profits and pay taxes, your ability to raise capital, and how you run the business.

Here are short descriptions of the various types of business forms.

Sole Proprietorship   This is the quickest and easiest way to start a business. Just check with a knowledgeable attorney about any licensing or legal requirements, and you're in business. In a sole proprietorship, profits and losses are simply included on your individual tax returns. On the downside, if someone sues your business, they may be able to sue you personally, and your personal assets are subject to those claims. Depending on the type of product or service you plan on offering through your online business, this might not be the best option in terms of your own protection.

Partnership   This type of business is an association of two or more people working as co-owners of a business with the intent of making a profit. The involvement of two or more people in the business generally increases the complexity and the amount of paperwork. Also, general partners can share unlimited liability, and each is usually responsible for the acts of the other. Depending on the type of product or service you plan on offering

Bright Idea
Consult with an attorney and an accountant before you decide what form to use for your new business. These professionals can advise you on tax advantages and which business form offers you the best protection of personal assets.

through your online business, this might not be the best option in terms of protection for the partners.

Corporation   A corporation is a legal entity that functions somewhat like an individual, legally and for tax purposes. Liabilities are held by the corporation, minimizing the personal liability for owners. The corporation operates as a business and can be owned wholly or partially based on registered certificates, called stock. Some of the responsibilities involved with setting up a corporation include filing an application for a legal name, paying a corporate franchise fee to the state in which you file, appointing a board of directors and corporate officers, and keeping minutes of periodic meetings of the board.

S Corporation   This is a unique type of corporation. It provides the advantages of a corporation but, unlike a corporation, is treated for income tax purposes as a flow-through entity. Income is reported individually by the owners or stockholders on their personal income tax returns. Also, the owners may deduct the corporation's losses against other sources of income. If your new business will have fewer than 35 stockholders, you may want to talk with your accountant and attorney about this option.

Limited Liability Corporation   This is another alternative, in which income and income tax are distributed among partners, but generally the partners are not personally liable for debts. This is a relatively new legal form of business. If you are interested in setting up such a corporation, be sure to consult a knowledgeable attorney.

To learn more about how incorporating can benefit you financially and legally, contact both an accountant and a lawyer. While there are many "kits" and online services that allow you to form your own corporation in minutes for a flat fee, your best strategy is to seek the guidance of a lawyer to help you with this process.

Other considerations involved with launching a business

Prior to selling any product or service online, you must first establish the infrastructure for operating your business. This requires establishing an office, filing the necessary legal documents to establish yourself as a business, and determining how incoming orders will be taken and processed.

Here are just a few of the questions you'll need to answer:

> Will you need a toll-free phone number for incoming orders?
>
> Who will answer the phone?
>
> Is it necessary to hire an independent order-taking or order-fulfillment house?
>
> Will it be necessary to accept credit cards as payment?
>
> How will your orders be shipped to customers?
>
> How much inventory will your need to keep in stock? Where will this inventory be stored?

Once an online business is established, there are specialized software packages designed to automate such tasks as order entry and processing, inventory

Timesaver
Business software packages such as Mail Order Manager (Dydacomp Development Corporation / 1-800-858-3666 / www.dydacomp. com) can cost several thousand dollars, but they can make the daily operation of an online/ mail-order business much more efficient.

Mail Order Manager is a software package designed to help mail order companies automate many of their daily operational tasks.

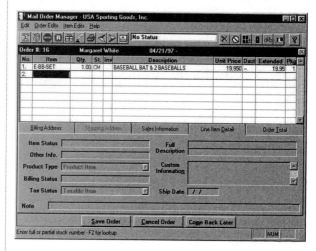

control, credit card authorization, ad tracking and management, bookkeeping, customer database management, and sales lead management.

Aside from the basic equipment and software you'll need to help your business get started, you'll also need various supplies, like company letterhead, business cards, envelopes, press kits/folders, invoices, packing slips, shipping labels, and packaging for your products, all of which should have your company logo imprinted on them.

One of the first things you'll need to do is develop a company logo and identity for your business. You can do this yourself using a graphics program on your computer, or you can hire a graphic artist.

As you design your letterhead, business cards, and other printed materials, keep in mind that these tools should all convey a highly professional image for your company. Also, you'll want all of your printed materials (as well as your online identity) to be consistent in terms of the look of your overall company image. Pay attention to continuity and detail.

What needs to be done before going online?

Here's a partial checklist of things you'll need to do in the planning stages of forming your online business (listed in alphabetical order, not necessarily in the order you should complete these activities). These tasks should be completed prior to your business's official start date:

- ☐ Calculate your start-up costs.

- ☐ Choose a local banker (after meeting several representatives and comparing services and rates).

- ☐ Choose a reliable lawyer and accountant. Have the accountant prepare the necessary tax forms for establishing your business.

- ☐ Conduct market research. Who will your customers be? How big is the market? Who are your competitors?

- ☐ Create a well-defined and detailed business plan.

- ☐ Determine your business's goals, mission statement, and objective.

- ☐ Determine your business's legal entity (sole proprietorship, partnership, corporation, or LLC).

- ☐ Determine your business's location and sign a lease (if necessary).

- ☐ Determine your financial resources.

- ☐ Develop a relationship with a shipping company (such as FedEx, UPS, or the U.S. Post Office)

Watch Out!
While you'll want to shop around for the best printing rates, don't cut corners by using cheap paper stock for your letterhead, business cards, and so forth. Remember that these items will represent your company in the eyes of your potential customers; make sure they look professional.

Timesaver
Take the time to
identify the risks
(financial or oth-
erwise) facing
your business.
Doing this might
not be fun in the
short run. But by
thinking ahead
to possible prob-
lems, you'll be
equipped to deal
with them effi-
ciently if they do
arise.

and determine exactly how you'll ship your products to customers.

☐ Develop a relationship with an Internet Service Provider. Make sure your site will be able to handle secure financial transactions.

☐ Establish your company's line of credit.

☐ Identify your personal strengths and weaknesses (as they apply to operating a business), and then the strengths and weaknesses of your business idea.

☐ Join the local Chamber of Commerce and/or professional organizations/associations.

☐ Line up your suppliers for inventory, manufacturing, and so on. Open accounts with these vendors or suppliers and apply for credit terms.

☐ Obtain a merchant account so your business can accept credit cards online.

☐ Obtain financing and raise start-up capital.

☐ Obtain the necessary local, state, or federal licenses or permits (most towns or cities require that you obtain some form of local business license). If you'll have employees, you'll also need an employee identification number.

☐ Plan and create your Web site (and hire the necessary talent in terms of programmers, graphic artists, photographers, and writers to assist you).

☐ Purchase or lease office furniture, business equipment, and related fixtures.

☐ Select an insurance agent and purchase all of the insurance you'll need (having the right insurance—and enough of it—is critical, for your own protection).

Planning your business operations

Once you have all of the pieces of your business's infrastructure in place, carefully determine how the day-to-day operations of your business will be handled. On paper (or using your computer), create detailed operating procedures for such things as order taking, order processing, Web site management (updating), accounting/bookkeeping, advertising and marketing implementation, credit card authorizations, shipping, inventory management and ordering, and whatever other tasks will be key to the success of your business.

Obviously, until your business is actually operating, you probably won't be able to anticipate every situation that will need to be dealt with. The more prepared you are in advance, however, the lower your risk will be in terms of having to compensate for mistakes and unexpected negative situations.

Setting up a merchant account

When it comes to shopping online via a secure Web site, one of the fastest, safest, and easiest ways for a customer to pay for his purchases is with a major credit card. During 1996, people charged over $886 billion in purchases. In the new millennium, this figure is expected to be significantly larger as our economy focuses less on cash and more on buying on credit.

In order to be competitive in cyberspace, being able to accept credit cards is an absolute necessity. To do this, you must obtain a merchant account through a bank, financial institution, or independent service organization. Using any Internet search engine, enter the search phrase "merchant account," and dozens of financial institutions will be

Unofficially...
As of June 1996, banks and other financial institutions worldwide had issued 525 million Visa cards, 367 million MasterCards, 50 million Discover cards, and 39 million American Express cards.

listed, each offering you the ability to accept major credit cards. This has become a highly competitive industry, so it's important to carefully research the services being offered and shop around for the best rates.

Let's look at how one company handles the process. According to Visa:

> *If you would like to accept Visa card payments, you'll need to establish a merchant Visa account through an acquiring financial institution. First, contact the financial institution that services your business accounts and tell them you want to set up a merchant Visa account. If you need to shop around, ask other companies in your area or line of business for referrals to their Visa acquiring institutions. (Visa itself is not a bank, but an association of banks…)*

Typically, to obtain a merchant account, you'll be required to fill out an application and pay a one-time application fee (of several hundred dollars). Assuming your application is accepted, there will often be an ongoing monthly fee to maintain your merchant account, as well as transaction fees. The transaction fee on each sale might be a flat rate, or it could be a percentage of the total sale.

In addition to evaluating a financial institution's process for applying for a merchant account, you need to pay careful attention to all of the fees, how quickly the funds will be available to you after the sale (if it's more than two days, look elsewhere), and what the steps are for processing credit card transactions. Will you be able to perform real-time and automated credit card processing from your Web site? What type of equipment will you need to lease or purchase? What special software will be required? Will you be required to use the financial institution's secure Web site to process credit card transactions?

Secure Electronic Transaction Protocol (SET)

Online security is one of the top concerns of people who shop online. When people enter their credit cards into an online order form, they want assurances that their credit cards and personal information won't be "broadcast" throughout the Web and available to hackers. Maintaining online security on your site involves adding some form of secure transaction capabilities.

Unless your Web site will offer secure transactions using the *Secure Electronic Transaction Protocol (SET)*, the SSL protocol, or another form of encryption/online security, don't even consider accepting credit card payments from your customers.

MasterCard maintains part of its Web site to deal with secure electronic transactions. The SET site (www.mastercard.com/shoponline/set) discusses SET and online security. According to MasterCard:

> *SET uses a system of locks and keys along with certified account IDs for both consumers and merchants. Then, through a unique process of 'encrypting' or scrambling the information exchanged between the shopper and the online store, SET ensures a payment process that is convenient, private, and most of all secure.*

Here are some of the benefits of SET:

- Your order and payment information is kept confidential.

Moneysaver
Despite all of the fees associated with accepting major credit cards, assuming you obtain a competitive rate, these fees should be considered a cost of doing business. They'll pay for themselves in the long run, if your business is successful.

- Through encryption, all transmitted data has increased integrity.

- You get the best security practices and system design techniques to protect all legitimate parties in an electronic commerce transaction. This means not only that your customers are protected against hackers, but that your own Web site and your company's ability to accept and process financial information are secure as well. It's important when dealing with confidential information, such as credit card information, that the data be kept secure throughout the entire online process, from the moment a customer fills out your online order form to the point where their credit information is processed and added to your company's record keeping and order processing software.

SET is an open industry standard developed for the secure transmission of payment information over the Internet and other electronic networks. This is one of the technologies available to online business operators that can be used to insure credit card transactions are secure. When you sign up with an Internet Service Provider, they'll be able to explain exactly how your site can incorporate this technology.

Obtaining a merchant account

Because your start-up business will be operating primarily on the Internet (with no retail locations), your local banks might not offer you a merchant account. If not, you'll need to use a financial institution or independent service organization that caters to mail-order and online-based businesses. The following is a partial list of merchant account services you'll find on the Web:

- First American Card Service (1stamericancardservice.com/basefold.html)

- American Merchant Resources (1-800-221-1392)

- Credit Merchant Account Services (203-483-5751 / www.merchantaccount.net)

- EDP Credit Card Services (1-800-968-5449 / www.apc.net/edp/cc.htm)

- Electronic Transfer, Inc. (1-800-459-0625, ext. 201 / www.paymentmall.com)

- Merchant Account Company (1-800-956-1990 / www.merchantaccount.com)

- Merchant Express (1-888-845-9457 / www.merchantexpress.com)

- Secure-Bank.Com (972-235-4772 / www.beseen.net/securebank)

- Superior Bankcard EZ Merchant (1-800-266-9650 / www.ezmerchantaccounts.com)

- USB Merchant Services (1-800-869-7170 / www.creditcards-atm.com)

The following companies are recommended by MasterCard if you're interested in acquiring a merchant account for your online business or e-commerce site:

Chase Merchant Services
1401 NW 136th Ave.
Sunrise, FL 33323
Phone: 1-800-622-2626

Comerica Merchant Alliance
P.O. Box 75000
Detroit, MI 48275-2430
Phone: 810-370-7162

"
[Your bank or credit card] will introduce you to professional services that can help you develop your Web site and get you on the Internet with applications for product display and ordering. They will also help you establish secure payment transaction systems based on MasterCard's SET protocol.
—MasterCard
"

Bright Idea
To learn more about the advantages of accepting credit cards, visit MasterCard's E-Commerce Merchant Model Web site and download the free interactive planning tool designed to help merchants evaluate the business potential of the Internet for their company. The site is located at www.mastercard.com/business/merchant/ecomm.html#top.

Harris Bankcard Center
700 E. Lake Cook Rd.
Buffalo Grove, IL 60089
Phone: 847-520-6405
www.harrisbank.com/smallbusinesses/
merchant/cihome.html

Keycorp
Merchant Services Customer Service
Department
55 Public Square, 7th Floor
Cleveland, OH 44113
Phone: 1-800-255-8425
www.keybank.com

Norwest Card Services
7000 Vista Dr.
W. Des Moines, IA 50266
Phone: 515-222-8163

Wells Fargo Bank
Merchant Card Services
1200 Montego Way
Walnut Creek, CA 94598
Phone: 510-746-4069

Financing your business

Securing adequate financing is a primary concern for most new businesses. Most people don't personally possess all the resources it takes to get a business up and running, but as a business owner you'll need to invest some of your own money. Putting your funds into a business venture helps prove your commitment to potential investors or other sources of financing.

Sources of financing include banks, the Small Business Administration (SBA), and private individuals. Be aware that many banks consider new business loans to be too risky, even when money is not tight. The SBA is usually eager to help new enterprises, but competition is keen for the SBA's limited loan guaranty support. Before applying for financing, you need to carefully prepare a thorough loan proposal.

Write up detailed figures on the capital needed, and be sure to include a salary for yourself and sufficient funds to cover start-up costs. A bank or SBA representative will review your business plan to be sure it's solid. Once you obtain a loan, you'll probably have to provide updated financial statements on a regular basis. As long as your business is profitable and you're making loan payments on time, you'll probably have minimum contact with the bank or SBA. Short-term loans may require closer bank monitoring.

No matter what type of business you plan on launching, it's going to require start-up capital (probably more than you think). Starting a business has a lot of expenses associated with it. After those expenses (which vary based on the type of business) are taken into account, you still need enough operating capital at the start to keep your business going for at least one year. Very few businesses become profitable immediately, and most of those that fail do so because there wasn't enough capital available.

Not every business has the same start-up expenses. Some of the costs you'll have to calculate into your budget and consider when creating your business plan include:

■ Accounting and consulting.

■ Advertising and public relations.

■ Business travel.

Bright Idea
You may consider seeking private investors who wish to have an equity stake in your business. Relatives or friends may be potential investors, too. Keep in mind, however, that these people may, understandably, expect to have a say in how the business is run. And if you tell them no, it can affect your relationship. Be sure you make the ground rules clear up front.

Watch Out!
Consult an accountant or lawyer to help you decide what legal form of business you want to establish. Making the wrong decision could lead to costly problems down the road, especially if your company fails or winds up being sued.

- Communications equipment (such as telephones, telephone service, cellular service, and pagers).
- Company cars and vehicles.
- Computer equipment and office technology (such as copy and fax machines).
- Custom-printed stationary, business cards, and envelopes.
- Insurance.
- Interest on loans.
- Internet Service Provider (ISP) fees.
- Inventory.
- Labor (salaries and payroll).
- Legal fees.
- Manufacturing equipment or specialized equipment.
- Marketing.
- Office furniture and fixtures.
- Office supplies.
- Order processing/shipping.
- Printing costs for brochures, press kits, and marketing materials.
- Recruiting.
- Rent.
- Salaries.
- Taxes.
- Utility bills (such as water, electricity, sewer, heat, and air conditioning).
- Web site design and maintenance.

After you've figured out exactly what it'll cost you to get your business up and running and fully operational for a least one year (although you'll eventually need projections for at least three to five years), you'll need to raise the necessary capital. Once again, you have many options available to you:

- Investing your own funds (using your savings, mortgaging your home, maxing out your credit cards, or taking out a personal loan)

- Seeking out independent partners and investors

- Obtaining small business loans from a financial institution

- Applying for state, federal, or private grants

- Borrowing money from close relatives or friends

- Winning the lottery (this is probably not a viable option, so don't rely on it)

Obviously, using your personal savings to launch your business provides you with the most freedom, but also exposes you to more risk if your business fails. Consult an accountant and lawyer to explore the various pros and cons of each option before deciding how you'll fund your business.

Just the facts

- For tax and legal reasons, you'll need to decide what form your business will take. Your choice of business form will affect your exposure to personal liability, how you draw profits and pay taxes, your ability to raise capital, and how you run the business.

- In order to be competitive in cyberspace, your business must accept credit cards by setting up a merchant account.

Timesaver
Save time when researching and narrowing venture capital options. Check out America's Business Funding Directory (www. businessfinance. com), an entrepreneurial database designed to match capital sources with people seeking funding. The service covers venture capital, equipment leasing, commercial real estate, SBA or SBIC loans, private investments, and more.

- Your business probably won't be profitable at first. Plan accordingly.
- Be sure you look into all the sources of financing available to you, including banks, the SBA, and your own funds.

GET THE SCOOP ON...
Choosing Web site creation software
▪ The basics of online graphic design
▪ Avoiding common Web design mistakes
▪ Using professionals

Planning Your Site

Chapter 4

The Internet's World Wide Web is packed with millions of Web sites. Some are interactive, highly professional, and eye-catching. Others look less professional, take too long to load, and offer poor design and layout, a bad choice of colors schemes, and ineffective or confusing text. These sites sometimes contain typos, are difficult to navigate, and have broken links or other problems that convey a poor image of the individual or company that developed the site. Even if such a site contains useful information or products, visitors probably won't stay long enough for the site to make any impact.

Making your site look professional

How do you make your site an attractive and useful one? Before you begin creating it, spend time surfing the Web looking for ideas. Determine what you think looks good and what Web site features you like, then figure out how you can incorporate those ideas into your site.

Timesaver
If you're looking for Web site design ideas, why not start by checking out the very best and busiest sites? Visit *PC Magazine*'s Top 100 Web Sites list at www.zdnet. com/pcmag/ special/web100/ index.html.

Even if you're not a programmer, don't know HTML (Hyper Text Markup Language) or Java programming, and aren't a graphic artist or a talented writer, you can still create an extremely impressive site using Web site creation software or services. Many commercial page-design software packages require no programming to create professional-looking Web pages. These packages (such as Microsoft FrontPage 98, FrontPage 2000, and Symantec's Visual Page) are bundled with predefined templates created by professional graphic artists. Templates make designing your basic site much faster and easier.

Using templates as a starting point, you can simply add your own text and graphics (and audio and video clips) to customize your site and make it look professional, with content that will interest potential customers.

There are also a growing number of complete e-commerce turnkey solutions available, such as Yahoo! Store (store.yahoo.com). These allow anyone to develop an online store quickly, using just a computer equipped with Internet access and Web browser software.

Whatever method you use, designing your site and creating the best content for it will take a considerable amount of time. Creativity is also important if you want to make your corner of cyberspace a unique, enjoyable, and informative place to visit.

Since your Web site is going be the primary way you interact with potential customers and clients, it's vital that your site convey a professional image. Your site must be:

- Easy to read and understand.
- Visually appealing.

- Simple to navigate through using any Web browser software.

- Fast-loading.

- Error-free (no broken links, misspellings, or inaccurate information).

- Loaded with the information your potential customers need and want.

Most importantly, your site must build up the confidence of your visitors, so they believe they're dealing with a highly reputable company. If you'll be taking orders for your products online, you must offer easy-to-understand order forms and make it clear to customers that they'll be participating in secure financial transactions online when visiting your site. This will make them more comfortable using their credit card to place orders.

Your site should answer the most common questions your customers will have, make full use of visuals to show off your products, and display your company's logo, address, e-mail address, and telephone number (preferably a toll-free number). Visitors should be able to contact you directly with questions and comments, or to place their order using an alternate method to online order processing.

While you might be tempted to load up your Web site with lots of flashy video and audio features, they can overwhelm visitors who aren't familiar with how to navigate the Web. In addition, the browser software many Web surfers use isn't equipped with the plug-ins that allow them to hear audio or see certain types of animated graphics.

Also, many people don't have the high-end video cards and monitors needed to display detailed *true color* (24-bit, 16-million color) graphics. If you attempt to incorporate high-resolution graphics

Unofficially...
True color or *24-bit color* is the color of a pixel on display screens using 24-bit value. This permits 16,777,216 different colors (2 to the 24th power). Many screens, however, can only accommodate eight-bit color, or 256 possible colors.

into your site, what many people will see is very different (and of much poorer quality) than what you intended.

As you develop your site, it's important to ensure that it is compatible with the major browser software packages (Microsoft Internet Explorer or Netscape Navigator). How your site looks when viewed with one browser may be totally different (in colors displayed and layout) from how it's displayed when viewed with another browser. The graphic resolution your visitor has set will also affect how she sees it. Some of the most common settings for graphic resolutions on a PC-based computer are 640 × 480, 800 × 600, 1024 × 768, 1152 × 870, 1280 × 1024, and 1600 × 1200. (Each has 256 colors, high color [16-bit] or true color [24-bit].)

People who can set their monitors to display graphics at higher resolutions have invested in high-end graphics cards and graphic accelerator cards. While this is changing as the price of high-end graphics cards and monitors decreases, most people use the 640 x 480 or 800 x 600 resolutions in 256 color mode.

If your online business will be targeting mass market customers on the Web, your best bet is to design your site so it can be easily viewed by the vast majority of Web surfers, without them having to adjust their display resolution or download additional plug-ins for their browser software.

Plug-in applications are programs that can be installed and used as part of your Web browser. For example, Adobe's Acrobat lets you view documents the way they look in print. Other plug-ins include RealNetworks' Streamvd player and Macromedia's Shockwave for Director, an interactive animation and sound player.

Bright Idea
For a list of popular browser plug-ins supported by Netscape Navigator, visit home.netscape.com/plugins/index.html. For information about the latest plug-ins supported by Microsoft Internet Explorer, visit windowsupdate.microsoft.com/default.htm?Page=productupdates, or use the Windows Update command found under the Tools pull-down menu of Explorer 4.0 (or later).

The first steps in developing your site

Before you start designing your site or putting it together, carefully evaluate and determine the exact purpose of your site. Ask yourself these questions:

- What messages or information do I want to convey?

- Will my site be an online extension of my existing business, used for customer service or technical support issues?

- Is the site being developed to enhance my existing company's image in cyberspace? Is it a marketing tool, public relations tool, sales tool, recruiting tool, or an all-purpose electronic commerce site?

- Will my site be an online catalog or interactive brochure for one or more products?

- What do I want visitors to be able to see and do when visiting my site?

- What is the overall goal of the site?

- Will I be accepting orders online?

- What features are important for my site to offer?

- How will my site be laid out and what will be contained in each of the pages? (Most sites contain a variety of individual Web pages.)

Developing your site's basic layout

One key ingredient to the success of any online business is the good design and simplicity of the site. When someone visits your site, she should find it intuitive to use and not at all confusing.

Unofficially...
When using product photos on your site, the pictures must be of professional quality and not look like they were taken with a Polaroid instant camera. Consider hiring a professional photographer to take photos and scan them. A graphic artist can also be used to create line art of your products, which will translate into smaller graphic files. Keep the image files as small as possible (for fast loading), but don't compromise on their clarity or quality.

The overall production values of your site will also go a long way toward boosting customer confidence. If a visitor to your site perceives it to be amateurish, she will leave and won't consider buying anything. In fact, the term "Web surfers" was coined because people exploring the Web have about the same attention span as a channel surfer watching television: short. If your Web site doesn't visually attract the attention of a visitor through high production values, the chances she'll stay long enough to read the text or look at the pictures is slim.

Thus, it's important to plan your site in advance, and determine what types of information will be available. You also need to think carefully about where and how that information will be conveyed.

Every Web site is comprised of text and images. Some images are photographs, while others are logos, line drawings, computer-generated graphics (bullets, arrows, lines), or animated graphics. The use of high-quality images is an absolute must on an e-commerce Web site or a site designed to generate business. As you choose which images will be incorporated into your site, keep in mind the file size of the image as well as the color scheme. For example, the background color of your product shots or the color of your logo should fit well into the overall color scheme of your site. Using colors that clash will detract from the professional appearance of your site.

Choosing the perfect content

You and the people helping you design your site are the only ones who can ultimately determine what the best content is for your site, because you know your company's products and services and who your target audience is. Remember, what you say, how you say it, and the graphic images you use will play a major role in the success or failure of your site. One advantage of the Web, however, is that things can be changed almost instantaneously; if something isn't working or you develop an idea that will improve something about your site, it can be fixed and uploaded quickly and easily.

Some of the important areas or pages of any online business (e-commerce) site include:

Home page When someone enters your Uniform Resource Locater (URL) (www. yourcompany.com) into their Net browser, they should be taken directly to your home page. Think of it as the main lobby of your store. It should list your company's name, display your logo, and immediately inform visitors what type of content is offered on the site. The home page can also be used to offer news items, such as information about a highlighted product or an item that's on sale. As an alternative to making the home page the first place a visitor to your site sees, you can start her at a "splash screen," a blank screen containing a short welcome message and/or your logo. A visitor must then click her mouse on the splash screen to enter the main areas of your site.

Company information/background Before people place an order with your company, they'll probably want to know something about your company—especially if they've never done business with you before. Use this page of your site to tell people about your company's background and boost their confidence in your company's products.

Product description pages   If you're developing an e-commerce site, these pages will describe each of your products in detail. In addition to offering detailed descriptions, prices, and ordering information, seriously consider offering a product photo and technical specifications, just as you would if you were creating a mail-order catalog or full-color sales brochure for the product. Using product photos in your site is an absolute must, but to keep the download time of your site short, use thumbnail images which a surfer can click on to see a larger version of the photo. A thumbnail image is a small-size photo which downloads very quickly. There's no need for someone to wait for a large photo to load if it's not something they're interested in.

News, sales, specials, and promotions   This page conveys company or industry-oriented news, late-breaking details about new or forthcoming products, information about special sales, or other information your visitors might be interested in. One way to keep people coming back to your site is to provide an ongoing and reliable source for information about a specific topic. Yet another way to get people excited about your site is to hold contests or special promotions, allowing visitors to win prizes.

Answers to common questions/technical support   Whether customers are shopping in a retail store or online, they'll have questions about the products you're offering, no matter how detailed your descriptions are. In a traditional retail store, a customer with a question can just ask the salesperson. In cyberspace, the

Watch Out!
Using large images, especially on your site's home page, may be a huge mistake because they take longer to load. (The size of the image refers to the file size in bytes, not the physical size of the photo as it actually appears on your site.) Instead, consider a series of small images.

customer should be able to call a toll-free phone number, send an e-mail message, or send the company a letter via fax or U.S. mail. If you tend to get people asking the same questions over and over, you might consider creating a Frequently Asked Questions (FAQ) page for your site. This document should be written in an easy-to-understand question and answer format, and address the most common questions and concerns among your customers. A well-written FAQ that's available on your site should reduce the number of questions and technical support inquiries your company receives.

Some of the questions you might want to address in a FAQ document as well as in the main body of your site include: What forms of payment does your company accept? How will the products ordered on your site be shipped? How long before shipping? What are the shipping costs? What are the shipping options? What is the sales tax policy of your online store? If a customer needs to speak with a customer service/technical support representative, how and when can someone be reached (and during what hours)? Does your site offer secure online ordering? Aside from ordering online, what other options do customers have? (For example, can orders be faxed, e-mailed, or called in?) What is your return or exchange policy? What guarantees and warranties does your company offer? Do you accept international orders? If so, what's the ordering procedure? What about additional overseas shipping charges and taxes? Will you meet or beat your competition's prices?

Watch Out!
If you use a carrier like FedEx or UPS that guarantees certain delivery times, part of the order-taking process should convey to the customers exactly when they can expect to receive the product they're about to order. Because Web surfers demand fast responses, it's important to be able to offer immediate shipping.

Customer testimonials   If you have a handful of highly satisfied customers who have written you letters, you might want to obtain permission to reproduce these letters online as part of your site. A potential customer will find it reassuring to read testimonials from other happy customers. Of course, if you have a celebrity endorsing your product, this, too, is an extremely powerful marketing tool that goes a long way toward boosting a potential customer's confidence. For example, if you visit the official Billy Blanks' Tae*Bo Web site at www.taebo.com (used to promote and sell Tae*Bo fitness products), you'll see a link on the site's main page leading to several celebrity endorsements as well as endorsements from non-celebrities.

Online ordering   One of the biggest challenges you'll face is designing an order form that's comprehensive, informative, and easy to understand. Otherwise, you risk scaring off a potential customer. Before designing your online order form, determine exactly what information you need to gather from the customer. This information might include the customer's name, title, company name, billing and shipping address (street address, city, state, zip), phone number, fax number, e-mail address, name of products they want to order, product numbers, quantities, sizes, and monogramming information. Your site may also need to be able to automatically calculate numbers, such as order subtotals, sales tax, and shipping charges. Finally, your order forms need to spell out exactly what forms of payment you accept, such as checks, cash, money orders, and credit cards. You must convince the customer that she's participating in a totally secure online transaction before she'll provide confidential credit card information. You might also want to develop a "shopping cart" feature into your site, so visitors can easily gather items to purchase, continue shopping, and then place their order for several items in one shot.

Order response screens/e-mail messages After someone places an order, she should immediately see an acknowledgement screen stating that her order has been received, what her order number is, and when she can expect her order to be shipped and to arrive. Of course, you also want to thank the customer for her order! In addition to this order confirmation screen, it's an excellent customer relations strategy to send the customer an e-mail, again thanking her and confirming the details of the order.

E-commerce, the sale of products and services on the Web, is still a relatively new industry, compared to retail stores or mail-order catalogs. Thus, no Web site design is guaranteed to work, and no e-commerce model is fool-proof. As you develop your site, plan to experiment and allow your site to evolve over time.

Just as with a printed document or advertisement, a Web page can be decorative, colorful, informative, nicely laid out, well-organized, and visually appealing. If you're not careful, however, it can also become a confusing hodge-podge of text, pictures, and graphics.

Bright Idea
No matter how
well you think
your site turns
out, plan on
updating and
modifying it
often if you want
people to come
back. If you can
get customers in
the habit of vis-
iting your site
daily or weekly
through offering
new content,
your chances of
repeat orders
increase
dramatically.

Throughout the design process, keep in mind that in most cases, your goal isn't to wow visitors with flashy graphics, but to provide a comfortable environment in which they can shop. Likewise, just as major department stores change their displays regularly to keep shoppers coming back, the content and even the design of your site should change periodically in order to keep people interested and keep the content fresh.

Once you've determined your target audience and the information about your company and product you want to convey, the planning of your Web site design is a highly creative process. Sure, basic rules of graphic design apply, but at the same time, there's plenty of room for creativity. As a general rule, however, keep the site simple. Only use pictures and graphics that add meaning or value to your site; use fonts, typestyles, and color schemes that are visually appealing and will appear consistent, no matter which browser software someone is using. The fonts and typestyles you choose to convey your text-based information should be readily supported by the most common Web Browser programs. This will ensure that your Web site design is actually displayed exactly how you want it to appear. If you incorporate an unusual font that a program such as Microsoft Explorer doesn't recognize, it will automatically be converted into a more familiar font, but that will change the overall look of your site.

Using color and art

Before you start creating your site, gather all of the visual assets available to you. This includes logos, artwork, images, sound clips, video clips, and any other elements that can be incorporated into your site. Once you know what assets are available, you'll be able to make intelligent and creative decisions to use these assets to get your key messages across to your site's visitors. Always be thinking about who your target customers are and how to address them.

Regarding color, most computers can display 256 colors. However, Mac and Windows browsers have a different set of 256 colors. And if you use a color that isn't part of the palette on your visitor's browser, the browser has to "dither"—attempting to match the color as closely as possible. Unfortunately, dithering can result in a grainy appearance and detract from the design of your site. So be sure to choose your colors from among the 216 colors that are common to both browsers.

Colors are like words; just as context can alter the meaning of a word or phrase, surrounding colors can make a central color look different to the human eye. Experiment and see what effects the colors have on one another. As you do this, consider the color of your text, backgrounds, supporting graphics, and so on.

PaletteMan (www.paletteman.com) is one color palette generation program geared toward Web designers. Using this site, you can select five colors from the 216-color web-safe palette and see how they look. You can also use Expressive Systems Group (www.eons.com/216color.htm). Other useful Web sites that help to explain the use of the "browser-safe palette" include Web Safe Color Palette (www.visibone.com/colorlab) and Commercial Photograph Library (www.photodisc.com/am/default.asp).

Watch Out!
When adding standard text to your site, use underlines as little as possible or not at all. On the Web, underlined text usually signifies a hyperlink. If text is underlined, a Web surfer expects to be able to click on that text in order to find out more information about a specific topic.

Choosing the best fonts

Fonts and typestyles play a huge role in the overall look of your site. The font you use can help set your site's attitude. Keep in mind, however, that using too many fonts on a single page can make reading any type of text confusing. Likewise, you want to avoid mixing too many type sizes, and avoid using too much bold, italics, or underlining. If you incorporate unusual or non-standard fonts into your Web site, the only way to assure that a viewer sees a particular font the way it's intended is to make the text actually a graphic. This, however, is very expensive in terms of memory. It's a trade-off.

In terms of deciding how text should appear on the screen, it's safe to follow the same graphic design rules you'd use for any type of traditional printed media. There are thousands of possible fonts to choose from, but for large amounts of text, it's best to stick with an easy-to-read font that looks good on the screen. To see samples of some of the fonts available to you, visit store.yahoo.com/vw/fonsam.html.

Keep in mind that every font has a variety of different typestyles that you can use to communicate with, including normal text, **bold** text, and *italic* text. There's also superscript and subscript. Since Web pages are displayed in full-color, you can also alter the color of your text, using bright colors (like red) to catch the readers' attention or emphasize a keyword or important point.

On a Web site, text can also be animated. You can make words flash on and off, rotate, shake, or do a wide range of other things in order to capture the reader's attention. The look of your text is as important as what the text says, if not more important. After all, if a viewer perceives your text as too wordy or confusing based on the layout, font size, or color, she's less likely to keep reading. It's important to balance readability with aesthetics when choosing the appropriate fonts and typestyles for your site.

Types of graphic files

Graphic files—whether a company or product logo, product photos, Web site backgrounds, small animations, Web buttons or bars—or anything else that's non-text-oriented can be created in several popular and well-supported formats for use on a Web page. The following is some detailed information about each popular graphic file format. In a nutshell, however, GIF images are excellent for displaying small graphic files, such as logos or pieces of line art, while JPEG images are better suited for displaying photographs and other types of highly detailed images.

TIFFs

Whatis.com is a Web site that offers definitions and descriptions of computer terms. The site is designed for non-technically oriented people and can be used to help you better understand technical lingo. This is a free service.

According to Whatis.com,

> A TIFF [Tag Image File Format] file can be identified as a file with a '.tiff' or '.tif' file name suffix [extension] …. One of the most common graphic image formats, TIFF files are commonly used in desktop publishing, faxing, 3-D applications, and medical imaging applications.

Bright Idea
To learn more about fonts and type-styles, visit the Adobe Web site at www.adobe.com. Another excellent resource is The FontSite (www.fontsite.com).

GIFs

Whatis.com reports,

> *The GIF…format is actually owned by*
> *CompuServe, and companies that make products*
> *that exploit the format [but not ordinary Web*
> *users or businesses that include GIFs in their*
> *pages] need to license its use …. There are two*
> *versions of the format, 87a and 89a. Version*
> *89a allows for the possibility of an animated*
> *GIF, which is a short sequence of images within*
> *a single GIF file. A GIF89a can also be specified*
> *for interlaced presentation. An interlaced GIF is*
> *a GIF image that seems to arrive on your dis-*
> *play like an image coming through a slowly-*
> *opening Venetian blind. A fuzzy outline of an*
> *image is gradually replaced by seven successive*
> *waves of bit streams that fill in the missing lines*
> *until the image arrives at its full resolution.*
> *Among the advantages for the viewer using*
> *14.4 Kbps and 28.8 Kbps modems are that the*
> *wait time for an image seems less and the viewer*
> *can sometimes get enough information about the*
> *image to decide to click on it or move elsewhere.*
> *GIFs are typically used for logos, and relatively*
> *flat color pictures. GIF compression retains the*
> *entire image, as opposed to JPEG images.*

Using an online utility called GifWizard (www.
gifwizard.com), you can greatly reduce the size of
your site's GIF files, making them load faster.

JPEGs

According to Whatis.com,

> *A JPEG (pronounced JAY-peg) is a graphic*
> *image created by choosing from a range of*

GifWizard is a tool that allows Web site designers to shrink the size of their graphic files and speed up download times for their Web pages.

> *compression qualities .... When you create a JPEG or convert an image from another format to a JPEG, you are asked to specify the quality of image you want.*

In order to obtain the highest quality graphic, you're going to create a file that takes up a lot of memory, which results in longer download times. It's possible to deduce the quality of the JPEG image, resulting in a smaller file size and faster download time, but you're making a trade-off. For the Web, it's usually not critical to have extremely detailed photographs. A lower resolution photo will usually work just as well. The higher the compression you use to compress a JPEG file, the more of the image is "thrown away". The process is not reversible, so be sure to save your original file in case you need to revert back to it later.

There are many online sources of free Web site graphics. Some companies also specialize in creating customized graphics and offer large libraries of precreated graphics that can be incorporated into

Timesaver
If you're looking for an extensive stock photo library, visit www.fotosearch.com. Here, you'll find thousands of photos that can be licensed and used on your site.

any e-commerce Web site. Webpromotions, Inc. (www.webpromotion.com) is just one company that offers a full range of graphic design and Web page design services. The company also offers a three CD-ROM artwork collection for about $100, containing over 100 animated graphic elements that can be used royalty-free. Free samples are available at webpromotion.com/propak3.html.

The Publishing Perfection Catalog (www. publishingperfection.com / 1-800-387-2164) is full of useful commercial software tools and CD-ROM-based graphic libraries available to Web site designers. One product in this catalog, WebSpice 1,000,000 (from DeMorgan), offers over one million buttons, arrows, rules, bullets, and other images that can be used within Web sites. Another library, WebSpice Themes for FrontPage 98, offers 1,250 themes and dozens of templates designed to make it easier to create a Web page with Microsoft's FrontPage software.

On the Web, you'll find a vast source of exciting public domain Web graphics you can download for free. Some of these graphics are animated (and called animated GIFs). Others are still images or graphics. Using any Internet search engine, type in the search phrase "Web graphics" or "animated GIFs," for example, to find graphics you can download for your site. One source of free Web artwork (including animated GIFs, backgrounds, and themes) is Webpedia Animation Archive (www. webpedia.com/animations). Other excellent clip art and graphic resources are Clip-Art.Com (www. clip-art.com) and Free Stuff Center (www. freestuffcenter.com/graphics.html).

While some artwork is free on the Web and can be downloaded and used in your site in a matter of seconds, keep in mind that a lot of the artwork you'll see on other sites is copyrighted. Thus, before using that artwork, you must obtain permission from the artwork's creator or the Webmaster of the site where you found the artwork. In Appendix D, information about copyrights and trademarks is provided.

How can you download a non-copyrighted piece of artwork you find on the Web? While using your Web browser software, position your mouse on top of the graphic you want to download. Next, click the right mouse button. Choose the "Save Picture As..." option, then choose the location on your hard drive where you want to save the graphic file. Once the file is on your hard drive, you can import it into any Web site creation software, adjust its size, position, and so forth, and then incorporate it into your site. Note that resizing an animated GIF image may render it motionless.

Graphics programs

To ensure that your site will look original, consider developing some of your own artwork. Computer graphics for use on a Web site can be created using a number of commercially available graphics programs, such as:

- Adobe PhotoShop 5.0 (www.adobe.com/ prodindex/photoshop/main.html).

- Paint Shop Pro 5 (http://www.jasc.com).

- Adobe Illustrator (www.adobe.com/prodin-dex/illustrator/main.html).

- Corel Draw 8 (www.corel.com).

- Corel Xara! 2.0 (www.corel.com).

- Macromedia Fireworks (www.macromedia. com/software/fireworks).

Moneysaver
Free download-able trial ver-sions of the graphics pro-grams listed here are available from each com-pany's Web site.

Using a graphics program to create your own graphics requires knowledge of how to use the software in addition to some artistic ability.

In addition to downloading graphic files from the Web, purchasing graphic libraries on CD-ROM, or creating your own images using a graphics program, other ways you can create or obtain photos or graphic images for your site include:

- Using a scanner to import printed images (photos, line drawings, and other artwork). A scanner will create a digital image saved in one of the popular graphic file formats that can then be incorporated into your site.

- Using a digital camera.

- Hiring a graphic artist to create customized banners, icons, backgrounds, or other Web graphics.

Choosing Web site creation software or another e-commerce solution

This section provides information if you'll be developing a start-up business online or developing a relatively small e-commerce site. To accomplish this, you can:

Custom-program your site from scratch using HTML and Java programming. This option could involve hiring a programmer, graphic designer, and/or writer. Programming knowledge is required. Once you understand the HTML programming language, all you need is a simple program, such as the Super Note Tab text editor (a shareware program) to begin writing code and creating your site. Many off-the-shelf Web site software packages allow you to program using HTML and/or Java.

Use commercially available Web site creation software, such as Microsoft FrontPage 98. With this, you can design a professional-looking site with little or no programming knowledge required.

Take advantage of a full service provider, which is a glorified ISP offering both Web site creation and hosting services. No programming knowledge is required.

If you're planning to start off with a major financial investment in the creation and marketing of your site, there are several high-priced (over $5,000) e-commerce solutions available, such as the services available from IBM Net.Commerce (www.software.ibm.com/commerce/net.commerce), iCat Professional Electronic Commerce Suite (carbo.icat.com/icat/business/register.icl), and Microsoft Site Server Commerce (www.microsoft.com/siteserver/commerce).

E-commerce software solutions for small online businesses

The following are inexpensive Web site design software packages. This is only a small sampling of the many software packages available to help you create a highly professional Web site for e-commerce applications.

Microsoft FrontPage 98/FrontPage 2000

FrontPage (www.microsoft.com/frontpage) is a popular Web site creation and management program. While FrontPage is an all-purpose Web site creation tool and includes a wide range of precreated templates, if you're planning on establishing a complete e-commerce solution based around

Unofficially...
While using
FrontPage doesn't
require any pro-
gramming knowl-
edge, it does
require some
familiarity with
the use of
Windows 95/98
and related pro-
grams, plus a
basic under-
standing of Web
page design.

the FrontPage software, you'll need an optional add-on module called JustAddCommerce from Rich Media Technologies, Inc. (www.richmediatech. com/jacmain.html).

FrontPage software is well supported by Microsoft and many third-party developers, so finding precreated templates is easy. You're also likely to find full compatibility with virtually all ISPs.

There are many books, videos, and other training materials available that can help you learn to use this program in order to develop and maintain highly professional Web sites. Microsoft also offers extensive online support, free Web site development tools and content, and a variety of other resources to help users of FrontPage. FrontPage 98 retails for under $200. (Pricing for FrontPage 2000 unavailable at press time.) A Macintosh version of this software is available.

Symantec Visual Page 2.0

Like FrontPage, Visual Page (www.symantec. com/vpage) from Symantec is an all-purpose Web design software package that can be used to create and maintain any type of Web site. The software is inexpensive, relatively easy to use, and offers a wide range of precreated templates and features.

Visual Page release 2.x has an estimated retail price of about $100. A free, 30-day trial version of the software can be downloaded from the company's Web site.

Additional inexpensive software packages for e-commerce

Buildashop Standard 6.0 Published by Rocketfuel Software (ignite.rocketfuel.com/

home), this software is priced under $100, but you're required to use the company's secure Web server as your ISP in order to accept secure order transactions. The company charges $1 per transaction, with a $10 per month minimum. The main portion of your site needs to be hosted by an independent ISP.

Online Merchant Published by Alpha Software (www.alphasoftware.com or www.onlinemerchant.com), this software is also priced under $100.

ShopSite Manager 3.3 Published by Open Market (www.openmarket.com), this program is priced just under $500.

Virtual Spin Internet Store Published by Virtual Spin (www.virtualspin.com), this software package offers a mid-priced e-commerce solution (starting at just under $400) to develop an e-store with up to 100 items. The price includes six months of service. A 12-month contract is available for just under $600.

WebBusiness Builder Published by IMSI Software (www.imsisoft.com), this software package sells for under $100. WebBusiness Builder uses a step-by-step multimedia tutorial to help even beginners create their own on-line store.

Timesaver
For reviews of many software packages designed to help you set up your online store, visit the C/Net Builder.Com Web site at www.builder.com/Business.

An up-close look at Yahoo! Store

One of the best and most flexible complete turnkey solutions for e-commerce comes from Yahoo! (store.yahoo.com). For an initial investment of about $100 per month, you can set up and operate

The popular Yahoo! Store offers an online-based, complete turnkey solution for online business operators of all sizes. It's inexpensive yet extremely powerful.

an online business, with no programming knowledge.

Using Yahoo! Store as your turnkey e-commerce solution offers many benefits. Everything is done online, without special software. In addition to providing design elements to help you create your site, Yahoo! lets you register your own domain name and URL. Yahoo! Store also offers a free service that other turnkey operations charge extra for—secure order transactions using industry-standard SSL (Secure Socket Layer) encryption.

Once your site is operational, your URL will immediately be listed with all of the major search engines if you've used Yahoo! Store. MetaTags will be added to your site. A MetaTag is a few lines of HTML programming incorporated into your site that make it easier for the various search engines to categorize your site and make it available to surfers. As you'll see, adding MetaTags to a Web site is easy, and doing this will help generate traffic to your site.

If you're a start-up company with a handful of products (fewer than 51), the price of using the Yahoo! Store service is $100 per month. There are no per-transaction fees, start-up costs, or minimum time commitments.

Thousands of companies use Yahoo! Store as their primary e-commerce solution. To see firsthand the capabilities of Yahoo! Store and how diverse the look of your site can be, check out some of the companies operating on the Web using this service. You should use the same procedure for any turnkey solution you are considering: Be sure to look at how they've served other e-commerce businesses and see if you are pleased with the results. Yahoo! Store's clients include:

Bugleboy	st2.yahoo.net/bugleboy
Buy.com	st5.yahoo.net/buycomp/
Cambridge Soundworks	st7.yahoo.net/ cambridgesoundworks/
Cirque du Soleil	st3.yahoo.net/ cirquestore/
Crabtree & Evelyn	st2.yahoo.net/ shopcrabtree/
Egghead.com	www.egghead.com
FAO Schwartz	st2.yahoo.net/ faoschwartz/
FTD Flowers	st1.yahoo.net/ftd/
International Male	st1.yahoo.net/intmale/
Lifetime TV	www.lifetimetv.com/ shopping/
Omaha Steaks	st6.yahoo.net/cc5892/
The Vermont Teddy Bear Company	st1.yahoo.net/vtbear/

Copyrighting

As you search through the Web gathering ideas, you may run across art, designs, photos, and texts you'd like to use for your own site. If you use these only as inspiration but create all new material for your site, copyright issues probably won't affect you directly. But if you are planning on taking some elements and directly incorporating them into your site, you'll need to brush up on your copyright law. In the appendix, we give you some detailed information on the matter. As a general rule of thumb, however, remember that when in doubt, assume the material is protected. It's always better to omit something you could have used than include it and find yourself bombarded with threatening letters from another company. Your incentive should be moral as well as legal. If you invest money on a good logo or good writing, you would think it unfair for your competitor to incorporate your work without paying for it. Apply the same standard to your own actions.

Avoiding the most common Web design mistakes

So far, we've talked about what you *should* do. It might be helpful, however, to look at things from the opposite perspective. There are certain common mistakes Web designers make when creating a site to be used for e-commerce or to generate business. By familiarizing yourself with them, you can learn not to repeat them at your own site:

- **Poor spelling, grammar, or punctuation.** Proofread all of the text in your site. There should be absolutely no editing mistakes. If necessary, hire a professional writer and/or copy editor to proofread your online content before making it available to the public. Don't just rely on the spell checker built into your word processor or Web site creation software. (As any writer can attest, sometimes you type in the wrong word, spelled correctly.)

■ **Excessive file size.** When choosing images for your site, make sure the file size of the electronic image isn't too large. Otherwise, it will take too long to load, and many Web surfers have no patience. They probably won't wait one, two, or three minutes for a Web page to load.

■ **Poor photo quality.** If you'll be using photographs on your site, make sure they appear crystal clear and in focus. The viewer should be able to make out visual details of the product. The quality of your photos will play a major role in building customer confidence. The overall professional image of your site is at stake. Avoid using photos that are out of focus, take too long to load, look amateurish, or add nothing to the overall content quality of your site.

■ **Incompatibility.** When choosing colors of backgrounds, text, and even graphic images, maintain continuity throughout your site, paying careful attention to making your site compatible with all of the popular Web browser programs. From a graphic design standpoint, the overall color scheme you choose should be friendly and easy on the eyes, and shouldn't clash.

■ **Frames.** Avoid using frames! They can be used so visitors can view several windows worth of information simultaneously. But this often

Unofficially...
To learn the basics about registering a trademark, an electronic brochure called *Basic Facts About Registering a Trademark* can be downloaded for free from the following site: www.uspto. gov./web/offices /tac/doc/basic.

makes a site confusing to look at and to navigate.

- **Poor directions.** While your goal is to get visitors to visit your main home page first and then navigate through your site from there, this doesn't always happen. Some Web search engines will send surfers directly to the page of a site that contains the keyword or search phrase they were looking for. As a result, they may find themselves visiting a sub-page of your site and not know where they are. To compensate for this, every page of your site should contain your company name and logo, a navigation bar or buttons, and an easy way for the visitor to return to your home page.

- **Hidden navigation icons.** Place your navigation icons for your site near the top of every page, so people don't have to scroll to the bottom of a page to determine where they should go next. This is referred to as placement "above the fold," using the phrase borrowed from newspaper publishing, where lead stories are placed in the top half of the front page, above where larger newspapers are folded. In this case, "above the fold" refers to the top half of the screen, where the icons are easily visible without the surfer having to scroll down.

- **Excessive scroll.** As you plan each page on your site, don't make the visitor scroll too much. Keep the information on each page short and to the point, then have her click on a "Next" icon to view another screen's worth of information, or a "Home" button to return to your site's home page. You can also offer buttons that will link to other areas of your site. The visitor

Watch Out!
Don't go overboard with Internet graphics technology. Remember that the point of your site is to convey information, inspire confidence, and convince the visitor to buy your product or service. Keep it simple and to the point.

should not have to look for these navigational buttons or read too much text to figure out what each page of your site is all about.

- **Poor targeting.** Make sure all of the content of your site is directed to your target audience. If you don't understand who your target customers are, what their needs are, and what they're looking for, you have little hope of providing a product that addresses their needs. Even if you have the perfect product for your target customer, make sure your site conveys this information clearly.

- **Too much information.** Unlike print materials and radio or television advertising, the Web is interactive. Make sure you reshape information from your traditional advertising to take full advantage of these interactive qualities. Instead of inundating the viewer of your site with tons of information on one page, spread it out, going from the general to the specific, allowing people to click on hyperlinks for more additional information about specific topics.

- **Sensory overload.** Too many Web sites add tons of bells and whistles, such as flashy graphics, audio, animation, video, too many fonts and typestyles, and busy backgrounds just to get a visitor's attention. This is overkill. Instead, focus on the facts you're trying to convey to the visitor, and use only those Web technologies and features that will help you to get your most important points across. For example, instead of several pages of text, perhaps a single color photograph will convey an important point. As the saying goes, "A picture is worth a thousand words." Also, it's easy to understand and takes

Bright Idea
As you're planning your site, develop storyboards or flow charts to help you graphically plan out the layout of your site and how each page will look. Remember, ease of navigation and continuity is important.

less time for the viewer to comprehend and digest.

■ **Shifting styles.** Once you choose a color scheme, background, and font group for your site, stick to it to maintain visual continuity. You don't want your site to appear overly busy or confusing because you used too many fonts/typestyles, or because each page has a totally different look, layout, and design. Set design standards for your site and stick to them.

■ **Poor choice of fonts.** Some fonts simply don't look good when viewed using Web browser software. Likewise, if the text is too small, it becomes very difficult to read. Stick with a basic font size of 10 to 12 points. The most common fonts to use include Helvetica and Times-Roman. They are easy to read and visually appealing.

■ **Being pushy.** Never force visitors to your site to register or provide personal information about themselves until they're ready to place an order. Likewise, if you're going to offer a free mailing list, encourage people to register to receive free information, but don't force them to register simply so you can build your mailing list.

Using outside creative talent

If you're making any type of financial investment in your online business, you might consider tapping the talents of professionals to help design and launch your site. This could mean hiring a Web site design service or individual programmers to create the site, graphic designers to develop the visual layout of the site, and/or hiring professional writers to create the text for the site.

Some companies and consultants work on a per-project basis, others get paid by the hour. You'll find an abundance of available talent using the Yellow Pages or any Internet search engine (enter a search phrase like "Web Site Design" or "Web Graphics" or "Web Site Programmer"). You might also consider soliciting referrals from other people. As you determine whom you might hire, ask to see specific examples of their work that relates to Web site design or specifically e-commerce Web sites. Also, have the agency or freelance person submit a formal written proposal and price quote based on your specific needs.

For a directory of Web site designers that are part of Yahoo! Store's referral program, visit store.yahoo.com/vw/partdir.html.

Just the facts

- Before you begin creating your own site, spend a considerable amount of time surfing the Web looking for ideas. Determine what features you like and how to incorporate them into your site.

- Avoid the temptation of overloading your Web site with flashy animated graphics, audio clips, and video clips. You don't want to overwhelm your visitors.

- Before you design or create your site, you must carefully evaluate and determine the exact purpose of your site and who it's targeting.

- Plan out your site. One of the first things a visitor to your site will notice is how well it's laid out and how intuitive it is to navigate through.

- You don't need a knowledge of Web design to create an online store or Web site. You can use

Moneysaver
The younger generation is computer-savvy. Consider tapping the talents of high school or college students familiar with Web site design, graphic design, marketing/advertising, photography, or journalism. A dedicated intern might well produce work as impressive as most professionals, if not better.

general purpose, commercially available software.

- As you begin creating your site, be careful that the content you add doesn't violate any other individual or company's copyrights or trademarks.

Getting Your Business Online

PART II

GET THE SCOOP ON...
Choosing the best domain name for your
online biz ▪ Researching and registering
domain names ▪ Costs ▪ When the name
you want is taken ▪ Where to get help

Selecting and Registering Your Domain Name

Chapter 5

What's in a name? When it comes to choosing the domain name for your online business, the name you choose is everything, so keep it simple. The domain name you choose becomes your identity on the Internet's World Wide Web. Ideally, you want a name that's very easy to remember, easy to pronounce, and easy to spell—one that people will instantly associate with your company, product, or service.

Internet commerce is poised to become one of the most profitable business opportunities in the twenty-first century, so it's important for your online business to be readily accessible by potential consumers. Even if you manage to come up with the absolutely perfect product to sell online and you also create an awesome Web site, if the domain name you choose isn't easy to remember and associate with your company, your online business will suffer.

Unofficially...
Forrester Research has projected that by the year 2001, over $546 billion in annual online transactions and sales will take place. That figure will only grow as more and more people throughout the world go online.

With all of the hype surrounding the Internet, rumors are flying that all of the domain names are being taken, and pretty soon there won't be any left. This is a major misconception! While it is true that many of the most desirable domain names ending with the *.com* extension have already been registered, there are still plenty of domain names available; moreover, many other extensions will be created in the future, as they become needed.

Understanding domain name syntax

While a domain name helps Web surfers find a Web site quickly and easily, the Internet itself and the Web browser software used to surf the Internet don't pay any attention to the alphanumeric name you register for your site. When a new domain name is registered, you'll be required to provide a numeric address, called the IP (Internet Protocol). An IP is a set of four numbers separated by a period that will be assigned by your Internet Service Provider (ISP). Each number can be between 0 and 255. For example, an IP address could be 129.52.0.203. This string of numbers is the actual address of your site, telling computers where your site can be found on the Internet.

When someone types your Web site's domain name into their browser software, the Domain Name System (DNS) automatically translates Web site names (such as www.your-domain-name.com) into the corresponding numeric IP address, which allows Web browser software to locate and access the Web pages.

Main URL features

A typical Web site's URL (uniform resource locator) looks something like this:

http://www.yourdomainname.com

or

http://www.your-domain-name.com

In reality, the domain name itself is divided into three distinct parts. The part that starts with *http://www* is common to most Web site addresses on the World Wide Web. This is the uniform resource locator (URL) used by Web browsers to find Web pages. The second part of the domain name is the part you actually get to choose. The third part of the domain name is the extension (e.g., .com, .edu, or .org). As you begin to think of the perfect domain names for your online business, consider the following:

- Only letters, numbers, and the hyphen (-) can be used in a domain name. Punctuation marks, such as a period, exclamation point, colon, and forward or back slash are not allowed. In addition, no spaces are allowed in the name. If necessary, use an underscore ('_') to indicate a space.

- A domain name can be up to 26 characters long, but this includes the extension at the end of the domain name (such as *.com, .edu, .org,* and *.net*).

- The domain name you choose must be unique and can't already be registered by someone else.

Domain names are not case sensitive, so you can't combine upper- and lowercase letters to create a unique domain name. As you promote your site, however, you can list the domain name using both

Bright Idea
Don't worry that "all the good names are taken." With the *.com* extension alone, there are 31,700,000,000 trillion possible domain names. At this time, only a few million of them have been used.

upper- and lowercase, since all Web browser software (such as Microsoft Internet Explorer or Netscape Navigator) will automatically translate the address entered into lower case. For example, to make your name more memorable, you can promote www.yourdomainname.com as www.YourDomainName.com. The name www.your-domain-name.com, however, is a totally different domain name that would need to be registered separately.

Many people surf the Internet and randomly type in Web site addresses based on the topics they're looking for, in hopes of luckily hitting a site that interests them. Thus, you want your domain name to be somewhat obvious. Network Solutions, Inc., calls this type of traffic "guess traffic" because you receive visits to your site from people who don't specifically know your Web address, but who find your Internet site by guessing. For example, someone looking to order flowers online might instinctively try to visit the Web site www.flowers.com or www.1800flowers.com. The first is an obvious choice, and the second might be used if that person had called 1-800-FLOWERS in the past and figured the company might also have a Web site.

Several million Web sites ending with the *.com* extension have already been registered. As a result, many of the one-word generic domain names you might think of to describe your company, product, or service might already be taken. You'll probably have better luck registering a domain name that combines two or three words.

Common extensions

All Web site addresses end with some type of extension, such as *.com, .net, .org, .gov*, or *.edu*. There are,

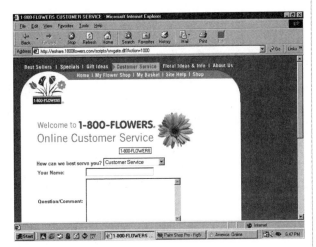

www.1800flowers.com (the Web site for 1-800-Flowers) is a good example of a domain name that is easy to guess and remember.

however, new extensions being created now that the Internet's World Wide Web has become an extremely busy and crowded place. Based on the type of Web site you're creating, there are guidelines for which extension you're supposed to use. The accompanying box gives a summary of what each U.S.-based extension means and what it can be used for (other extensions are available for domains registered in other countries). New extensions are always being created or adapted for more general use.

As this book is being written, additional extensions under consideration for adoption in the U.S. included: *.firm* (for businesses), *.store* (for e-commerce-based Web sites), *.web* (for sites emphasizing activities related to the World Wide Web), *.arts* (for Web sites with content relating to cultural- and entertainment-oriented activities), *.rec* (for Web sites relating to recreation), and *.info* (for Web sites providing information).

Bright Idea
The *.com* Web site extension has been around since 1985, and most Internet surfers automatically enter a *.com* extension when surfing, out of habit. Thus, it's an excellent idea to have your domain name end with this extension, even though others are available.

EXTENSION	DESCRIPTION
.com	Designed for use by commercial businesses.
.net	Designed for network-related organizations.
.edu	Designed for four-year degree-granting educational institutions (or other educational organizations).
.gov or **.mil**	Available to United States Government agencies, including the U.S. military. For more information, visit www.registration.fed.gov or www.nic.mil.
.us	Available to local, regional, or state government agencies, in addition to K–12 schools, community colleges, technical/vocational schools, private schools, and libraries.
.org	Available to non-profit organizations.
.to	This is a relatively new alternative to the *.com* extension. It can be used for virtually any purpose. For more information about this extension, visit: ssl2/domainhost.com/internic/reg/to/toinfo.html. (The *.to* extension was originally the country extension for Tonga.)
.ca	Refers to sites originating from Canada.

Choosing your domain name

There are three basic approaches you can take when deciding upon a domain name for your online business. First, you can use your company name (www.yourcompany.com). When someone is looking for a specific company's Web site, they instinctively try a Web address that includes the company name. There are countless examples of companies whose Internet presence can be located using its company name. The following are just a few examples:

1-800-Flowers	www.1800flowers.com
AT&T	www.att.com
Brooks Brothers	www.brooksbrothers.com
Honda Motors	www.honda.com
Microsoft Corporation	www.microsoft.com
MTV	www.mtv.com
National Football League (NFL)	www.nfl.com
Nike	www.nike.com
Sony Corporation	www.sony.com
The Gap	www.thegap.com
The Walt Disney Company	www.disney.com
US Airways	www.usairways.com
Visa	www.visa.com

Moneysaver
Unless you have a lot of money to invest, avoid using non-specific names for your domain name. It's expensive to create a connection in the minds of your customers between a made-up or random word and your product.

If your online business involves selling a product or service, your domain name can also be the name of that product or service. For example, Lefkey International sells computer keyboards for left-handed computer users. The company has several domain names, including www.lefkey.com and www.lefthandedkeyboard.com. Pharmative Corporation sells vitamins and other nutritional supplements on the Web. This company's domain name is www.vitamin.com.

Being creative

As you kick around domain name ideas, think about new and unique names that describe your product/service. CD Now, Inc., is an online music superstore. Here customers can choose from thousands of audio CDs and videos and order them directly over the Internet using a major credit card. The domain name for this company is www.cdnow.com. If you're looking to buy the latest computer game, www.gamedealer.com calls itself the Internet's game superstore. Based on the domain name, someone not familiar with the company will have a pretty good idea of what this company offers.

You can also follow in the footsteps of several major online businesses and choose a domain name that sounds somewhat non-specific and that can apply to anything at all. These typically are coined names that don't necessary mean anything. Coined names are easy to trademark and protect, but as a small business owner, they're difficult to promote, especially if your online business will be catering to a potential worldwide market.

Amazon.com, for example, started out selling books online. The company now offers books, music, videos, auctions, and software, and continues to grow. Based on the name, a consumer would have no clue what product "Amazon.com" offers—it has nothing to do with the South American river or a mythical tribe of statuesque warrior women. It's only because the company has spent millions of dollars on marketing that Web surfers know about Amazon.com, allowing it to become one of the most successful online businesses in America.

Another example of an online business with a generic-sounding domain name is Beyond.com. This company classifies itself as an online superstore for computer software, video games, and other forms of electronic entertainment. Again, without a huge marketing effort, people wouldn't know what Beyond.com is or what it sells.

While choosing a generic-sounding domain name allows for future growth into other areas, it also requires a tremendous amount of marketing and advertising in order to inform people about what your online business offers. If your online business will be starting out small and without a multi-million dollar advertising campaign, consider a less generic and more descriptive domain name.

Coming up with the perfect name for your business may take a lot of thought and creativity. As you kick around ideas in your head, seek out the advice of friends, relatives, and other people you respect. Also, consider carefully what you are naming. Consider characteristics, features, advantages, and anything else that comes to mind when you think about the products or services you'll be offering. Acronyms can also be the basis for a company or domain name.

What are the goals of the company you'll be starting? Is there an image you're trying to convey? Who is your target audience? Using a pad of paper (or your computer), keep a running list of ideas and potential company/domain names. After you've compiled a list, narrow it down by selecting only those names that you really like. Next, you'll need to

Watch Out!
Make sure the name you choose won't accidentally be offensive to someone. Does the name you're considering mean something totally different in another language? Is there any chance the public will associate anything negative with the name you're considering? Doing your homework upfront can save you misery down the road.

determine if the domain names you like are available and if they violate any existing trademarks or copyrights.

Getting help

If you're still having trouble coming up with potential domain names, seek the help of professionals. Consider hiring an advertising and or marketing agency that specializes in helping companies create names and slogans. The NameStormers (512-267-1814 / www.namestormers.com) is just one company offering a selection of software tools and consulting services designed to help entrepreneurs and business owners create catchy company names, slogans, and domain names.

The NameStormers offers a Windows-based software package called NamePro ($495) that uses a computerized approach to developing new and unique product and company names. Many URLs incorporate the "namesmithing" techniques and databases the NameStormers have developed over the past decade.

Instead of purchasing the software, a less powerful online edition of the program, called NameWave, is available at the company's Web site (httpds.dmans.com/namewave). By answering a few questions and choosing from a variety of categories, this Web site will generate up to 200 domain name ideas per online session. Each session costs $15.

If your company name and product name differ, or you'll be selling multiple products/services through your online business, consider registering and using multiple domain names that lead to the same Web site. Having multiple domain names will entitle you to have multiple listings on the major Web search engines, and can be used in your specialized marketing campaigns to provide target

Unofficially...
Registering a domain name doesn't give you ownership of it. This process gives you the exclusive rights, however, to use the domain name (the Internet address) as long as you pay your annual fees to InterNIC. The concept is very similar to having a regular telephone number.

audiences with a domain name that's easy to remember, based upon their interests.

Domain parking is available: plan ahead

You're not the only entrepreneur hoping to create a successful online business. In addition to the thousands of start-up electronic commerce sites created every month, huge companies and corporations are also constantly expanding and enhancing their online presence. As a result, thousands of new domain names are registered every week. If you anticipate expanding your online business into new areas or believe that sometime in the future, you may have a need for additional domain names, now is the best time to register those names—before someone else does!

When you register a domain name that won't immediately be used, it's called *parking* the domain name. You have the rights to it; however, the address isn't active and doesn't lead to a Web site. Internet Service Providers often offer complimentary "holding services," allowing you to reserve a domain name without having to put a Web site online.

Finding if a domain name is available: InterNIC

Okay, you've had your brainstorming session and you've come up with several possible domain names that would be absolutely perfect for your business—congratulations! What you need to do now is determine if anyone has already registered your potential domain names.

First, connect to the Internet and try to access the domain name you've selected. If your Web browser software is able to connect to that Web site,

Bright Idea
Need help thinking of a domain name? Consider using a thesaurus. You can find one online at www.thesaurus. com.

Network Solutions is the primary online registration service for all .com, .org, and .net domain names. Shown here is the service's home page (www. networksolutions. com).

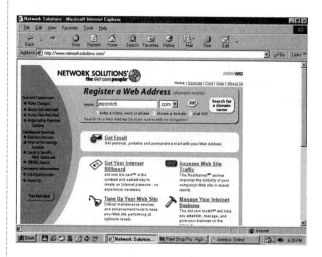

the name is obviously taken. Even if the domain name you like isn't currently active, that doesn't mean someone else hasn't already registered it. To determine if a domain name is available, visit the InterNIC Web site (www.internic.net). This will take you directly to Network Solutions Registration Services site.

Getting started

At Network Solution's (InterNIC) main Web page, go to the area that says, "Search the database of registered domain names using WHOIS:" and type the domain name you're interested in researching. Note: You should only enter the "domainname.com" portion of the domain name, not the "http://www." part.

Next, click the "Search" icon, located next to the field where you entered the domain name to research. The WHOIS database will now be searched. The process typically takes less than one minute.

You might see the message "No match for '(your domain name).com.'" This message means nobody has registered the domain name and you are free to register it immediately. From Network Solutions' (InterNIC) main Web page, choose the "Register a domain name" option.

If the domain name entered is already registered, information about the registrant, including the registrant's company name, address, phone number, e-mail address, domain name, administrative contact, billing contact, and domain servers will be listed. You now have the option to contact the domain name's owner directly. If he isn't using the domain name, you may be able to purchase or lease it from the current registrant. (See below for more details.)

If you receive a response from the WHOIS database indicating the domain name you've entered in "On Hold," this means one of the following things, according to Network Solutions/InterNIC:

- Payment for the domain is not current.

- The domain name is involved in a dispute with a trademark owner.

- Name server activation is pending.

- Another administrative or technical matter is pending.

Registering with Network Solutions/ InterNIC: step-by-step

If the domain name you want isn't already taken, registering one is a relatively quick and easy process. We'll be discussing InterNIC here, but this service is also offered by many Internet Service Providers (ISPs) that you hire to host your Web site/online business. (See appendix for how to contact InterNIC.)

Unofficially... Network Solutions/ InterNIC reports over 125,000 new domain names are registered every month, and that number continues to grow as the Internet becomes more popular.

Watch Out!
If you choose to have your ISP or another agency or service register a domain name on your behalf, make sure the information provided to InterNIC is actually your information so that you obtain control over the domain name. If you're concerned about having your domain name "stolen" before it can be registered by you, follow the steps in this chapter and register it yourself.

From Network/Solutions/InterNIC's main Web page, follow these steps.

Contact the Internet Service Provider (ISP) that will be hosting your Web site. From the ISP, obtain their server's IP addresses and host names. You'll also be required to provide a valid e-mail address for yourself or your organization. You'll need this information to continue with the online domain name registration process.

Click on the "Register a domain name" link found on Network Solutions/InterNIC's main Web page.

When the Domain Name Registration screen appears, you'll need to provide the general information that's required, including your e-mail address and the domain name you're attempting to register. In the "Your e-mail address" field, type your complete e-mail address. The domain name should be entered as the domain name, followed by the extension. It should not include the "http://www" portion of the URL. Finally, on this initial screen, you'll be asked to choose one of three options: "New Registration," "Modifying Existing Domain," or "Delete Domain." Since you're registering a new domain name, select this first option and click the "Proceed" icon found near the bottom of the screen.

The second screen in the Domain Name Registration process requests the following information:

> **New Domain Registration for:**   Your domain name should appear
>
> **Organization Name**
>
> **Organization Address**
>
> **City, State, and Zip**

Country

Comments   This field should only be completed if registering a *.edu* domain or when requested by Network Solutions. For *.edu* registrations, you'll need to summarize the subjects taught and degrees awarded.

Administrative Contact/Agent   Here you can enter your assigned NIC handle or enter the contact person's full information, including his name, type of contact, organization, street address, city, state, zip, country, phone number, fax number, and e-mail address.

Technical Contact   Here you enter your assigned NIC handle, identify the technical contact as the same person as the supplied administrative contact, or choose to enter the contact person's full information.

Billing Contact   Here you can enter your assigned NIC handle, or identify the billing contact as being the same person as the administrative contact or the technical contact. You also have the option of entering the contact person's full information.

Name Server Information   In this section of the online domain name registration form, you'll be asked for your primary server hostname, primary server netaddress, secondary server hostname, and secondary server netaddress. This is information supplied to you by your ISP. Additional fields are provided to input information about secondary servers hosting your site. These fields can be left blank, unless you're instructed otherwise by your ISP.

Watch Out!
In an effort to make registering a domain name easier, Network Solutions/ InterNIC continues to revamp its site and change the format of the online registration process in terms of the visual layout of the site. The information you'll need to provide, however, remains consistent with what's outlined in this section.

Once all of the information requested by the Domain Name Registration form has been entered, click the "Submit This Form For Processing" button located at the bottom of the form.

A message confirming the form has been submitted will appear on the screen. Usually within minutes, you'll receive an e-mail message from InterNIC containing the Domain Name Registration Agreement. This is a legal document, so read it carefully. If you agree to the terms, you must cut and paste the e-mail message (containing the agreement) into a new e-mail message and send it back to InterNIC using this address: hostmaster@internic.net.

Once the Domain Name Registration Agreement has been returned, it will be followed by another automatic relay e-mail message from InterNIC/Network Solutions. This message will contain a tracking number for your registration. Any correspondence with InterNIC/Network Solutions in the future must contain this tracking number in the "Subject" line of your e-mail message. The tracking number will be in the following format: NIC-YYMMDD.# (NIC-year, month, day, plus a unique number assigned to your registration). If you don't receive an additional confirmation of your registration within 48 hours, contact the InterNIC Help Desk by calling 703-742-4777, or send an e-mail message to hostmaster@internic.net.

As soon as your registration form has been processed, you will receive yet another e-mail message confirming that your domain name has been registered. You will then be mailed an invoice for the registration fee. The section below explains these fees in greater detail.

Costs of obtaining and registering domain names

Bright Idea
As you register your domain name, consider registering all of the alternatives to your domain name as well. Examples include domain names with similar spellings, the same name but with different extensions, or your domain name with and without hyphens. This will keep your competition from using a domain name similar to yours.

The cost of registering each new domain name through InterNIC/Network Solutions is $70. This fee covers the initial registration and most updates to the domain name's database record for a period of two years.

After the initial two-year period, the annual renewal fee of $35 covers one year of maintenance for the domain name record. The annual renewal fee is assessed each year on the anniversary of the initial registration.

Upon successfully registering a new domain name, within seven days after the name activation an invoice will automatically be sent to the billing contact for your domain name. This invoice will be sent via both U.S. Mail and e-mail (you only need to pay one). Payment is due within 30 days. If payment is not received within this period, the domain name registration will be deactivated and deleted. Likewise, within seven days of the annual renewal being due, an invoice will be sent to the billing contact for the domain name. The registrant then has 30 days to pay the invoice or run the risk of having the domain name deactivated and deleted. Payments can be made by check, money order, or by any major credit card.

Internet Service Providers and other organizations that register large numbers of new domain names on an ongoing basis can establish a debit account with InterNIC Registration Services.

Registering your domain name with WorldNIC

WorldNIC (1-888-642-9675 / www.worldnic.com) is another division of InterNIC/Network Solutions offering personalized domain name registration services for computer novices. In addition to registering a domain name, the WorldNIC service includes ".com" e-mail addresses and can include Web site hosting and site creation services. Toll-free technical assistance is also available. Just as with InterNIC, WorldNIC can be used to register a domain name with a *.com, .net, .org,* or *.edu* extension. The initial costs are $119 for the first two years of a domain name's registration (including one ".com" e-mail address). Additional e-mail boxes cost about $60 per year.

There are other domain name extensions aside from *.com, .net, .org,* and *.edu* domain name extensions, but to register your domain with an alternate extension, you'll need to contact that extension's registrar directly.

When the domain you want is taken

Unfortunately, millions of domain names are already taken. If the domain name you were hoping to obtain as the online address and identity for your business has already been registered by someone else, you have several options—including choosing another name, which is the easiest, fastest, and cheapest alternative. If the domain name you want is taken, select another one that's not and register it.

As mentioned earlier, when you do a domain name search using the WHOIS database, if the name you're researching is already taken, you'll be provided with that domain name's registrant information. You now have the option to contact that individual or company and offer to purchase or lease the domain name. This, however, can become a costly endeavor.

Unofficially...
Many businesses do nothing but register hundreds of domain names and then sell these names to the highest bidder for a profit. One example is iGoldRush.com (www.igoldrush. com). Other companies act as "middlemen" between buyers and sellers of domain names, such as DomainMart (www. domainmart. com).

Exactly how much is a domain name worth? This is a question with no easy answer. The price range for domain names sold on the secondary market is anywhere from $100 to $150,000 or more.

If an individual or company has registered a domain name that's not in use and you wish to buy it, try contacting the domain name registrant directly and inquiring about the domain name's availability. You will most likely have to engage in a negotiation process if the registrant is open to giving up the domain name ... for a price.

Getting help registering your domain name

The best place to seek out personalized help when it comes to registering a domain name is to contact your ISP directly. If you sign a long-term Web site hosting agreement with an ISP, they may offer to register your domain name free of charge or for a small fee.

An alternative is to try to reach someone at InterNIC's Help Desk by telephone (which typically requires sitting on hold for a while), or using one of the many domain name registration services on the Internet. From any Internet search engine, type in the search phrase, "Domain Name Registration." Typically, these services charge a one-time fee (in addition to InterNIC's registration rates); however, they handle all of the e-mail correspondence and related paperwork. This type of service shouldn't cost more than $100, since it usually takes less than 15 minutes to register a new domain name.

Just a few domain name registration companies available online include:

WorldNIC	www.worldnic.com
Direct Line Domain Name Registration	www.siteleader.com/ domain-registration
Domain Name Registration.Com	www.domainnameregistration. com
A+ Domain Name Registration Center	www.aplus-domain.com
Instant Domain Registration Center	www.instant-domain.com
Name.Space	name.space.xs2.net
Domain Name Registry	www.domainnameregistry.com
Domain Bank	www.domainbank.net
Internet Domain Bureau	www.idbnet.com/idb-home. shtml
Domain Agency	www.domainagency.com

Just the facts

- Your online business's domain name gives you an address on the Web and an identity. Choose your domain name wisely.

- Try to choose a domain name that's easy to remember, pronounce, and spell—one that people will instantly associate with your company or product.

- If your company name and product name differ, or you'll be selling multiple products or services through your online business, consider registering and using multiple domain names that lead to the same Web site.

- To determine if a domain name is available, use InterNIC's WHOIS database (www.internic.net).

- The cost of registering a domain name is about $35 annually. Consider acquiring domain names with similar spellings or different extensions.

GET THE SCOOP ON...
What's an ISP, anyway? ▪ The cost of
going online ▪ Getting necessary
services, affordably ▪ Technical support
▪ Computer equipment

Selecting Your Host: The Ins and Outs of ISPs

Chapter 6

An Internet Service Provider (ISP) is your business's gateway to the Internet. Once you create your Web page, it's necessary to hire either an ISP or a separate Web site host to get your site on the Net. This means the data files you create (the individual Web pages, artwork, and related files that comprise your Web site) will be uploaded to the host's server, where they will be made available to anyone surfing the Net.

It takes a lot of time and effort to create and then launch your online business. To actually get it online, however, you'll need to register a domain name with InterNIC (see Chapter 5, "Selecting and Registering Your Domain Name") and create your Web site. You'll also have to develop a relationship with an ISP, as we'll discuss in this chapter.

After you've read this chapter, be sure to refer to Chapter 14, "The Experts Share Their E-Commerce

66

Web hosting is the term that refers to the service involving the placement of your Web site onto the Internet through a computer server. Once this is done, anyone, from anywhere in the world, is able to access those Web pages and view the information that is provided there for them.
—Mindspring Internet Services (www. mindspring. net)

99

Knowledge and Experience." It includes an interview with Sandy Bendremer, the cofounder of Galaxy Internet Services. He'll offer additional advice about choosing a host that's best suited to meet your company's needs.

The costs associated with going online

There are several different fees associated with setting up a Web site and getting it online. As discussed in Chapter 5, you'll need to register your domain name(s) with InterNIC. This will cost about $35 a year per name.

Your company will also be responsible for whatever fees are involved in creating and designing your Web site. This may mean purchasing Web page creation software. Creating your actual Web site may also require you to hire programmers, graphic artists, writers, photographers, and other professionals—either full-time, part-time, or on a freelance basis. These costs will vary greatly. You could create a basic Web site in under an hour and by spending little money, using just your own artistic ability and a Web page creation program or service. The professional look of your site will probably be lacking, however. Your level of artistic ability and the time you spend creating your site will impact its overall look.

Finally, to get your site online, it's necessary to sign up with an ISP (unless you have the Web server equipment to host your own site in-house). For businesses, this typically means paying a one-time set-up fee plus an ongoing monthly fee to an ISP, which also will vary greatly based on your needs and what services are offered. Some ISPs charge a flat monthly fee as low as about $20 per month, but then charge you for additional services, such as tech support, maintenance, or updating.

If your online business will be handling credit card transactions, it'll be necessary to use an ISP offering secure transactions. This typically costs more. In some cases, if you use certain e-commerce Web page design software packages, you may need to also hire a second ISP (one that supports your software package) to handle secure financial transactions such as order taking. There may be additional per-transaction fees associated with processing secure transactions, as well.

The ISP/Web-hosting business is extremely competitive, so be sure to shop around for the best rates and the highest level of service/technical support you can find. Finding a reliable ISP is as easy as:

- Seeking out a reference from someone you know.

- Surfing the Internet, using a search engine and a search phrase, like "ISP" or "Web Hosting."

- Checking the Yellow Pages.

- Calling any of the ISP services listed later in this chapter.

Keep in mind that some ISPs are national companies, which means they offer dial-up access through cities nationwide and cater to companies like yours located anywhere in the country. These nationwide providers tend to offer less personalized service (because they're large), but highly competitive rates. If you decide to affiliate yourself with a national ISP, you also run less of a risk that the ISP you ultimately choose will suddenly go out of business (due to the competitive nature of the business).

Unofficially...
Many ISPs offer anyone dial-up access to the Internet. Only some offer Web page hosting services. A growing number of ISPs that offer Web page hosting services are starting to offer secure online transactions to accommodate e-commerce sites.

Choose an ISP that offers the services you need, such as server extensions. Also, make sure you maintain an offsite backup of your site to which you have 24-hour access. Even if the ISP provides a backup, it's an excellent strategy to be able to restore your site at another location should this become necessary.

A local ISP is one that caters to companies in a single city or region. These services tend to be a bit more expensive; however, you'll receive much more personalized service. If the ISP/Web-hosting service you choose doesn't offer dial-up Internet access or the ability to maintain your site over the Web, you may be required to dial a long-distance phone number to update or maintain your Web site.

Services you need at prices you can afford

Choosing an ISP is a lot like choosing a long-distance phone company. All of the long distance companies (such as AT&T, Sprint, and MCI/Worldcom) offer long-distance services of the same basic quality, but each has a different pricing plan, different levels of customer service, and different incentives to get you to sign up with them. Typically, you can also save money by signing up with a little-known long distance phone service.

The same general rules that apply to choosing a long distance company apply when choosing an ISP. Most offer the same basic services, but with subtle differences and at different price points. This is why it's important to determine exactly what you need and then shop around for the best rates and services.

Some of the things you should inquire about when investigating a possible ISP/Web-hosting service include the following:

■ **Rates.** This includes set-up fees, monthly rates, and extra charges.

■ **Phone lines.** Does the ISP offer nationwide dial-up access or just local or regional access? Does the service support your modem speed? If you're using a 56K modem, it's important your ISP can handle connections at this speed. The 56K connection has become an industry standard; however, if you'll be using an ISDN connection or another type of high-speed Internet connection, the ISP you select may not be compatible.

■ **Types of accounts offered.** For Web hosting, you'll probably need a SLIP/PPP account, which are the most common types of dial-up accounts.

■ **Amount of storage space.** When you sign up with an ISP to host your Web site, you may be limited to a specific amount of file storage space on their server—typically 10MB or 20MB, which should be plenty of space for most sites.

■ **Passwords.** As the customer of the ISP, can you control/select your log-on passwords?

■ **Domain name registration services.** Does the ISP offer this? If so, make sure your domain name is registered with your company name and you are listed as the owner of the domain name.

■ **E-mail.** Does an ISP's Web-hosting services include e-mail boxes so you can easily accept e-mail messages from customers, clients, and others? How many e-mail boxes do you receive? Is there an extra fee for e-mail boxes?

Moneysaver
ISPs are cost-effective. Connecting directly to the Internet using your own server can cost at least $2,000. You'll also need to establish a direct connection to the Internet (24 hours a day, 7 days a week) via a T1 phone line or ISDN phone line. This can cost hundreds or thousands of dollars every month.

Watch Out!
Some ISPs offer free Web site hosting. This, however, typically means you'll be required to prominently display ads for their company or their sponsors. This can potentially look amateurish and be annoying to the visitor. While this is okay if you're operating a personal Web page, it's not suitable for an online business/e-commerce site.

- **Special software.** Does the ISP offer special software for maintaining your Web site or monitoring traffic to your site? If so, is there an additional cost of this software? Are you able to use your own software?

- **Compatibility.** Is the Web site creation software you'll be using compatible with the ISP?

- **Backup services.** What type of backup services does the ISP offer? How often does the server go down? When it goes down, how long does it typically take to fix?

- **Secure services.** Does the ISP offer secure services such as Netscape Commerce Server for online transactions?

- **Bandwidth.** Does the ISP have sufficient bandwidth to accommodate the level of traffic your Web site will be receiving? Or will visitors to your site experience lags?

- **Terms of the contract.** What are the contract terms you'll be required to sign with the ISP? Is there a minimum length of service (three months? Six? Twelve? Twenty-four?)? What are the penalties if you choose to end your service agreement sooner?

- **Additional services.** What additional services does the ISP offer, and at what cost?

- **Extra modem services.** Does the ISP support modem shotgunning so you can achieve a faster Internet connection? *Shot-gunning* refers to the use of two different modems to establish one faster Internet connection.

- **Tracking.** Does the ISP offer traffic reports or other information you can use to keep track of who is visiting your site, when they're visiting, which site they linked from, which pages of your site they visited, and so forth?

- **Other Web site help.** Does the ISP offer Web site design and creation services for an extra fee?

- **Data transfer.** How much data transfer/traffic comes with the account, and what are the charges for additional data transfer?

All-in-one turnkey solutions

Instead of having to invest in Web site creation tools (software), hire an ISP, and figure out the ins and outs of secure Internet connections to handle credit card processing and order transactions, services like Yahoo! Store (store.yahoo.com) offer a one-stop and relatively inexpensive solution. For a monthly fee starting at about $100, Yahoo! Store will help you create an e-commerce Web site, host your site, and handle all secure transactions. Services like these are also easily expandable as your business grows.

Yahoo! Site (site.yahoo.com/site) is another Web page creation and hosting service. It isn't e-commerce-oriented, but it can be used by businesses looking to create an online presence. The pricing for Yahoo! Site is a flat fee of about $30 per month. This fee includes:

- An easy-to-use site builder.

- As many addresses as you want.

- Hosting on Yahoo!'s servers.

- 25 Megabytes of disk space.

- Unlimited bandwidth (you are entitled to an unlimited number of hits).

Bright Idea
As you investigate ISPs, don't be afraid to ask lots of questions. If you can't get your questions answered in a prompt and friendly manner when the ISP is first trying to get your business, just imagine what the ISP will be like once you're a customer and need technical support!

66

[In] dial-up access ... you use your computer's modem to call up an Internet Service Provider and log onto the Internet. Most Web-hosting companies do not offer dial-up access because it takes up server capacity that they would rather dedicate to Web-hosting clients.
—Host Index.Com

99

- Search engine submission. Yahoo will submit your site to the major search engines.

- Detailed updates daily.

Getting technical support from your ISP

By this point, I hope, you've asked several of the questions mentioned above. But let's face it—as you get your online business up and running, you're going to have many more questions. Being able to get your questions answered quickly, easily, and as accurately as possible will save you time and money. How much technical support you'll need will depend on how much you know about creating, publishing, and managing your Web site.

As you investigate ISPs, make sure you ask about the availability of technical support. Specifically, you should ask:

- What types of technical support are available?

- During what hours can you speak with a human?

- Does the ISP offer toll-free technical support, or will you rack up large phone bills each time you call and are forced to sit on hold?

- How much does telephone technical support cost?

- Are you limited to how much technical support you're entitled to?

- What other forms of technical support are available (such as online, e-mail, and fax-on-demand)?

- What is the procedure for reporting problems?

There are a variety of Web-hosting companies, in terms of size, services offered, and price. By asking a lot of questions, you should be able to winnow out companies who can't offer you what you need.

Finding an ISP

Here's a partial list of the country's largest Web-hosting services, in alphabetical order:

Timesaver
When you're deciding on your ISP, be sure to find out how long you will typically have to stay on hold in order to speak with a human. If the ISP is under-staffed and makes you wait for help, you waste time you could be using for other tasks.

America Online
www.aol.com

AT&T WorldNet
www.att.net

Bell Atlantic Internet Solutions
www.bellatlantic.net

CompuServe
www.compuserve.com

EarthLink
www.earthlink.net

Galaxy Internet Services
www.gis.net

GTE
www.gte.net

IBM Internet Connection Services
www.ibm.net

MCI/Worldcom
www.internetmci.com

Microsoft Network
www.msn.com

MindSpring
www.mindspring.com

Netcom
www.netcom.com

Prodigy Internet
www.prodigy.com

Earthlink from
Sprint is one of
the country's
largest Internet
Service Providers
(ISPs)

Yahoo!

site.yahoo.com

Bright Idea
When looking at
ISPs, don't forget
to compare the
access speeds
each allows to
be sure you get
the speed you
need.

The following are free online services designed to help people find a reliable ISP to meet their needs. These services rate, review, and list hundreds of ISPs; they're sponsor-supported, however, and many of those sponsors are ISPs. So once you find an ISP you might be interested in working with, refer to the questions listed earlier in this chapter to help you evaluate what's being offered.

Find-A-Host.Com
(www.findahost.com/hosts/default.cfm)

Host Index (www.hostindex.com)

HostReview.Com (hostreview.com)

HostSearch.Com (www.hostsearch.com)

InternetList.Com
(webhostlist.internetlist.com)

The List: The Definitive ISP Buyer's Guide
(thelist.internet.com)

Galaxy Internet Services is a fast-growing ISP. Read the interview with one of the company's founders in Chapter 14.

Microsoft-registered Web presence providers

If you're using Microsoft FrontPage to create your site, consider using a Registered Web Presence Provider (WPP).

According to Microsoft,

Over 600 registered Web Presence Providers worldwide, including most major ISPs, currently support the FrontPage server extensions. A Web presence provider is an Internet Service Provider that has registered with Microsoft to offer support for the FrontPage server extensions to its customers.

Hosting your Web site with a registered Web presence provider for FrontPage ensures that the dynamic features of your FrontPage-based Web site are fully supported, such as the Search and Hit Counter components and the ability to remotely author and manage your site directly across the Internet. WPPs are Web-hosting and

Unofficially...
The cost of a
low-end multi-
media system
will start at
under $600.
Newer model PC-
based computers,
equipped with
Pentium II or
Pentium III
processors, will
give you the
computing power
you need for Web
site creation and
management.

Internet services providers who manage the Web server hardware and software required to make your Web site available on the Internet. You essentially rent space on their Web servers. Additionally, WPPs may provide customer technical support, training and consulting services, 24-hour site monitoring, maintenance and traffic reporting, security management, and other Web-based services.

To access a listing of Microsoft's WPPs, visitmicrosoft.saltmine.com/frontpage/wpp/list.

The computer equipment you need in-house

Depending on whether you're using Web page creation software or an online solution such as Yahoo! Store, the core system requirements for creating and maintaining your Web site will be slightly different. If you're planning to host your own Web site, the equipment you'll need will be more extensive and costly.

The core system requirements needed to actually create and then manage your Web site will depend in part on the Web site creation software and graphics development software you'll be using. For a PC-based system, this typically means at least a Pentium 166 computer that's fully multimedia compatible and has a good-sized hard disk (at least five gigabytes).

Visit any computer store to see the various computer models and system configurations offered. Choose a system that will be able to handle your applications, but that offers you the ability to upgrade your system as needed. Stay away from PC-based systems that offer "closed architecture." These systems are typically cheaper, but can't be upgraded, so you may wind up having to purchase new equipment sooner than planned.

As you shop around for a computer, keep in mind that technology is changing very quickly. Within one year to 18 months, it may be necessary to upgrade your PC with newer and faster technology, such as a better video card, faster CD-ROM drive, more memory, or a better microprocessor. Within three years, you might need a new PC altogether to keep up with the current technology trends.

Before shopping around for a PC system, carefully define your needs. Ask yourself what the computer will be used for. You should also determine, in advance, what primary software applications you plan on running, and what types of accessories and peripherals you'll be connecting to the computer. In addition to creating and managing your actual Web site, you might be using the computer to manage other aspects of your online business, such as accounting, bookkeeping, order processing, contact management, inventory control, credit card processing, and package shipping processing.

Speed

Since you'll definitely need access to the Internet to surf the Web, send and receive e-mail, and maintain your Web site, you want the fastest connection possible. Some options for Internet access include a standard dial-up connection at 28.8K or 56K baud rates. You can also purchase a special type of modem and obtain access (in many cities) to the Internet via an ISDN or T1 connection.

A growing number of cable TV companies, such as Media One (www.mediaone.net), now also offer

Bright Idea
Useful equipment you may consider investing in based on your Web page design needs include a digital camera and flatbed scanner for creating and importing graphics; a powerful graphics program to edit the graphics you import; a Microsoft IntelliMouse with Wheel (for navigating and scrolling around the Web).

access to the Internet at high speeds using a cable modem. It's also possible to access the net at high speeds using a wireless connection via satellite (this service is available from DirectPC, www.direcpc. com. Many technologies on the horizon will make fast Internet access cheap and readily available.

As you're shopping for a computer, you'll need to determine a core system configuration for your computer. To do so, look at the system requirements of the software you plan to use. For example, the minimum system requirements for MultiActive's ecBuilder Pro e-commerce Web site creation and management software (www.multiactive.com) include a Pentium 90 processor (or higher) with 16Mb Ram and at least 50Mb of hard disk space. A CD-ROM drive, VGA monitor, Internet access, and Web browser software (Internet Explorer or Netscape) are also required.

Retail versus mail-order

Buying a computer from a retail store or computer superstore has several advantages, especially if you don't know a lot about computers. For starters, the in-store salespeople and technical staff will be able to address your needs and answer your questions on the spot. Also, if the computer turns out to be defective, you can return or exchange it locally. The drawback to buying your computer equipment from a retail computer store is that you'll typically pay higher prices, possibly including state sales taxes. Your buying decisions will also be limited to the PC brands carried by the retail stores you visit.

The alternative is to buy your computer equipment through mail order or from an online merchant. While you'll have to pay shipping to receive your purchase, the prices are generally lower. Refer to publications such as *Computer Shopper*, a monthly magazine full of ads from computer mail-order companies. The trick to saving money when shopping via mail order or online is to determine your exact needs and then shop around for the best prices. For reliable computer hardware reviews, visit the C/Net Web site at www.cnet.com.

To learn more about the popular name-brand PC computers, check out these PC manufacturers' Web sites:

Acer	www.acer.com
Compaq	www.compaq.com
Dell	www.dell.com
Gateway	www.gateway.com
IBM	www.ibm.com
Micron	www.micron.com
Packard Bell	www.packardbell.com
Sony	www.sony.com

The need to surf the Web and FTP Files

HostIndex.Com reports that while it's necessary to upload your Web site files to your ISP, not all ISPs have a local access number or offer dial-up access.

This is a very common problem for those exploring the idea of getting a domain hosting account. First, you need a local dial-in access account, available throughout North America for around $20 per month. Having a local access account with an ISP gives you access to the Internet. It also gives you the connection needed to make use of an FTP [File Transfer Protocol] program on your computer which in turn is used to upload (publish) your Web site-related files to a server anywhere in the world.

For example, perhaps your Web hosting company is located in Florida. However, you live in

Unofficially...
Fast modem con-
nection (56K
minimum) is one
of the most
important fea-
tures for your
online business.
In addition to
ISDN and cable
modems, other
new technologies
offer fast
Internet access.
For one example,
see FatPipe
from Ragula
Systems, Inc.
(http://www.
fatpipeinc.com).

*California. How do you get your Web pages
from your computer in California to your virtual server in Florida? All you need to do is to
dial-in to your local access provider and once
your Internet connection is established, simply
launch your FTP application and upload your
files to your server. Many Web site creation tools
have a built-in FTP application.*

Sending Web site files created on your PC to
your host is an easy process using an FTP application. Several such programs are available as shareware or in the public domain (for free) from services like American Online or Download.com.
Making the connection between your PC and your
ISP or Web site host can be done using any Internet
connection.

See chapter 13, "Analyzing Your Site," for details
on file transfers and FTP applications.

Just the facts

- To actually get your site online, you'll probably
  have to sign up with an ISP/Web-hosting service.

- The ISP/Web-hosting business is extremely
  competitive, so be sure to shop around for the
  best rates and the highest level of service/tech-
  nical support you can find.

- Before shopping around for a PC system, carefully define your needs.

- The alternative to buying your computer equipment from a retail computer store is to shop via
  mail order or from an online merchant. While
  you may have to pay shipping to receive your
  purchase, the prices are generally lower.

An Internet Presence for Existing and New Businesses

PART III

Expanding Your Existing Business into Cyberspace

Remember high school? There were the "in crowd" and the "uncool kids." If you wanted to be part of the in crowd, you had to dress how others dressed and act exactly how others did.

Chances are you graduated from high school a long time ago, but some things never really change. If you're reading this chapter, perhaps you operate your own traditional business. But when it comes to succeeding in today's business world, no matter what type of business you own or operate, it's becoming increasingly important to join the in crowd by establishing an Internet presence for your business. The "in crowd" in today's business world can be found on the World Wide Web.

Some established businesses identify an immediate benefit for creating an Internet presence, whether it's to sell products to a potential worldwide audience, offer potential customers information

Chapter 7

66

Although the lat-
est Greenfield
Online Shopping
2000 study
shows 39 percent
of Net surfers
say they visit
shops less often
because of their
ability to buy
online, the data
also show that a
local store is still
the preferred
place to buy in
most instances.
But the Web is
often favored
over catalog
shopping.
—The Industry
Standard, April
6, 1999 (www.
thestandard.
com).

99

about these products, or offer improved and more convenient customer service. Other companies are establishing themselves on the Internet now, because business operators understand that having an Internet presence will soon be critical, and they want to be prepared. They also want to reserve or register the best domain names for their business, before those domain names are taken by the competition. The general philosophy is to learn how to operate in cyberspace now, before the stakes become too high and being online becomes an absolute requirement.

Establishing an Internet presence doesn't necessarily mean you have to invest a fortune to create a state-of-the-art Web site. If you currently operate a traditional retail store, service business, consulting business, or other traditional (non-virtual) business, a Web site can be used for a variety of purposes. For several hundred dollars, a basic Web site, capable of communicating information about your company and its products, can be created in a matter of hours or days, depending on your knowledge level and how much planning and preparation you've already done.

As millions of people from around the world gain access to the Internet and begin surfing the Web, their buying habits are changing rapidly. If you're looking to buy a major appliance, for example, you no longer need to spend hours driving from one appliance dealer to the next to learn about the latest models, their features, or their cost. You can research products and comparison shop online in far less time and without having to deal with pushy salespeople or find a parking spot at each store. Best of all, as a consumer, you can do your shopping any time, day or night, without ever leaving your home.

Using this example, if you're an appliance dealer, you could miss out on many sales if your business isn't represented on the Web and easy to find using a search engine.

Whether you operate a local retail store or a service-oriented business, the Web allows you to offer your products or services to a worldwide market via the Web, as opposed to just the people located in your business's immediate geographic area. By expanding your potential marketplace, your sales can increase and profits for your business can grow dramatically.

Many established businesses are using the Internet simply to improve their customer service and cut costs. For example, if your business receives many phone calls from potential customers requesting information (sales brochures) for your products, there is a cost associated with printing those brochures, dealing with customer phone calls, and then mailing out the requested information. Once your Web site is established, those same brochures can be re-created online. Then, your company can simply promote its Web site's URL, and potential customers can almost instantly obtain the information they want.

No longer is it just a small group of high-income, computer-savvy people who shop online. More and more consumers, from all walks of life, are turning to the Internet to find products and services they need or want, and this trend is growing extremely quickly.

If you are a traditional business operator, an online presence can be used to complement your existing marketing, sales, information distribution, or customer service efforts. And don't be intimidated by the thought of expanding into the

Watch Out!
If you operate a medium- to large-sized traditional company, don't take a "trial and error" approach and attempt to design, build, and manage your Web site in-house. Hire professionals. They'll know how to make your site easy to use and integrate it with your company's corporate identity, brand, and reputation.

Internet. There is no need to abandon your existing business model. Unlike starting a virtual business, adding an online component to your traditional business can be done over time, with a relatively low financial investment, and without having to reorganize your existing business.

The basic steps for creating an Internet presence for your existing business are pretty similar to starting a virtual (online) business. For both, you'll need to:

- Register a domain name.

- Plan your Web site's content.

- Actually create your Web site.

- Develop a relationship with an ISP.

- Manage the day-to-day operation of your site and keep it updated.

- Promote and market your Web site and generate traffic to it.

Other chapters of this book go into great detail about each of the above steps. The purpose of this chapter is to focus on a handful of additional steps and considerations necessary for establishing an online presence for an existing company based in the "real" world.

How virtual and traditional businesses differ

A virtual business is one that was created for the sole purpose of doing business online, typically using e-commerce technologies. A virtual business will most likely be operated from a business office or home office, but its primary existence is in cyberspace. This type of business is very different from a retail store, a traditional mail-order business, or a service-oriented business involving in-person contact between customers and product/service providers.

In reality, an online-based business could be operated from anywhere, by someone using a laptop computer to access and maintain a site being hosted by an independent ISP. Just as there are many types of traditional businesses, there are different types of virtual businesses. With a virtual business, however, the primary communication between the business operator and potential customers is done online.

Creating an online presence for a traditional business

When someone decides to start an online-based business, it's necessary to create an entire infrastructure for that business in advance, before going online. Until all the steps are completed—from incorporating the business to creating a company logo to developing a Web site to establishing procedures for order fulfillment—the virtual business shouldn't go online; it shouldn't "open" to the public. Aside from registering a domain name and planning and creating a Web site, a virtual businessman needs to follow many of the same steps already completed when establishing a traditional business. Thus, as a traditional business operator, you've already done much of the initial groundwork.

The biggest challenge you're going to face is seamlessly integrating your new online presence with the rest of your business, without compromising your existing business's reputation or brand. A main reason for going online is to make it easier for your customers to take advantage of the products or services you already offer and possibly increasing

Bright Idea
To avoid many of the common mistakes made by existing companies creating an Internet presence, subscribe to e-commerce newsletters or publications, such as *Web Commerce Today* (www.wilsonweb. com/wct). Instead of trying to reinvent the wheel, learn from the success and mistakes of other companies.

Timesaver
Visit Network Solutions' Web site (www. networksolutions. com) and use the WHOIS feature to determine if the domain names you like have already been taken. If your company's name is a registered trademark and someone else has the domain name registered, you may have legal rights to that domain name, so contact your lawyer.

your customer base. Thus, to keep your existing customers happy and to cater to a potential new audience, you want to take full advantage of your traditional business's reputation, corporate identity, and brand recognition—something a start-up virtual business needs to create from scratch.

For an established business looking to go online, one important consideration is the domain name you choose. The domain name should be your existing company's name, easy to remember (and spell) and intuitive. Avoid using an extremely long domain name or one that is complicated to spell. If the spelling of your company name is confusing, consider registering multiple domain names for your site, and include the most common misspellings or name alternatives. The object is to make it very easy for people to find you online. For example, if you were IBM and you were planning to create a Web site for your company, the most obvious domain name to register would be www.ibm.com.

People who choose to find you on the Web will discover your domain name in one of three ways:

- They'll obtain your domain name from your company's advertisements or traditional marketing materials.

- They'll use an Internet search engine to find your domain name, usually by typing the name of your company or the product they're looking for as the keyword or search phrase.

- They'll experiment, use common sense, and enter your company name as part of the URL when trying to find you. Back to the IBM example, if you want to find IBM's Web site, the most obvious URL is www.ibm.com, so that's what most people will try.

While still in the planning stages of the online presence for your existing company, determine as early as possible:

- What the purpose of the Web site will be.

- What services or features you'd like to offer visitors.

- What visual assets you already have available (company/product logos, product photos, and other artwork).

- What printed materials (such as brochures), you'd like to make available online, and in what format.

- What content needs to be created from scratch or adapted from existing materials currently not in electronic formats.

Your established corporate and brand identity should remain completely consistent as you develop your Web content. This means, for example, that the color schemes you use on your Web pages should be consistent with the look of your traditional printed materials. The look of your company/product logos should remain constant, and the overall "attitude" of your site should be consistent with your corporate image.

In terms of your Web site's content, if you have a well-established business, avoid using precreated or generic Web site artwork—such as animated GIFs or clip art)—or preformatted Web site design templates. To enhance your company's corporate identity, you're better off having original artwork and custom Web site design. Obtaining precreated or generic artwork or Web page templates is easy, because these assets can be downloaded free of

Watch Out!
Not maintaining a strong continuity will actually be detrimental to the great efforts and expense you've already incurred in developing your corporate and brand identity in the offline business world.

charge, purchased on CD-ROM or licensed, but they won't be exclusive to your site.

Developing original artwork and a unique Web site design from scratch will cost a bit more, but having a unique-looking site that builds your corporate image is beneficial and will help boost customer confidence.

Almost any graphic artist or professional Web site designer will be able to create original artwork and visual assets for your company's Web site that will maintain continuity with your existing business's overall image and brand.

IBM's e-business solution (www.ibm.com/e-business) is one tool to help traditional businesses use the Internet effectively. What the company says about their own product is applicable to other related services:

> *E-business isn't about reinventing your business.*
> *It's about streamlining your current business*
> *processes to improve operating efficiencies, which*
> *in turn will strengthen the value you provide to*
> *your customers—value that cannot be generated*
> *by any other means, and value that will give*
> *you a serious advantage over your competition.*

IBM's e-business solution involves helping companies translate what they're already doing into the Web, while looking for ways to usefully expand basic business services. IBM recommends you start your quest to go online by first identifying which of your core business processes are most suitable for, or most in need of, conversion to e-business. An especially good place to start is customer relationship management. This means identifying how you can enhance your business relationships with your existing customers by offering services or products online via the Web. What services can you offer online that can save you or your customers time and money? For example, on the Web, perhaps you could offer 24-hour technical support, when your company currently offers technical support only during business hours in your time zone.

Converting hard copy assets into an electronic format

During the life of your existing business, you've probably created or acquired a variety of artistic assets, such as logos, product photos, line art, and other materials that could easily be incorporated into your Web site to maintain continuity between your company's online and offline branding and overall image.

Instead of having to have electronic versions of your various artistic assets recreated from scratch, there are a variety of ways to create electronic versions of existing assets using a flatbed scanner, photo/negative scanner, or digital camera.

If you need to scan a large number of photos or negatives in order to create electronic GIF or JPEG files for use on the Web, consider investing in a photo scanner, such as the Hewlett Packard S20 PhotoSmart scanner (suggested retail price of about $500). This unit connects directly to a PC via a USB interface and can be used to scan 35mm film strips (positive or negatives), 35mm mounted slides and negatives, and photographic prints up to 5" × 7". The unit comes with the necessary software for manipulating and editing the photos once they're scanned and made into electronic files. Once these images are created, you'll still want to use a file size-reduction service to speed up the download time for each image.

Timesaver
If you have traditional negatives of a photo you want to add to your site, but don't have direct access to the necessary scanning equipment or the time to do the work yourself, many services are available to translate the negative into an electronic file.

Bright Idea
Do you want to learn more about electronic photography? Hewlett Packard offers a free, informative Web site offering all sorts of information about electronic photography and creating electronic images. Point your Web browser to www.photosmart.com.

For creating product photos from scratch, you can use a traditional camera and then have the images scanned to create electronic files, or you can use a high-end digital camera. Since product photos on a Web site must look totally professional, it's an excellent idea to hire a professional photographer or advertising agency to have these photos created. Your product suppliers or manufacturers may already have artwork suitable for use on your Web site, which will save you money.

For Web site art, you'll want to create GIF or JPEG files that can easily be added to your Web pages. As always, you'll want to pay careful attention to file sizes (which impact download times) as you select which artistic files you choose to add to your site during the design phase.

Thanks to Adobe Acrobat and Acrobat Reader software (www.adobe.com), you can easily and inexpensively take your existing printed materials, such as full-color brochures, advertisements, and annual reports, and have them transferred into the popular PDF format. This allows Web surfers visiting your site to load and read electronic files which are exact replicas of traditionally printed and typeset files. Many companies use this software to offer downloadable versions of existing product brochures and sales information via their Web site.

What your business could offer on the Web

Depending on the type of business you operate, the services and features you can and should incorporate into your Web site will vary greatly. The most important thing to consider before adding any features or content elements to your site is to analyze what each addition offers to visitors. If what you're planning doesn't directly help the visitor gather the information they need or serve a definite purpose (other than provide a bit of flash or glitz to your site), skip it.

The best way to determine what your particular Web site should offer is to spend time surfing the Web and examine what other businesses in your field or industry have done. You may also glean some good ideas from the Web sites of other types of businesses. While you don't want to steal content for your site, it's important to gather ideas and determine what works online and what doesn't. Soliciting ideas from your existing customers can also be very beneficial.

Some of the features you might consider offering on your existing company's Web site include:

- **Product information**　Sales brochures, technical specifications, product photos, product videos, and downloadable software demos.

- **Online order processing**　Web sites can be transformed into fully functional e-commerce sites if you choose to add order processing features, shopping cart modules, and/or credit card processing to your site. Instead of having your site simply act as an interactive brochure, you might want customers to be able to place their orders online. If your business already has a merchant account, contact the company you work with to determine how to adapt this account so you can process online orders.

- **Technical support/Customer service**　Consider allowing your customers to e-mail their questions directly to your technical support staff. You could also offer a detailed frequently asked

Unofficially...
As you plan your site's content, your primary concern should be ease of use (simple navigation), fast downloading times, and content that provides exactly what the visitors to your site will be looking for.

questions (FAQ) document that provides answers to the most common questions your potential customers have. If your company offers software or computer hardware, you could offer downloadable patches or bug fixes online. One current trend is for company Web sites to offer live, real-time technical support via an online chat room incorporated into a site. Offering top-notch online customer service will help build customer loyalty and make it easier for your customers to get their questions answered and their concerns addressed in a timely manner.

- **Company or investor information**   Every company Web site should offer a detailed company background, executive bios, company press releases, investor information (if applicable), and other related documents.

- **Online recruiting**   If your company hires employees or has job openings available, post them online. To learn about job opportunities, one of the first places job seekers look these days is on the Web sites of the companies they're interested in working for. Recruiting online via your Web site could save you money in recruitment-related advertising.

- **Contests or promotions**   One way to build customer loyalty and get people to visit your site repeatedly is to offer them an incentive. Some companies offer free shipping on orders placed online. Others offer a discount to online shoppers, while some companies offer ongoing contests to keep potential customers coming back to their site.

Bright Idea
If you already operate a successful traditional business, find ways you can enhance the services you offer to your customers using the Web. The ability to shop 24 hours a day, obtain technical information about a product, or get questions answered promptly are all value-added services you could offer online.

■ **Building brand awareness** A Web site is an excellent tool for building brand awareness for any type of company, product, or service.

Unless you are extremely knowledgeable about Web site creation and programming, don't invest a fortune trying to create the ultimate state-of-the-art Web site, no matter what type of business you're in. Even if you happen to have a totally original Web site creation/design idea and you invest a fortune to make the idea a reality, it'll be ripped off within a matter of days (or even hours). While it's important that your site look original and contain original content, designing special features for your site that involve complex programming isn't usually the best approach or best use of your time and financial resources.

Spreading the word about your online presence

There are many ways to spread the word that your business now has a Web site. The following are a few ideas for promoting your site's URL to your existing customers, once it's online:

■ Add the URL (Web site address) to every piece of printed sales and marketing material your company uses. This includes all of your traditional advertising, such as print ads, radio and TV ads, and billboards. In a prominent space on these materials, add a phrase like "Visit us on the Web at www.(your company).com" or "For more information, check out our Web site at www.(your company.com)." Wherever your company's address and phone number is listed, add a line that displays your Web site's URL.

Unofficially...
Services like Service Metrics (www.servicemetrics.com) help Internet businesses measure Web site performance, pinpointing and solving critical performance issues. These can include knowing when people are accessing your site, which pages of your site they're accessing, and what keywords or search phrases have led them there.

- Add the URL to your company's letterhead, envelopes, business cards, sales receipts/ invoices, and press releases and press kit folders. If you're a retail store, consider having the URL printed on your shopping bags. Large retailers, such as The Gap and Barnes and Noble, display large signs within their stores encouraging people to visit their Web site.

- Knowing when people are accessing your online business, particularly what pages of your Web site they're accessing, and what keywords or search phrases they used to find piece of information on your site are all pieces of information that can help you better manage your online presence.

- List your URL prominently in your company's catalogs or direct mail pieces.

- If the products your company sells includes packaging or manuals, add your company's URL to these materials.

- If your business has an "on hold" message when people call you, announce your Web site as part of this message.

In addition to all of these methods for attracting your existing customers to your Web site, be sure to promote your site to new (potential) customers. Many Web site promotional methods are described in detail in Chapters 9, "Generating Revenues from Your Site," and Chapter 10, "Promotion Is the Key to Success." These methods include paid online advertising, ad banner exchanges, creating an affiliate program, registering your site with the Internet search engines, online-based public relations efforts, e-mail marketing, and establishing link exchanges with other sites.

One way to help get people to visit your site, especially if you're a well-known and established company, is to focus on your company's reputation and brand. People feel comfortable shopping online with merchants they're already familiar with and have positive offline experiences with. If you're The Gap, for example, a customer who is already familiar shopping at The Gap's retail stores will be more comfortable shopping on The Gap's Web site (www.thegap.com), as opposed to some unknown company selling jeans and T-shirts on the Web. People who buy clothing from The Gap are already familiar with the company's products and product quality. If your company already has a positive reputation in the traditional business world, be sure to exploit that reputation in the online world in order to boost the credibility of the online aspect of your business.

Just the facts

- A virtual business is one that was created for the sole purpose of doing business online.

- The biggest challenge a traditional existing business faces is integrating its new online presence with its established business, without compromising its reputation.

- An established business going online should choose its domain name carefully. The domain name should be your existing company's name, or one that's easy to remember and spell, and intuitive.

- Your established corporate and brand identity should remain consistent on the Web. The overall "attitude" of your site should be consistent with your corporate image.

- IBM's e-business solution (www.ibm.com/
  e-business) is designed specifically to help traditional businesses get the most out of the
  Internet.

- Once your Web site is online, start off by promoting it to your existing customers and clients
  using the methods outlined in this chapter.

GET THE SCOOP ON...
Your child's needs ▪ Your family's needs ▪
Key decisions and how to make them ▪
Preparing your child for care ▪ What to expect
the first day

Fine-Tuning Your Business Before Going Online

A s we've emphasized in earlier chapters, before you can take your online-based business idea and launch it into a profitable company, it's critical to do your homework. You need to know exactly what you're getting into, what type of time and financial commitment will be needed, and what to expect once your site actually goes online. It's necessary to become an expert in your field, become familiar with every aspect of how a traditional business operates, and also get to know what's involved with launching a business on the Web. This means truly understanding what the Web is all about.

Research—the key to success

Once you're convinced your business idea is sound and you've begun developing your Web site and putting the infrastructure of your business in place, but before going online, it's vital to develop

Bright Idea
As early as possible, discuss with your business partners or lawyers who will be responsible for designing and maintaining your Web site. It might be helpful to have one person be the "go-to" person, the resident authority for questions that arise.

well-thought-out answers to the following questions. To obtain honest and accurate answers to the these questions, research will be required. This will probably mean making a time commitment on your part. Think of the time you spend now doing research as an investment in your company's future success, because the more prepared you are right from the start, the better your chances will be for success once your online-based business is actually launched and fully operational.

Some of the important questions you want to consider include:

- What is the market potential for your products/services?

- Who are your customers?

- Who is your competition?

- What is the current and projected size of the market and what is its growth potential?

- How will you reach your customers?

- Are your advertising, marketing, and promotional plans well thought out? Are your expectations of how well these plans will work realistic?

- How will you harness the power of the Web?

- What Web technologies are available to help you achieve your goals?

- Which ISP/Web host provider will you use?

- Once you receive orders, how will they be processed and shipped?

- What are your options for receiving payment from customers? Which of these options will be used on your site, and how?

- How will you obtain inventory? Who will be your main suppliers?

- How much initial investment capital is needed to help make your online business successful?

- How will you manage the day-to-day operations of your business? How automated will it be? What software is available to assist in your business's management?

Unfortunately, nothing can replace the need to do research as you prepare to launch any type of business. If you've already developed a business plan, hopefully you've already done much of the necessary research and the above questions have been answered.

In order to gather accurate and timely information, do as much research as possible online, and be sure to use industry-oriented magazines and newsletters as a resource. Also, don't just rely on one source of information when doing research. Whenever possible, try to confirm whatever facts and figures you uncover using multiple reliable resources.

Nobody is an expert in every aspect of business. Some people are more adept at business-related finance and bookkeeping, while others have a knack for marketing, product development, customer service, or management. Once you know exactly what will be required to make your business successful, carefully analyze your own talents, knowledge base, and skills. Determine what you're good at and what you know, and pinpoint the areas where you'll need to seek guidance.

For example, if you've never designed any type of Web site and you have no knowledge of HTML or Java programming, chances are you should hire an expert to design and manage your online business's Web site until you get up to speed on how this is

Watch Out!
If you don't have
answers to rele-
vant questions
before launching
your online busi-
ness, go back
and do some
fine-tuning in
order to avoid
problems down
the road.

done. Likewise, if you're highly computer literate and have an excellent idea for an online business, but you lack the knowledge to manage a traditional business, you might want to partner with someone with business-related skills and experience.

If your online business is simply a part-time activity and you're already financially stable thanks to a full-time job, it's a bit safer to take the learn-as-you-go approach to operating your own start-up business. However, if you're making a significant financial and time investment in the launch of your business, and you're relying on this business to generate your income, there's no substitute for doing research about every aspect of your business and acquiring in advance as much knowledge as possible.

There are millions of reasons why new businesses fail, and an equal number of mistakes you could make that might lead to serious problems. Competition is fierce out there, and customers are becoming increasingly more savvy and demanding. Unless you have the infrastructure and knowledge in place to deal with every situation that might arise, think twice about actually launching your business, because you're unprepared. If you don't already have a long list of potential problems your business could run into (and know how you'll deal with these situations), you haven't done enough research and preparation. Lack of preparation and lack of funding are some of the common reasons why start-up businesses of any kind fail.

In the business world, chances are there will always be someone you perceive to be smarter than you operating a competing business that's better funded than yours. It's your job to take full advantage of the assets, skills, and knowledge available to you and make the most of them. When it comes to traditional business, in certain situations your chances of competing successfully are slim to none—for example, if you were to open a small sporting goods shop or pharmacy a block away from a Wal-Mart. The Internet, however, offers a much more level playing field, because your presence on the Web can evolve into something just as professional-looking, functional, and engaging as your competition, no matter how big the competition.

Every well-run business on the Web has a fairly equal chance for success, provided that the people operating the business know what they're doing. Of course, if you're planning to launch an online business like Amazon.com to compete head-on with traditional bookstore chains like Waldenbooks and Barnes and Noble, it will take a significant amount of investment capital. But millions of online entrepreneurs have already been successfully launching online businesses that are smaller in scale and that target a niche market with a specialized or customized product.

If you have a unique idea (or at least a really good idea) for an online business, you develop a professional-looking Web site, and you know exactly who your target audience is and how to reach them successfully, your chances for achieving success will be excellent. Starting any type of business involves taking some risks, careful planning, conducting extensive research, and making a significant time and financial commitment.

Becoming a niche marketing expert

Unless you have millions of dollars to invest in an online business that will cater to the masses and

Watch Out!
If you've made the decision to launch an online-based business, dedicate yourself to doing it right and putting in the necessary effort, or don't bother. Doing it halfheartedly will doom you to failure.

compete head-on with the big players, your best chance for success in launching an online business is to cater to a niche—or specialized—market. The audience for a niche-oriented product is typically a group with a very well-defined interest, need, or desire. Your job is to determine who these people are and exactly what their interest, need, or desire is. Next, you must figure out a way to convey to this audience that you have a product that caters directly to their wants.

By carefully defining your company's niche market, determining who the people are that make up the market, determining what their needs and wants are, and then pinpointing a way to cater to the market with a unique product or service, you'll soon become a niche-marketing expert. At the very least, you'll become an expert in the niche market your business is catering to.

If you don't truly understand who your target audience is and how your product meets their wants, your sales will suffer. Likewise, if you don't truly believe that what you're offering to your target audience is a solution to a problem or answer to a need, you won't convince a potential customer that what you're offering has any value whatsoever.

Just because you have a Web site that's selling a product you believe is useful doesn't mean the rest of the world will share your belief. Like a sales brochure, TV commercial, or print ad, your Web site should be a powerful sales tool, designed to educate visitors about your product and how it offers something a potential customer wants.

As you analyze your niche market, consider carefully if these people are typical Web surfers and whether or not they have the ability to order products online using a major credit card. Young adults, kids, and teens are more apt than their elders to be computer savvy and comfortable surfing the Web. They also typically have a high level of disposable income (or a lot of influence over their parents' buying habits). But as a rule, younger surfers don't have credit cards to place orders online. Older people, on the other hand, also have a lot of disposable income, but a relatively small percentage of people over the age of 55 are comfortable shopping online.

The online buying habits of people are changing rapidly as more and more people, from all walks of life, gain access to the Web. Without making assumptions, ensure the niche audience you're trying to reach is, in fact, online and able and willing to make purchases on the Internet.

Identifying the needs and wants of your potential customers

Once you determine what product your online-based business will be offering and who the target market is, it's your job to get to know your potential customers. Defining your target market means determining some or all of the following information:

- Age range
- Income level
- Gender
- Occupations
- Level of education
- Hobbies
- Interests
- Religion
- Buying and spending habits

Bright Idea
Don't forget to think about your competition when you plan your Web site. Your site needs to convey not just why a potential customer should buy from you, but also why your product tops what's available from your competition.

- Internet surfing habits

- Special interests, needs, and concerns

- Club, association, or group affiliations

Only by truly understanding your target audience will you be able to design a Web site that caters to them. Once you have developed a profile of who your potential customer is, you must determine what her needs, interests, and wants are as they relate to the product you plan on offering. Will your product solve a problem, meet a need, save the customer time or money, help her achieve a goal, or provide her with something she really wants?

As part of your business plan and overall business practices, you must figure out exactly what it is about your product or service that someone will be interested in. Next, you must use a combination of the resources available to you using the Web (such as text, graphics, audio, video, animations, and interactivity) to inform your target audience about your product in a way they'll find engaging, informative, and easy to understand.

The more defined your niche market is, the easier it will be to find ways to reach these people and promote your Web site and products to them. Later in this book, you'll read about several start-up business ventures, including LefKey International (www.lefkey.com), an online-only business that sells computer keyboards designed for left-handed computer users. This is a relatively small market to begin with; however, LefKey has been successful in targeting specific groups of left-handed individuals, including those with jobs involving a lot of hands-on computer work (such as accountants, programmers, and office support personnel). LefKey knows exactly

Watch Out!
If you conduct surveys online, remember that visitors are often hesitant to provide personal information about themselves until they're ready to place an order for your product. In addition, unless you give them an incentive—such as offering a discount or free gift—they probably won't want to take the time to answer your questions.

who its target audience is and uses its marketing dollars to specifically reach this niche.

Understanding your target market is vitally important when developing your Web site. It's also important when determining how and where you'll be marketing and promoting your online business. Whatever money you allocate toward marketing, advertising, and promoting your business will be spent best if those funds allow you to directly reach the group of people your business is targeting.

Knowing who your audience is and what their needs and wants are will make it much easier for you to sell your products to these people. In advance, you should come up with an extensive list containing all of the reasons why someone in your target audience will want your product, and then develop a list of objections or reasons they might have for not buying your product. Using your list of objections, come up with solutions or a sales pitch that addresses each objection, and determine the best way to communicate this information online.

Conducting formal or informal market research, interviewing focus groups, and/or sending out questionnaires to customers will help you better understand your target audience.

As your online business begins to take form and you sit down to plan out and design your Web site, make sure you're catering every aspect of the site to your target audience.

Beware of get-rich-quick schemes

Anyone with an e-mail address, fax machine, U.S. mailbox, TV, or access to some of the less reputable business publications is constantly bombarded with offers to get rich quick while working from home or

Bright Idea
Any information or content on your site that's not directly addressing a concern or providing useful information to the potential customer should either be removed or reworked, in order to make your site as informative, user-friendly, and clutter-free as possible.

using the Internet. Con artists have devised all sorts of scams, pyramid schemes, and multilevel marketing plans. These initially appear to be extremely attractive, but in reality, they're complete ripoffs or business opportunities for which the profit potential has been greatly exaggerated.

Yes, people have been successful establishing Web sites to sell legitimate multilevel marketing products. But there are many Web-based get-rich-quick schemes, franchises, and business opportunities that you should definitely avoid. As a general rule, if the offer sounds too good to be true, it is. If you receive unsolicited e-mail (spam) offering an extraordinary business opportunity, be wary.

Tips for avoiding pyramid schemes

When it comes to determining if you're about to get caught up in a pyramid scheme and perhaps get ripped off, the Federal Trade Commission (FTC) recommends following these basic rules:

- Beware of plans asking you to spend money on costly inventory.

- Be cautious of claims that you will make money by recruiting new members instead of on sales you make yourself.

- Beware of promises about high profits or claims about "miracle" products.

- Be cautious about seemingly unsolicited testimonials to the effectiveness of the program; they could be from shills hired by the promoter.

- Don't pay money or sign contracts in a high-pressure situation.

- Check out all offers with your local Better Business Bureau or state Attorney General.

66

Over a quarter of the investment dollar losses reported to a federal-state database between March and October 1995 involved high-tech 'information super-highway' scams, with paging licenses and 900 numbers among those reported most often. Individual investment losses reported by the FTC ranged from $2,900 to as much as $400,000.
—The North American Securities Administrators Association (NASAA)

99

Scam artists from around the world are becoming computer savvy themselves and are cashing in on the Internet's potential by selling fraudulent Internet-related business opportunities. Many of these scams are targeted to individuals who are not technologically savvy. Many pitches are designed to take full advantage of a would-be entrepreneur's Internet innocence.

The FTC urges you to investigate Internet-related business opportunities as carefully as you would check out any business opportunity. It suggests that before you invest or buy into any online-based business opportunity, you should do the following:

- Realize that seminar "trainers" or "consultants" often are there to sell you a business opportunity, not teach you Internet basics. In fact, they may be counting on your lack of experience with computers or the Internet.

- Investigate all earnings claims. Talk to others who have purchased the opportunity to see if their experience verifies the claims. Whenever possible, visit them in person.

- Demand to see the company's claims in writing. Get all promises in writing.

- Ask for a disclosure document if you are interested in a franchise. This document is required by law. It should provide detailed information to help you compare one business to another. Be skeptical of companies that do not have disclosure documents.

If you run into trouble, you can file a complaint with the FTC by contacting the Consumer Response Center by phone at 202-FTC-HELP (382-4357); by

Unofficially...
Although the Federal Trade Commission cannot resolve individual problems for consumers, it can act against a company if it sees a pattern of possible law violations.

mail at Consumer Response Center, Federal Trade Commission, Washington, DC 20580; or through the Internet at www.ftc.gov/ftc/complaint.htm.

The FTC reports e-mail boxes are filling up with more offers for business opportunities than any other kind of unsolicited commercial e-mail. Many of these offers are scams. In response to requests from consumers, the FTC asked e-mail users to forward their unsolicited commercial notices to the agency for an inside look at the bulk e-mail business. The FTC discovered that, more often than not, bulk e-mail offers appeared to be fraudulent, and if the recipients had pursued them, they could have been ripped off to the tune of billions of dollars.

Twelve common scams

In a press release issued by the FTC, the organization identified the top 12 scams that are most likely to arrive in consumers' e-mail boxes.

Business opportunities

These business opportunities make it sound easy to start a business that will bring lots of income without much work or cash outlay. The solicitations trumpet unbelievable earnings of $100 a day up to $1,000 a day or more, and claim that the business doesn't involve selling, meetings, or personal contact with others, or that someone else will do all the work.

Many business opportunity solicitations claim to offer a way to make money in an Internet-related business. These messages usually offer a telephone number to call for more information. In many cases, you'll be told to leave your name and telephone number so that a salesperson can call you back with the sales pitch. You may also be asked to dial a 900 number to learn details about the business, while paying $3.99 (or more) per minute.

Bulk e-mail

Bulk e-mail solicitations offer to sell you lists of e-mail addresses by the millions, to which you can send your own bulk solicitations. Many companies offer software that automates the sending of e-mail messages to thousands or millions of recipients. Others offer the service of sending bulk e-mail solicitations on your behalf. Some of these offers say, or imply, that you can make a lot of money using this marketing method.

Sending bulk e-mail violates the terms of service of most Internet Service Providers. If you use one of the automated e-mail programs, your ISP may shut you down. In addition, inserting a false return address into your solicitations, as some of the automated programs allow you to do, may land you in legal trouble with the owner of that domain name.

Sending bulk e-mail to recipients who have specifically requested you to send them information or put them on your mailing list is an entirely different story. Using bulk e-mail to reach this type of audience is a powerful and acceptable marketing tool.

Incidentally, using cookies (refer to Chapter 12, "Making Your Site Look and Sound Great") and online questionnaires and order forms, you will probably be gathering information about your customers or Web site visitors. So it's wise to include a *Privacy Statement* somewhere on your site, indicating that any information gathered by your company will be kept confidential and that you won't be selling their information to other companies. Visit several

Watch Out!
Several states have laws regulating the sending of unsolicited commercial e-mail, which you may unwittingly violate by sending bulk e-mail. Few legitimate businesses, if any, engage in bulk e-mail marketing for fear of offending potential customers.

different established online businesses to see how they word their own privacy statement.

Chain letters

With chain letters, you're asked to send a small amount of money ($5–$20) to each of four or five names on a list, replace one of the names on the list with your own, and then forward the revised message via bulk e-mail. The letter may claim that the scheme is legal or that it's been reviewed by a lawyer, or it may refer to sections of U.S. law that legitimize the scheme. Don't believe it. Chain letters—traditional or high-tech—are almost always illegal, and nearly all of the people who participate in them lose their money. The fact that a "product" such as a report on how to make money fast, a mailing list, or a recipe may be changing hands in the transaction does not change the legality of these schemes.

Work-at-home schemes

Envelope-stuffing solicitations promise steady income for minimal labor—for example, you'll earn $2 each time you fold a brochure and seal it in an envelope. Craft assembly work schemes often require an investment of hundreds of dollars in equipment or supplies, and many hours of your time producing goods for a company that has promised to buy them. You'll pay a small fee to get started in the envelope-stuffing business. Then, you'll learn that the e-mail sender never had real employment to offer. Instead, you'll get instructions on how to send the same envelope-stuffing ad in your own bulk e-mailings. If you earn any money, it will be from others who fall for the scheme you're perpetuating. And after spending the money and putting in the time on the craft assembly work, you are likely to find promoters who refuse to pay you, claiming that your work isn't up to their "quality standards."

Health and diet scams

Pills that let you lose weight without exercising or changing your diet, herbal formulas that liquefy your fat cells so that they are absorbed by your body, and cures for impotence and hair loss are among the scams flooding e-mail boxes. These gimmicks usually don't work. The fact is that successful weight loss requires a reduction in calories and an increase in physical activity. Beware of case histories from "cured" consumers claiming amazing results; testimonials from "famous" medical experts you've never heard of; claims that the product is available from only one source or for a limited time; and ads that use phrases like "scientific breakthrough," "miraculous cure," "exclusive product," "secret formula," and "ancient ingredient."

Free goods

Some e-mail messages offer valuable goods for free—for example, computers, other electronic items, and long-distance phone cards. You're asked to pay a fee to join a club, then told that to earn the offered goods, you have to bring in a certain number of participants. You're paying for the right to earn income by recruiting other participants, but your payoff is in goods, not money. Most of these messages are really pyramid schemes, operations that inevitably collapse. Almost all of the payoff goes to the promoters and little or none to consumers who pay to participate.

Investment opportunities

Investment schemes promise outrageously high rates of return with no risk. One version seeks

Unofficially...
The trendiest get-rich-quick schemes offer unlimited profits exchanging money on world currency markets; newsletters describing a variety of easy-money opportunities; the perfect sales letter; and the secret to making $4,000 in one day.

investors to help form an offshore bank. Others are vague about the nature of the investment, stressing the rates of return. Many are Ponzi schemes, in which early investors are paid off with money contributed by later investors. This makes the early investors believe that the system actually works, and encourages them to invest even more.

Promoters of fraudulent investments often operate a particular scam for a short time, quickly spend the money they take in, then close down before they can be detected. Often, they reopen under another name, selling another investment scam. In their sales pitch, they'll say that they have high-level financial connections, they're privy to inside information, they'll guarantee the investment, or they'll buy back the investment after a certain time. To close the deal, they often serve up phony statistics, misrepresent the significance of a current event, or stress the unique quality of their offering—anything to deter you from verifying their story.

Cable descrambler kits

For a small sum of money, you can buy a kit to assemble a cable descrambler that supposedly allows you to receive cable television transmissions without paying any subscription fee. The device that you build probably won't work. Most of the cable TV systems in the U.S. use technology that these devices can't crack. What's more, even if it worked, stealing service from a cable television company is illegal.

Guaranteed loans or credit on easy terms

Some e-mail messages offer home equity loans that don't require equity in your home, as well as solicitations for guaranteed, unsecured credit cards, regardless of your credit history. Usually, these are said to be offered by offshore banks. Sometimes they are combined with pyramid schemes, which offer you an opportunity to make money by attracting new participants to the scheme. The home equity loans turn out to be useless lists of lenders who will turn you down if you don't meet their qualifications. The promised credit cards never come through, and the pyramid money-making schemes always collapse.

Credit repair

Credit-repair scams offer to erase accurate negative information from your credit file so you can qualify for a credit card, loan, or job. The scam artists who promote these services can't deliver; only time, a deliberate effort, and a personal debt repayment plan will improve your credit. The companies that advertise credit-repair services appeal to consumers with poor credit histories. Not only can't they provide you with a clean credit record, but they also may be encouraging you to violate federal law.

Vacation prize promotions

Electronic certificates congratulating you on "winning" a fabulous vacation for a very attractive price are among the scams arriving in your e-mail. Some say you have been "specially selected" for this opportunity. Most unsolicited commercial e-mail goes to thousands or millions of recipients at a time. The cruise ship you're booked on may look more like a tug boat. The hotel accommodations likely are shabby, and you may be required to pay more for an upgrade. Scheduling the vacation at the time you want it also may require an additional fee.

Other online scams to watch out for

Internet Fraud Watch (www.fraud.org / 800-876-7060), operated by the National Consumers

Watch Out!
If you follow the advice of credit-repair services by lying on a loan or credit application, misrepresenting your Social Security number, or getting an Employer Identification Number from the Internal Revenue Service under false pretenses, you will be committing fraud.

League, reports that Internet-related fraud complaints have increased 600 percent since 1997. Online auction complaints were the No. 1 fraud complaint in 1998. Auctions were first in 1997 with 26 percent of the total frauds reported, but increased to 68 percent in 1998.

The IFW's research shows that the majority of fraudulent payments (93 percent) were made offline by check or money order sent to the company. "Requesting cash is a clear sign of fraud," says Grant. "If possible, pay by credit card because you can dispute the charges if there is a problem."

Rounding out the top ten scams, in order (according to the Internet Fraud Watch), are:

■ general merchandise sales,

■ computer equipment/software,

■ Internet services,

■ work-at-home, business opportunities/franchises,

■ multilevel marketing/pyramids,

■ credit card offers,

■ advance-fee loans, and

■ employment offers.

> 66
> More people are online, and more people are getting scammed .... Consumers need to remember that con artists are everywhere—even in cyberspace.
> —Susan Grant, Director of the Internet Fraud Watch
> 99

Some online auction services, such as eBay.com, are wholly legitimate and very successful online businesses that allow anyone to buy and sell virtually anything. The problem people run into using these auction services is not the services themselves but certain sellers who use these service to sell their products. Such people, who are not affiliated with the online auction, are dishonest and sell products that aren't as described (such as an illegally pirated copy of commercial software that is described as an unopened retail version).

Always pay attention to details

If you ask small, Web-based business owners what makes their business successful, one of the top answers you'll hear repeatedly is paying careful attention to detail. When designing and maintaining your business, attention to detail means:

- Correcting spelling and grammatical mistakes before your Web site goes online.

- Making sure there are no dead links on your site.

- Making sure your site is optimized to work with each of the popular Web browser programs.

- Ensuring you obtain the information you need on your order forms in order to process orders accurately.

- Ensuring that your site is easy to navigate, and that all of the navigational icons and toolbars are clearly visible and intuitive.

- At the bottom of each page, there's a "Back" or "Main Page" icon allowing someone to quickly and easily link back to your site's main page.

- Your company's contact information (such as e-mail address, toll-free phone number, and fax number) is clearly displayed on each page of your site.

Moneysaver
Make sure your site contains accurate product information, statistics, and product numbers. Otherwise, you risk losing sales—and money.

Many online tools add special features to your site and assist in site maintenance. One such Web site is BigInfo.net (www.biginfo.net/pages/OnlineTools), which offers links to dozens of other useful sites for Web page designers and Webmasters.

Designing a Web site can get a bit confusing if your site offers too many links. NetMechanic (www.netmechanic.com) offers free online utilities to check a Web site for broken links, spelling mistakes, Web browser software compatibility, and average download times. These are all details that need your attention on an ongoing basis.

Making online ordering fast, easy, and secure

In addition to having the capability to process secure transactions, your Web site's online order forms need to be easy to understand and require as few keystrokes or mouse clicks as possible. Your site should automatically calculate subtotals, shipping charges, sales tax, and so forth, and display this information in a format your customers will be able to understand.

Before designing your own site, visit several e-commerce sites and see what other companies have done to make their online ordering procedures as quick and easy as possible. Using the "shopping cart" approach, your customers should be able to easily add and delete items before checking out and processing their order.

Placing an online order is often the most intimidating aspect of shopping online for the average consumer. If your site doesn't put customers at ease, chances are they won't place their order there. Before requiring someone to enter any personal information, it's an excellent strategy to clearly display information regarding your site's security measures and policies to help boost customer confidence. Always give someone the option to print out an order form and fax it to you, or to place the order by calling a toll-free phone number.

Some companies sell specific software packages online (which can be downloaded once an online payment is processed), where there is no company/customer contact other than via the Web site. Many of these software packages are designed for use by computer-savvy individuals who are comfortable placing an online order and downloading software which they purchase.

Just one example of a fully automated e-commerce site is Bonzi.Com Software (www.bonzi.com), which offers a variety of downloadable Internet utilities, including Voice E-mail 4.0, Internet Boost '99, and Intruder Alert '99. This site offers easy online ordering using what the company calls its "Secure Immediate Delivery System," which is explained in very simple terms on the actual site, helping to boost customer confidence in the company.

Make building customer confidence a top priority

In addition to providing useful information about your products on your Web site, it's useful to provide related information your visitors will perceive to be valuable. As you attempt to convey your message, it's important to build up the confidence of your visitors by positioning yourself as a reputable company, selling top-quality products at a fair price.

Some of the things you can do to enhance confidence in your company are:

1. Display your company logo on each of the Web pages throughout your site.

2. Prominently list a toll-free number people can call for more information or to place orders if they're not comfortable placing an order online.

3. Offer a "Company Information" or "Company Background" page on your Web site.

Bright Idea
Design your Web site's online order forms for a computer novice who has never purchased anything online before. The interface should be intuitive.

4. Make it clear your company offers totally secure online order processing.

5. Offer a guarantee of satisfaction, such as a "30-day, no-questions-asked, money-back guarantee" on all orders.

6. Include detailed descriptions and photos of your products.

7. Add a page to your Web site containing customer testimonials.

8. Add a page or an FAQ document to your site that answers all of the frequently asked questions people have about your company, products, ordering procedures, payment methods, online security, and so forth. This document can be written in a question and answer format. Be sure to provide detailed and easy to understand answers to questions you would have as a customer visiting your site for the first time.

Security and privacy: every Web surfer's concern

As an e-commerce site operator, become familiar with the potential hesitations Web surfers (your potential customers) have, and address these concerns directly on your site. To help build up consumer confidence, consider forwarding the following advice from the FTC to your site's visitors. At the same time, address each issue in terms of explaining how and why your online business offers a secure environment and is reputable.

The FTC offers this advice to Web surfers:

■ **When placing orders, always use a secure browser.** This is the software you use to navigate the Internet. Your browser should comply with industry security standards, such as Secure

Unofficially...
The Internet Alliance (www.internetalliance.org) is a trade association representing companies involved in online commerce. Along with the National Consumers League, it sponsors Project Open to help consumers get the most out of going online. Visit this site for ideas on how to boost the confidence of your site's visitors.

Sockets Layer (SSL) or Secure Electronic Transaction (SET). These standards encrypt or scramble the purchase information you send over the Internet, ensuring the security of your transaction. Most computers come with a browser already installed. You also can download some browsers for free over the Internet.

■ **Shop with companies you know.** Anyone can set up shop online under almost any name. If you're not familiar with a merchant, ask for a paper catalog or brochure to get a better idea of their merchandise and services. Also, determine the company's refund and return policies before you place your order.

■ **Pay by credit or charge card.** If you pay by credit or charge card online, your transaction will be protected by the Fair Credit Billing Act. Under this law, consumers have the right to dispute charges under certain circumstances and temporarily withhold payment while the creditor is investigating. In the case of unauthorized use of a consumer's credit or charge card, consumers are generally held liable only for the first $50 in charges. Some cards may provide additional warranty or purchase protection benefits.

■ **Keep a record.** Be sure to print a copy of your purchase order and confirmation number for your records. Also, you should know that the federal Mail or Telephone Order Merchandise Rule covers orders made via the Internet. This means that unless stated otherwise, merchandise must be delivered within 30 days, and if there are delays, the company must notify you.

Many companies with privacy practices post this information directly on their Web site. A company's

Bright Idea
Keep your passwords private. Be creative when you establish a password, and never give it to anyone. Avoid using a telephone number, birth date, or a portion of your Social Security number. Instead, use a combination of numbers, letters, and symbols.

privacy policy should disclose what information is being collected on the Web site and how that information is being used. Before you provide a company with personal information, check its privacy policy. If you can't find a policy, send an e-mail or written message to the Web site to ask about its policy and request that it be posted on the site. As an online business operator, you should be prepared to respond to these requests promptly and professionally.

Just the facts

- Nothing can replace solid research as you prepare to launch any type of business.

- Once you know what is required to make your business successful, analyze your own talents, knowledge base, and skills, then pinpoint the areas where you'll need help.

- If you have a unique (or innovative) idea, develop a professional-looking Web site, and know how to reach your target audience, your chances for achieving success will be excellent.

- Figure out exactly what feature of your product or service would interest someone. Then use Web resources to inform your target audience about your product in an engaging way.

- Watch out for scam artists who sell fraudulent Internet-related business opportunities.

- Placing an online order can be intimidating to the average consumer. Be sure your site puts customers at ease.

GET THE SCOOP ON...
The pros and cons of selling or trading
online advertising space ▪ Income
from downloadable products ▪ Charging
for site access

Generating Revenues from Your Site

Chapter 9

Whether you're developing a Web site to promote an existing business or you're planning to use your site for selling your product or service, there are many ways you can generate income from the site. These include:

- Taking orders for your product or service online using automated credit card processing.

- Using your site as an interactive brochure and encouraging people to visit your retail store, call your toll-free number, or send a check to make a purchase.

- Offering software or information that can be paid for online and downloaded on the spot.

- Selling online advertising space to other companies.

- Selling access (membership) to your site.

We'll discuss all of these issues in this chapter.

Using your site to accept purchase requests

The purpose of many online businesses is to encourage visitors to make purchases directly from the site, typically paying by credit card. Depending on the product or service sold, you might then ship the product via a traditional courier such as U.S. Mail, FedEx, or UPS.

If the customer is purchasing software or information that can be downloaded, your e-commerce site can become a fully automated business; someone can pay by credit card and then download the software or information they purchase directly from the site. Offering information for sale in the form of electronic books or documents is relatively easy, especially using Adobe Acrobat 4.x software. This software allows you to create electronic documents in the Portable Document Format (PDF). PDF is the open de facto standard for electronic document distribution worldwide, which can be accessed and printed by any type of computer or Web browser when special software (available free to the document reader) is used.

Selling advertising space

Once your online-based business becomes established and you have a steady flow of visitors that fall into a specific niche market or demographic, you can sell banners or advertising space on your site to other companies interested in reaching your audience.

Unless your site receives hundreds of thousands of hits per week, you probably won't get rich selling ad space. You may, however, be able to defer some of the costs involved with maintaining the site itself. There are many independent services that can be used to monitor Web site traffic. It is these independent services which advertisers use to verify Web traffic and determine ad rates.

If you plan to sell advertising space on your site, you'll need to develop specifications, be able to track the number of visitors to your site, and develop fair ad rates. Many agencies specializing in online advertising can help you sell your available ad space on a commission basis.

Membership fees

Another way companies generate revenues from their Web site is by charging a time-based membership fee to access the specialized information on the site. If you're planning to make people pay to access your site, it's necessary to provide them with information or services they perceive to be valuable and not readily available elsewhere. Many sites that specialize in distributing online adult-oriented material have become extremely successful by charging an access fee.

Mainstream businesses that have attempted to charge membership, subscription, or access fees for content have had a much more difficult time getting people to pay for access to Web content, however. Many Web users believe surfing the Web should be free (once they pay for Internet access through an ISP). In addition, they believe that no matter what type of "premium information" or content your site charges people to access, chances are good that similar content is available elsewhere on the Web for free. Whether or not this belief is true is irrelevant; what matters is that people believe it and therefore resist paying access fees. So the success of such a site will depend on how well you're

Bright Idea
Niche marketing can generate extra income. If the visitors your site attracts fall into a well-defined niche market, you may find some advertisers will be willing to pay a premium in order to target your audience by advertising on your site.

able to alter this popular perception, at least among your target audience.

Affiliate programs have become another powerful revenue generation tool for online businesses. These programs are relatively simple to participate in and are described in greater detail later in this chapter.

Selling and trading online advertising space

Selling advertising space in the form of banner ads or sponsorships on your site is a way to generate revenue; however, many people visiting your site may be turned off by being involuntarily exposed to additional advertising over and above the marketing information they're receiving about your business's product or service.

If, however, your site offers information your visitors perceive to be valuable or unique, they'll be more willing to accept seeing the ads from which you derive income. Also, if you spread the advertising throughout your site and keep it relatively subtle, people will be much more accepting of it. For example, placing a banner ad just at the very bottom or top of a page can be effective.

Choosing to accept paid advertising on your site adds an assortment of additional management responsibilities, ranging from carefully calculating traffic to your site, preparing reports for your advertisers, selling the advertising space, and doing the financial paperwork associated with selling advertising. You'll also need to set advertising specifications for what types of advertising you'll permit on your site (such as the size of the ads, length of the animations, and the ad's content).

Watch Out!
The last thing you want to do is annoy or turn off a potential customer by exposing them to too much online advertising. Use advertising creatively, but avoid overkill.

It's always better to have advertising that somehow relates to your online business, so that you're offering visitors additional links to information, products, or services they are likely to be interested in.

In terms of the design and management of your site, building and maintaining a high level of customer confidence in your business should be a top priority. The advertising you display will affect how the visitors to your site perceive your company, and can either help or hurt your company's image and brand. Displaying on your site banner ads from large, well-known companies with excellent reputations creates a very different impression than offering banner ads from adult-oriented sites or poorly designed ads from small online businesses that people have never heard of.

As you outline your ad specifications, some of the things you'll need to spell out for potential advertisers include:

- **Accepted file formats**—GIFs, JPEGs, etc.

- **Banner dimensions**—A typical banner is 486 x 60 pixels; however, you can also offer vertical banners, advertising buttons, and smaller or larger banners.

- **File size limit**—You'll want to spell this out so you limit the time it takes for a visitor to download your entire page. Each graphic you add increases the overall download time. Most Web sites choose a maximum banner ad size of 32K (32,000 bytes) or 15K (15,000 bytes). By including the image size (in pixels) in the HTML code, you will decrease the download time.

- **Animation length**—This determines how long a particular animation lasts per cycle before

Bright Idea
Create an "Advertise Here" link on your home page, allowing potential advertisers to obtain specifications about your ad rates and target audience. Be clear about the types of advertising you will accept, and make sure the advertiser supplies his own artwork (banner ads) that meets your approval.

repeating. You'll want to keep animation lengths under five seconds so that the file size isn't too large.

■ **Tag line text**—This is one line of text, usually a maximum of five to eight words, that is displayed directly under the actual banner ad. It can be used to convey an advertising slogan, etc. It's your decision whether or not to accept tag lines and, if you do, to determine their allowed length, font size, and so forth.

■ **Target URLs**—Make sure you have full approval over the site your visitors will be linked to if they click on the ad. Also, remember that if a banner ad is animated, there may be a different link associated with each frame of the animation, so you'll want to review each one to see if it is appropriate for the image you're trying to convey for your own site.

Watch Out!
To avoid potential misunderstandings with advertisers, clearly spell out that your business has full approval over what types of advertisers and advertising content you will accept. Consider rejecting advertising for liquor, tobacco products, pornography, or products or services competing with your own.

■ **Signed insertion order required**—This indicates that you require a signed order, in writing, from the advertiser. It's an excellent idea to create a written contract/insertion order for your advertisers to sign.

Make it perfectly clear that all advertisements are subject to approval by your company's management, and that you maintain the right to refuse any advertiser, graphic, text description, or URL.

You'll also need to list your rates. Online advertising rates are typically based on a predetermined number of impressions or page views, and are measured in cost per thousand impressions (CPM). Your rate card should list the number of impressions you're willing to sell and the CPM. You may consider offering a discount to advertisers who purchase higher numbers of impressions. You'll also need to offer a discount to recognized advertising agencies purchasing advertising space on behalf of clients.

Your actual ad rates should be based upon how specialized your audience is and how many unique impressions an advertiser can expect to obtain. For example, if an advertiser pays for 100,000 impressions, but you only have 10,000 unique users visiting your site, each visitor will see the ad 10 times. If, however, you can guarantee at least 50,000 or 75,000 unique users based on 100,000 impressions, this makes your audience more attractive to many potential advertisers, because when an individual has seen an ad a number of times, new viewings of the ad are less likely to get him to click on it or buy the product or service it features.

Once you choose to accept online advertising, you'll need to provide advertisers with up-to-the-minute traffic reports on your site, so they can calculate the number of impressions in a particular time period and determine the click-through rates of their ads. To enhance your credibility with advertisers, consider using an outside service to compile traffic information to your site. In fact, larger advertisers and most advertising agencies purchasing ad space on behalf of a client will insist on this.

DoubleClick (www.doubleclick.com) is one of several well-established companies that helps Web sites manage their online advertising. Their products include:

- **DoubleClick Select** This service offers publishers ad sales and management. DoubleClick's ad management technology will manage your ad inventory and provide you with reports of site performance.

Unofficially...
Of course, you don't want your banner to get too few impressions—this will result in a message not getting properly communicated. But avoid "banner burnout," the point at which a banner stops delivering a good return on investment because it is seen too many times by an individual and gets stale.

- **The DoubleClick Network** This service is designed to help Web site publishers realize revenue from ad space inventory.

- **DoubleClick DART** Once you begin selling online advertising space, this service offers ad management service. It will handle your site's targeting, ad delivery, reporting, and billing.

DoubleClick Network is a collection of the most highly trafficked and premium-branded sites on the Web (for example, AltaVista, Dilbert, US News, and Macromedia).

Comprehensive online reporting lets advertisers know how their campaign is performing and what type of users are seeing and clicking on their ads. This high-level targeting and real-time reporting is one advantage Web-based companies have over other medium, like television, radio, billboard, or traditional print advertising.

Before you can begin selling online ad space to potential advertisers, it's important to learn the basics of how the advertising industry works. Numerous print and online-only publications target advertising professionals and people who buy and sell media. Some of these publications include:

Bright Idea
For a listing of other online-based businesses that offer services similar to DoubleClick, point your Web browser to www.internetadvertising.org/resources/networks.shtml.

Advertising Age*	www.adage.com
Advertising Law Internet Site	www.webcom.com/~lewrose/
AdWeek*	www.adweek.com
ChannelSeven	www.channelseven.com
Click Z	www.clickz.com
Forrester Research	www.forrester.com
Infoscavenger	www.infoscavenger.com
Interactive Week*	www.interactiveweek.com

Internet Advertising Resource Guide	www.admedia.org
Media Information	www.mediainfo.com
SRDS Online*	www.srds.com

* also offers a print edition

Another useful resource for helping you learn about buying and selling online advertising is cob.jmu.edu/wrightnd/buyingsellingadsmay98. htm. For a list of some advertising agencies specializing in Web advertising, point your Web browser to www.internetadvertising.org/resources/agencies. shtm.

If you have an established Web site that's already receiving a respectable level of traffic and you're looking to sell advertising space, you can hire an agency to represent your site to potential advertisers instead of having to solicit them yourself. CyberReps (www.cybereps.com) is just one example of an agency that works with Web site operators looking to sell advertising space.

Cybereps is one of many agencies recognized for the ability to develop distinctive sponsorship and promotional campaigns in addition to traditional advertising buys. The company offers media clients and advertisers several different sales and marketing choices, including media sales, marketing, and promotional programs. Cybereps clients include The Internet Movie Database, ClickZ Network, FreeRealTime.com, and Stewart Cheifet Productions.

Affiliate programs

Affiliate programs have become an extremely popular way for online businesses to generate revenue. You can choose to participate in another company's affiliate program, or you can establish your own.

Timesaver
If you're interested in selling advertising space to other businesses who want to reach your niche market, Ad-Guide (www.ad-guide. com/Media_ Buying_and_ Selling) is a Web site directory and search engine devoted to advertising and marketing services and resources.

Make sure, however, that the affiliate programs you choose are of interest to the people visiting your site. Likewise, the program you launch should attract affiliates that will really be able to generate traffic to your site.

According to LinkShare Corporation (www. linkshare.com), one of the Internet's leading affiliate program facilitators, if you choose to participate in another company's affiliate program, here's how it works:

> *Affiliate programs are a way for site owners like you to be compensated for driving traffic to online merchants' sites. You drive traffic by putting links on your site that, when clicked, send visitors to a merchant's site.*
>
> *Some merchants will pay you a percentage of all the sales they make when visitors from your site click on a link, go to the merchant's site, and buy something. Other merchants will pay you simply for sending the traffic their way, on a per-click or per-thousand click basis. Still others will pay for impressions. Merchants may also offer to pay you for a combination of these. It's a win-win partnership, because you get increased revenue and merchants get increased traffic.*

Revenue can be generated by your site by becoming an affiliate with companies that offer such a program, such as 1-800-Flowers or Amazon.com. If you display a 1-800-Flowers banner on your site, for example, each time someone links from your site to 1-800-Flowers and places an order, you will earn a commission on the sale. Displaying advertising banners from highly respected companies such as 1-800-Flowers, Amazon.com, The Disney Store Online, or

"
An Affiliate is a Web site that partners with an online merchant. The affiliate places links on its site to promote the merchant's products. In exchange, the affiliate receives a commission for all valid transactions it has referred.
—LinkShare Corporation
"

LinkShare is an affiliate program management service that allows Web site operators to participate in the affiliate programs of other companies. If you don't mind posting banner ads from other companies on your site, this is a good way to generate revenue from your site.

The Sharper Image, for example, can help boost your company's credibility among visitors to your site. When a visitor to your site sees ads from respected and nationally known companies, he will believe that these big companies have chosen to advertise on your site.

By operating your own affiliate program through a recognized service such as LinkShare or Yahoo! Store, you can generate traffic to your site and hopefully generate sales without having to pay any fees in advance. You'll only be obligated to pay your affiliates a commission based on sales generated by their referrals. For companies with a limited advertising and promotions budget, establishing an affiliate program is an excellent way of boosting traffic to your site, and a marketing tool online businesses of all sizes have found useful.

Later, in Chapter 16, "Successful E-Commerce Entrepreneurs Speak Out," you'll read an interview with Cara France, the founder of ArtisanGifts.com, who established her own affiliate program through Yahoo! Store and credits this decision with helping her business grow.

Bright Idea
Make sure your expectations are realistic. The click-through rate for banner ads is low, so don't expect to get rich quick by participating in this type of program. Participating in an affiliate program should be just one part of your overall marketing, advertising, and revenue generation plan.

LinkShare, like other reputable companies, provides clients with technology to make this type of program relatively easy. The company's software allows online merchants to alter, update, and improve their merchandising techniques.

Another respected service helping companies implement and manage affiliate programs is Revenue Avenue, a service of MSN Link Exchange (revenue.linkexchange.com). Using this service, you'll be able to increase site traffic and create qualified leads or generate sales. If you choose to establish your own affiliate program, you'll need to determine what incentives you'll pay your affiliate partners.

Just as if you were to participate in another company's affiliate program, you must decide if you'll offer your partners a pay-per-click, pay-per-lead, or pay-per-sale commission. Revenue Avenue, Linkshare, Yahoo! Store, or whatever service you choose to help you implement your affiliate program will offer you assistance in determining your pay rates, commissions, and/or incentives.

Another potential traffic booster is to participate in a Web ring, which is a group of sites based on a similar topic or area of interest that refer Web surfers to each other. For more information about Web Rings, visit www.webring.org. Participating in a Web Ring is also free of charge. The drawback is that you have to promote the Web Ring itself and other sites affiliated with it.

Selling software or other downloadable goods

When you think of the ultimate online business model, being able to sell downloadable software or information is ideal. There are no products to ship and no inventory to maintain. After you develop a

Watch Out!
One potential drawback to getting involved with affiliate programs or pay-per-click programs is that you must include other banners on your Web site. You want to avoid cluttering your site with too many ads from organizations or companies that aren't your own, or you could take attention away from what you're trying to sell on your site.

software package to sell online or create an electronic document, your Web site can be used to promote it. The site will accept and process real-time credit card payments, and then allow the customer to instantly download the software or information they've purchased—directly from your site. In most cases, there will be no in-person, fax, e-mail, or telephone communication with the customer. Your business is truly virtual, and once it's set up, almost entirely automated.

By operating this type of business, your primary objective once the site is operational is to promote the site's URL and drive potential customers to the site. This type of online business model works well if you have a unique software program (or utility) or information people will be willing to pay for and will want almost instantly. Since most people don't have broadband Internet connections, the size of the downloadable file needs to be kept within reason to make this type of business model viable.

If you have a printed book, brochure, instructions, or other document you want people to be able to purchase and download, one easy way to assure the printed document will maintain its layout and design when transformed into an electronic file is to use Adobe Acrobat 4.x (www.adobe.com).

Using Adobe Acrobat 4.x, you can take your printed (or desktop published) document and save it in the PDF format. A PDF file can be read by any type of computer or Web browser using a free program from Adobe (Acrobat Reader) your customers can download.

Three examples of successful online businesses that follow a business model involving the sale of downloadable goods are:

Unofficially...
Among many other innovative uses of Adobe's software, it permits the *Los Angeles Times* to provide readers with an online version, complete with color, photos, and headlines, exactly as they appear on the printed page. Many other newspapers, magazines, and newsletter publishers also use this software to distribute their documents via the Web.

- **Bonzi.Com (www.bonzi.com)** A software developer selling popular utility programs online; people can pay using a major credit card and then download directly from the company's Web site.

- **PetFish.Com (www.petfish.com)** This small online business sells a selection of virtual pet fish people can "adopt," pay for using a major credit card, and then download to their computer.

- **Beyond.Com (www.beyond.com)** Using a business model similar to Amazon.com, Beyond.com calls itself an online software and video game superstore. In addition to allowing customers to purchase thousands of software products online and then have their purchases shipped to them, a growing selection of software titles can be purchased and downloaded directly from Beyond.com's Web servers.

Charging visitors for access to your site

One of the most popular business models used by sites dealing in various types of adult-oriented material is based upon membership to a Web site. The online business operator sells a renewable membership, issues a password to access that site, and then provides unlimited access to the site during the membership period.

Some industry-oriented publications or high-priced newsletters also use this business model to distribute information to customers, subscribers, or members who are willing to pay for it on an ongoing basis.

Watch Out!
If you plan on offering downloadable software or electronic documents for sale on your Web site, make sure the ISP you choose to work with is capable of handling this type of online business transaction.

This type of business model works well if the information you'll be offering on your site changes regularly and people will be returning to your site often to obtain the information.

An example of a family-oriented Web site that uses a paid subscription-based business model is Disney's Club Blast (disney.go.com/preview/preview.html), an interactive Web-based activity center and online magazine published by The Walt Disney Company.

The Wall Street Journal Interactive Edition (www.wsj.com) is another example of a subscription-based online business model. Subscribers pay a flat annual fee for access to the electronic edition of the *Wall Street Journal*, which is constantly updated with new news stories and other features.

The Electric Library (www.electroniclibrary.com), another example of a paid subscription-based Web site, makes it possible to conduct research over the Internet, using a database of reliable sources.

With The Electric Library, any person can pose a question in plain English and begin a comprehensive search of several media, including hundreds of full-text newspapers and magazines, maps, photographs, newswires, and classic books. The content is updated daily.

By visiting the online businesses described within this section, you'll discover firsthand some of the options available to you when customers, members, or subscribers pay for the privilege of accessing Web site content. Speak with your ISP to determine exactly what programming and technology is available to help you implement this type of pay-for-access service.

Just the facts

- To sell online advertising space on your site, you need to develop advertising specifications, track the number of visitors to your site, and develop fair advertising rates.

- Choosing to accept paid advertising on your site adds an assortment of additional management responsibilities.

- Affiliate programs have become popular revenue generation tools among online-based businesses and e-commerce sites. Launching one can be an excellent way to drive traffic to your site with few or no up-front costs.

- Being able to sell downloadable software or information fits the ideal online business model—there are no products to ship and no inventory to maintain.

Promoting Your Site

GET THE SCOOP ON...
Paid and free promotion ▪ Banner
advertising ▪ Newsgroups and mailing lists
▪ Why you should avoid using spam
▪ Using traditional advertising ▪ The power
of public relations

PART IV

Promotion Is the Key to Success

A s we've discussed in earlier chapters, Web page design is a crucial part of starting your own online business. But it's not the whole story.

You can have all the greatest ideas in the world for the online presence for your business. You can even spend a fortune hiring the world's best Web page designers and writers to produce an awesome online presence. If potential customers can't find your site online, however, or don't even know of your business's existence, all your efforts will be in vain. An online business is no different from a traditional business, in that marketing, advertising, and public relations play major roles in the overall success of your venture.

You may not have the financial resources to launch an advertising and marketing blitz, with network television ads, national radio spots, billboards, print ads in national magazines, and extensive online ads/banners. But you can implement an aggressive grassroots marketing effort on almost any budget.

Next to developing an online presence for your business that's informative, visually appealing, easy to understand, and intuitive for user interface, it's critical that you develop innovative ways to promote your online business in order to generate traffic—and ultimately orders—for your product.

This chapter will explore some of the ways you can promote your business, with a focus on what can be done online with a relatively small budget. This includes online promotional, marketing, and public relations ideas.

The importance of promoting your online biz

If you're making a substantial financial investment in your business and have a large advertising and marketing budget, seriously consider hiring an advertising and/or public relations agency to help you develop an advertising, marketing, and PR campaign.

The target audience

As you're developing your business's Web site, begin articulating what your marketing strategy will be, focusing specifically on determining who your targeted audience is and the various ways you can effectively reach this audience. Once your business goes online, you want to drive as much traffic to your site as possible. At the same time, however, you need it to be the right kind of traffic.

Defining your target

A target audience can be any group of people with a specific need or desire to have your product or service. Your audience might be made up of primarily:

Bright Idea
You want the people visiting your site to be interested in your subject matter along with your product. This means you need to choose a target audience and market directly to it.

- Males.
- Females.
- Adults (ages 18–49).
- Teens (ages 14–17).
- Married couples.
- Singles.
- Seniors.
- People with a specific interest or hobby.
- High-income professionals.
- Homemakers.
- Home office workers (telecommuters).
- People with a specific career.
- People with some type of physical disability.
- Any other group of people you can define and reach through a targeted marketing, advertising, and PR effort.

Of course, your business may have several distinct target audiences. If so, you'll probably find it easier to implement one targeted marketing effort at a time. As you define your target audience, determine early on if these people are active Internet users. After all, it's only in the past few years that the Internet has become readily accessible to mass market consumers. The majority of the people currently online and active on the Web continue to be well-educated, middle- to upper-class professionals who are computer literate.

Once you've determined your target audience, decide exactly what message you're hoping to get across to this audience. What will you be trying to accomplish with your marketing, advertising, and PR? Are you trying simply to make people aware of your company or brand? Do you want them to visit

Unofficially...
Students make
up a good por-
tion of the
online popula-
tion, but when
marketing to this
younger demo-
graphic, keep in
mind that they
typically don't
have credit
cards.

your Web site? Is your goal for potential customers to actually order your product online? For example, Abercrombie and Fitch, the clothing company (www.abercrombie.com) has a strong online presence which specifically targets the college-age audience and provides information about the clothing as well as promoting the overall attitude of the company and the image of the clothing. The company uses its Web site to build upon the image it creates in its other forms of advertising and promotions.

How you convey an advertising or marketing message can mean the difference between a 1 percent and 10 percent response rate. The wording you use and the visual impact of your ad (including the colors, fonts, and ad size) will play a major role in getting potential customers to respond to your message.

If you don't have a well-defined target audience, it will be extremely difficult to reach the people on the Web who will be most interested in what your online business has to offer. Knowing your audience, however, is only the first step in developing an effective promotional campaign for your online business.

Reaching your target

After defining your target audience, the second step is to do extensive research to determine the best ways to reach them. We discussed in earlier chapters some of the concerns you'll have to keep in mind. What are their needs and wants? Are you solving a problem? Offering a benefit? Will your target audience save time or money using your product? Determine exactly what feature of your product your audience will be most interested in, and then develop a marketing message that will catch their attention.

Having defined your target audience and your message, the next step is to discover the best ways to get your message across to them. Does your audience tend to visit specific Web sites, read certain magazines, attend specific events or functions, or have well-defined buying habits?

Being able to effectively market any type of product requires such skills as the ability to communicate and a very good understanding of your audience. In addition, you need to understand at least the basics of how various media outlets work and the benefits of advertising on them, including television, radio, newspapers, magazines, direct mail, e-mail, online advertising, billboards, and PR.

Spend time learning who the major players in the various media are and the terminology used. Unless you hire an advertising agency to do your media placement for you, it'll be your job to determine the best ways to spend your advertising, marketing, and PR dollars in order to generate the most impact.

Since you'll be launching a new online-based company, you'll probably want to experiment with different marketing messages and use different promotional vehicles to determine what works best. Each time you execute any form of marketing campaign, it's important to carefully track the results to determine what works best and generates the most positive results.

Once your site is established, but before you begin promoting it, one of the first things you must do is develop a strong understanding of what your site is all about. Figure out exactly how to convey this information to others. On a sheet of paper, write your site's title, URL address, and contact information for the person responsible for handling

Watch Out!
Make sure the advertising medium you use fits the volume of traffic your site can handle. Running a television ad can spur millions of simultaneous attempts to contact you. An ad in a monthly magazine, however, seen by the same number of people, will cause orders to trickle in over time.

the advertising and marketing of your site. Then write a list of 25 keywords that can be used to classify your site.

Now write a 25-word, 50-word, and 75-word description of your site. Choose the wording carefully, so your description catches the attention of the reader, describes what your online business is all about, and encourages the reader to visit your site.

This information will prove crucial when registering your site with the various search engines, as well as when you send out press releases announcing your site to the media and general public. You can also use this information to attract people's interest when you begin participating in newsgroups and mailing lists.

Later, when it comes time to find sites on the Web where you can advertise or exchange banner ads or links, use the same list of keywords you just compiled to find other sites of interest to a similar audience.

Promotional and advertising opportunities available online

When it comes to promoting an online business, you don't necessarily have to go any further than the Internet to reach potential customers. Of course, the best ways to reach customers for your product will vary based on the type of business you're operating. The Internet does, however, provide a variety of different promotional opportunities that can be used to target mass groups or very specific demographic audiences, depending on your needs.

If you've spent any time surfing the Web or exploring online services such as America Online, you've seen banner advertising. Online ad banners are typically rectangular display ads (which may be

Bright Idea
Using e-mail can be a highly effective way to reach a target audience. But use a list of e-mail recipients who *want* information from your company. Randomly spamming strangers by the thousands, while inexpensive, is considered rude and unprofessional, and it often annoys the recipient.

animated) that viewers can click on in order to visit whatever Web site is being promoted. You'll discover in Chapter 11, "Tapping the Power of Internet Search Engines and Portals," that purchasing banner ad space on the major search engines is an effective and widely used way to generate traffic to your site.

You can also purchase or trade banner ad space on other Web sites or online services that cater to the audience you're trying to reach. If you don't have a large budget to spend on online advertising, you can take advantage of services like Link Exchange, networks of Web sites that trade banner ad space.

In June 1997, the Internet Advertising Bureau (www.iab.net) commissioned Millward Brown Interactive to conduct the IAB Online Advertising Effectiveness Study. Regarding online banner advertising, his study concluded that Web ad banners can "remind consumers about brands for which they are already aware [and] inform users about products that were not previously on the consumer's radar."

The study attributed most of the increased recognition on the simple presence of the banner, whether or not the visitor clicked on it.

Banner advertising can be extremely effective if your banner ad message is appropriate, catchy, and placed on sites where people interested in your product or service are surfing. There are also many other online promotional and advertising opportunities available, including:

- Internet newsgroups.
- Internet mailing lists.
- ListBot and SparkList electronic mailing lists.
- E-mail broadcasts (spam).

Unofficially...
Advertising Age, the advertising industry's top magazine, offers an online edition featuring news and articles of interest to anyone involved with online advertising. To access the online edition, visit www.adage.com.

- Electronic press release distribution.
- Sponsoring and participating in online chats.

Internet newsgroups and mailing lists

Newsgroups are one of the most used features on the Internet. Their exact structure varies somewhat from group to group, but Microsoft's definition is still the most useful explanation. According to Microsoft,

> *A newsgroup is a collection of messages posted by individuals to a news server. News servers are computers maintained by companies, groups, and individuals, and can host thousands of newsgroups. You can find newsgroups on practically any subject. Although some newsgroups are monitored, most are not, and messages can be 'posted' and read by anyone who has access to that group. There are no newsgroup membership lists or joining fees. Your Internet Service Provider must have a link to a news server for you to set up an account with that news server .... After you set up an account, you can read and post messages on any of the newsgroups stored on that news server. When you find a newsgroup you like, you can 'subscribe' to it .... Newsgroups can contain thousands of messages, which can be time-consuming to sort through. Many newsgroup readers ... have a variety of features that can make it easier to find the information you want in newsgroups.*

Newsgroups and Internet mailing also provide promotional opportunities for your online business.

An Internet newsgroup is very similar to a public bulletin board or discussion group that focuses on a specific topic or caters to a specific audience. Anyone can start a newsgroup or participate in the "conversation" happening there.

Some newsgroups are moderated, which means someone acts as a gatekeeper and reads and sometimes edits each text message posted to a newsgroup in order to ensure that the material is relevant. Unmoderated newsgroups often get cluttered with spam and other messages that have no relevance to the newsgroup's main topic. The difference between a newsgroup and an online chat forum is that newsgroups don't happen in real time.

Since newsgroups cater to very specific audiences and focus on particular topics, becoming an active participant in newsgroups will allow you to reach potential customers with specific interests. To effectively use newsgroups, it's important to consider netiquette and avoid posting messages in the interactive discussion that are blatant ads for your product or service. Instead, by becoming active in the conversation, you can mention your online business as a resource and answer questions from others.

There are literally thousands of different newsgroups in existence, and new newsgroups are created daily. Some newsgroups have thousands of active participants who generate dozens or perhaps hundreds of messages per day, while others are less busy.

To obtain a complete listing of Internet newsgroups, visit www.liszt.com/news. Listz's "/news/" offers several methods for locating Usenet groups of interest.

Bright Idea
Check out I-ADVERTISING (www. internetadvertis ing.org), a definitive resource for information on the Internet advertising industry. This site and its accompanying e-mail discussion list will provide you with valuable resources and current information about the Internet advertising industry.

Internet mailing lists

Internet mailing lists are similar to newsgroups, except that messages posted to a mailing list are automatically sent to an e-mail in-box. According to Listz's homepage,

> *Internet mailing lists ... are (usually) just communities of people sitting around discussing one of their favorite topics by e-mail. For example, fans of bluegrass music can join BGRASS-L, and meet other bluegrass fans, and talk about bluegrass via e-mail.*
>
> *The mailing list format lends itself to calm, mature discussion, where relationships between the list members grow and deepen over an extended period of time. Most Internet experts feel that the mailing list format is the most civilized type of online community. Another common type of Internet mailing list is the newsletter or announcement format, where a single writer (the list owner or moderator) broadcasts a periodical e-mail to a willing audience (and the audience doesn't participate directly.)*

If you're interested in establishing an Internet mailing list to communicate with clients or customers, there are several free or inexpensive services to help you do it. For example, eGroups.com (www.egroups.com) provides alumni groups, support groups, sports teams and their fans, small businesses, and thousands of other organizations an integrated package of free net services for effective group communication.

LinkExchange's ListBot and ListBot Gold (www.listbot.com) are similar services designed for anyone interested in establishing and managing an Internet mailing list.

As an online business operator, you can communicate with your clients, customers, or anyone else using a one-way Internet-based mailing list. This allows you to broadcast newsletters, online fliers, and other information people you associate with are interested in. Creating an online mailing list and communicating with customers (or potential customers) can be an extremely powerful way of generating business, providing the people you're distributing your information to requested that information, and you're offering these people something of value or information they're interested in.

One service that can be used to manage and distribute one-way electronic newsletters or other correspondence to customers is SparkNet, which offers the SparkList service. According to SparkNet, "An 'announcements list' is a one-way list/communication where the list-owner sends a message to SparkLIST and SparkLIST sends the e-mail to everyone on your list (one by one). This is very similar to a fax-blast service, but for e-mail."

SparkNET Interactive is the leader in e-mail list hosting, promotion, management, moderation, and purification/merging/purging. According to SparkNET, there are several different ways online businesses can use a service like this one to distribute information to a large group of people online. These uses include:

1. E-mailing a company newsletter to your customer base

2. Sending new product announcements to existing customers

Timesaver
To search newsgroup content quickly, visit www.dejanews.com/=liszt or www.remarq.com. Both services work like Internet search engines, but you can search newsgroup titles and message content.

3. Distributing press releases to important media contacts

4. Building a mailing list of visitors to your site

5. Providing additional information to your customers via email. You can also offer special deals or promotions.

Paid online advertising versus free promotion

You'll discover from this chapter and the next that there are many different ways to advertise and promote your online business. Some promotional opportunities involve a financial investment on your part, to pay for things like online advertising, a graphics artist to design your ads, or an ad agency. Other opportunities are free, and simply require a time commitment on your part.

To establish your online business and generate an ongoing flow of traffic to your site (comprised of new potential customers as well as existing customers returning to your site), you'll need to invest time and money into advertising, marketing, PR, and promotion. Simply running a few banner ads or sending out a press release concerning your Web site isn't enough to keep your business thriving. As we've noted before, successfully marketing and promoting your business will take creativity, time, financial resources, and the willingness to experiment in order to determine what works best for your particular type of business.

Whether you have an advertising budget of several thousand or several hundred thousand dollars (or more), don't neglect the free promotional opportunities available on the Net, such as the use of banner exchanges, participation on newsgroups and mailing lists, and the use of e-mail.

The ins and outs of banner advertising

Perhaps the most common form of Internet advertising is the use of banner ads. These are display ads, often animated, that are placed on other Web pages and act as links to your site. Banner advertising can be used to enhance name, product, or brand recognition, or to lure potential customers to your site.

Online advertising is different from any other form of advertising, such as billboards and ads on TV, print, and radio. One major advantage to online ads is that the people seeing the ads can respond instantly and get more information about what's being advertised simply by clicking their mouse to link to a Web site created by the advertiser. Another distinct advantage to online advertising is that it works 24 hours a day, every day, and ad campaigns can be launched, modified, or stopped almost instantly. This gives you, the advertiser, total control over who, when, and where the public sees your ad.

To use banner advertising, the first step is to develop your advertising message and determine the specific audience you're trying to target. Next, develop the actual banner ad artwork to be placed online. It may be helpful to hire an advertising agency that specializes in Web advertising to assist you in the creation and placement of your banner ads; however, this is something you can do yourself with relatively little artistic or programming ability. In Chapter 11, "Tapping the Power of Internet Search Engines and Portals," information about creating a banner ad is offered.

Unofficially...
Click-through rate (CTR) is the response rate of an online advertisement. It is usually given as a percentage. For example, if an ad is seen 10,000 times and generates 50 responses, it would have a CTR of 0.5.

Unofficially...
Button ads are similar to banner ads. They're graphic-based, appear online, and can be animated, yet are smaller than banner ads (typically over 70 percent smaller). The most popular use of button ads are for links to instantly download software, such as Microsoft Internet Explorer or Netscape Navigator.

For a banner ad to help you generate business, it has to be catchy. Its job, just like a traditional print ad, is to capture the attention of the reader and, in this case, encourage her to click on the ad in order to visit your site.

Chapter 11 describes in more detail the most common ad banner sizes and shapes. As you create the artwork for your banner ad, keep size specifications in mind and tap your creativity to determine the best way to take full advantage of this advertising space using features such as color, fonts, artwork, text, and animation. Keep in mind that while from a creative standpoint it's easy to develop a flashy, in-your-face banner ad, research has shown that the simplest banner ad messages often have the greatest impact on viewers.

As you develop your banner ad, remember that only a small portion of people who actually see the ad are going to use it as a hyperlink to access your site. Research shows that on average, only about 2.5 percent to 3.5 percent of the people who see a banner ad will respond by clicking their mouse on the banner. This is called a "click-through." Your goal is to establish the highest possible click-through rate. This means developing an ad that's visually attractive, eye-catching, and informative, one that creates a sense of urgency, need, or excitement. What you say in your banner ad, how you say it, how the ad looks, and where the ad is placed will have a major impact on your click-through rate and, ultimately, the success of your business.

Ad placement is another key issue. Through research, you must determine who your customer base is and the best places on the Web to advertise in order to reach this base. Of course, you'll have to work within your advertising budget. Once you pinpoint where the best places for your banner ad are, it's important to determine the best position on a site for your ads to appear. The position on the page can have an impact on response rates.

One of the great features of online advertising using banners is that you can track the results instantly. As soon as your ad goes online, you can begin measuring how many exposures your ad receives and how many people visit your site as a result of seeing your banner ad. Based on this information, you can fine-tune your ad message or alter the placement of your banner ads to reach a more targeted audience.

The cost of banner advertising varies from a few cents per day to thousands of dollars per day, depending on the popularity of the sites where you're advertising. Rates are usually based on the number of impressions your banner ad receives (you pay for 10,000, 50,000 or 100,000 or more impressions), or the length of time your ad is displayed on a Web site. If your advertising-space purchase is based on time, it's important to request specific information about how many hits the Web site in question receives; also be sure to analyze how the site is promoted, to ensure it will continue receiving that level of hits while your ad is running.

When deciding where to buy online advertising space, do plenty of research. Part of your research should include surfing the Web looking for sites that would be appropriate for your ad and that cater to the needs of your potential customers. As you pinpoint individual sites, contact the Web master and request advertising information and rates. Often, at the bottom of a commercial Web site, you

Bright Idea
To learn about current online advertising rates for popular Web sites and search engines, visit the Ad Resource Online Marketing Web page at www.sisoftware.com/html/web_advertising.html. Or see the Interactive Advertising Source Guide, from Standard Rate and Data Service (www.srds.com).

Moneysaver
To save money when buying online ad space, visit Ad Auction, a company that provides a business-to-business e-commerce service for buying and selling media. They offer discounted ad inventory on quality, branded Web sites. Register on the company's Web site at www.adauction. com, or call (415) 575-0860.

will see a link that says something like "Advertise Here" or "Advertising Information." By clicking on these links, you can learn more about the advertising opportunities on the site. Once again, if you're having trouble determining the best places to buy online ad space, consider hiring an ad agency that specializes in Web advertising. These agencies have most likely already done the research and will know how much it costs to advertise on the various sites that will help you reach your audience.

In addition to search engines and special interest commercial and non-commercial Web sites, look into advertising under "E-zines" or "zines," which are online-only magazines catering to specific audiences. You can find these electronic publications using any search engine. To access a directory of popular "E-zines," visit www.dominis.com/Zines. The majority of these special interest publications accept paid advertising in the form of banner ads and buttons.

One alternative to doing this research is to take advantage of an advertising agency. One example is 24/7 Media, Inc. (www.247media.com), one of the largest Internet media companies. One benefit to using this type of agency is that you'll receive expert help developing your placement strategy, and your Account Executive will monitor your results and provide you with a full report to ensure maximum impact for your ads.

Finding an advertising agency you can hire is as easy as opening the Yellow Pages, using a search engine, or visiting the Web site sponsored by The American Association of Advertising Agencies (www.aaaa.org).

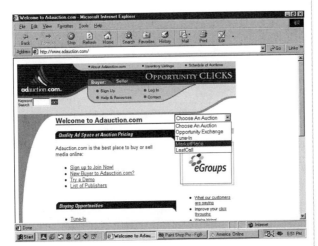

AdAuction.com is an advertising sales service that allows Web site operators to purchase online ad space at a discount. If your online business's advertising budget is small, this service is worth investigating.

Banner ad trades—the ad barter system

If your business is considered a start-up, you're probably trying to keep your overall costs down, while attempting to generate as much exposure as you can for your online-based business. One way to take advantage of banner advertising without having to pay for it is to trade banner ad space with other commercial or non-commercial Web sites. This means that you offer another Web site banner ad space on your site in exchange for ad space on their site. No money changes hands, yet both sites receive the benefits of cross-promotional advertising.

Obviously, your site's traffic may be lower than an already established site, so you may have to negotiate with other Web site operators to determine a fair exchange of banner ad space. For example, you may offer four weeks of banner ad space on your site in exchange for one week's worth of ad space on another site. If you can track exposures, you may agree to keep each other's banner ads on your

LinkExchange is one of several banner exchange services that allow you to promote your Web site using a banner, without paying for online advertising space on other Web sites.

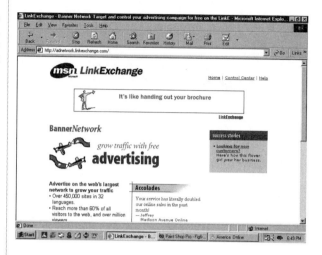

Watch Out!
Before signing up to participate in any banner exchange programs, make sure that you have control over the types of banners that will be displayed on your site. For example, make sure no sites promoting or advertising cyber sex or pornography will be displayed on your site.

respective sites until they receive a predetermined number of exposures (such as 10,000, 50,000, or 100,000).

There are several well-established online services, such as LinkExchange (a service of MSN.com, www.linkexchange.com), which help businesses trade banner ad space. At the time this book was written, LinkExchange had over 400,000 participating Web sites. There is no cost for using the service, and anyone can begin promoting their site within a matter of days. In exchange for incorporating banner ads for LinkExchange (or participating Web sites) on your site, the service will automatically display your banner ad on other sites.

Once you sign up to participate in the LinkExchange service, you'll be able to purchase highly discounted banner ad space on popular commercial Web sites, such as Yahoo!

Other banner-exchange services on the Web include:

▪ **Banner 123**   www.123banners.com.

- **One For One Banner X-Change** www.1for1.com.

- **Ad-Xchange** www.ad-xchange.com.

- **BannerSwap** www.bannerswap.com.

- **Exchange-It** www.exchange-it.com.

- **I-Stores Banner Exchange** www.i-stores.com/bannerx.

- **MS-Links Exchange** ms-links.com.

Press release distribution

A press release is a document (usually between 500 and 1,000 words) about your company designed to make a newsworthy announcement to the media. A press release is a key tool for public relations professionals. This type of document has a highly defined style and format, and in a nutshell answers the basic questions on the minds of reporters who might be interested in reporting on the topic of your press release—who, what, where, when, and why.

For tips on how to write a press release, visit Aid4 Writing a Press Release at: y4i.com/pressreleasewriting.html, "pertinfo" or the Gebbie Press Web site at pertinent.com/pertinfo/business/gebbiePress1.html. Online-based public relations firms, such as PressFlash (www.pressflash.com), or traditional PR firms can also be hired to write and distribute your press releases to the media for a fee.

Press releases can be distributed to the media (such as newspapers, magazines, radio news outlets, television news outlets, and online publications) via U.S. Mail, fax, or e-mail. Once you have a press release announcing your business (or some other newsworthy event relating to your business), your goal is to get it into the hands of the editors,

Watch Out!
Using any search engine, enter the search phrase "Banner Exchanges." A listing of other services similar to LinkExchange will be displayed. By visiting the sites for these various services, you can determine which ones offer you the best opportunities to target your niche audience.

reporters, and journalists responsible for covering your industry or type of business. This can be done by manually gathering your own media contact list by reading bylines in newspapers and magazines, or by purchasing a media directory. To help you compile your own customized media list, consider visiting the Web sites sponsored by *Editor & Publisher* (http://www.mediainfo.com), *Media Online Yellow Pages* (www.webcom.com), or The National Press Club (npc.press.org).

Broadcast Interview Source (www.yearbooknews.com, 202-333-4904) publishes a variety of media directories which list the contact names, phone numbers, addresses, fax numbers, and e-mail addresses of writers, reporters, producers, editors, and radio/television hosts. One of the books published by this company, called *Web News Selects*, spells out how to get in touch with the most influential editors and search engines on the Internet. This is a complete, up-to-date manual of phone and fax numbers—plus the still-crucial snail-mail addresses for online media.

The company also publishes *Talk Show Selects*, which profiles the most influential radio and television talk shows in the nation, as well as *Power Media Selects,* which profiles more than 700 of the most influential print and broadcast media outlets and organizes them in a single volume.

The Gebbie Press's *All-In-One Directory* (www.gebbieinc.com) lists contact information for over 23,000 media people from TV and radio stations, newspapers, magazines, African American and Hispanic media, news syndicates, networks, and AP/UPI bureaus.

Other media directories are published by:

- **Bacon's Media Directories** www.baconsinfo. com.

- **Burrelle's Media Directories** www.burrelles. com.

If you choose to save money and handle your own public relations efforts, consider using the press release distribution services of PR Newswire (www.prnewswire.com), Newsbytes News Network (www.nbnn.com), or Global Internet News Agency (www.gina.com). You supply the press release and pay the company's fee, and your release gets distributed to media representatives that you designate based on area of interest, industry, or a specific topic.

As you compile the list of media outlets to send your press releases to, don't forget to include:

- Television shows (especially those that cover your industry).

- Talk radio and news stations.

- Newspapers.

- Magazines.

- Trade journals.

- Newsletters.

- Online publications.

- The Webmasters at sites catering to your target market's area of interest.

- Special interest groups/clubs.

Bright Idea
Make sure the URL for your online business is listed prominently in your press release. This will help ensure it gets listed in any article your press release helps generate.

Using traditional PR efforts to reach both online and other media outlets in order to obtain free editorial coverage is a powerful way to reach potential customers. In order to generate the best possible publicity for your business, make sure your press releases contain only newsworthy information the media would be interested in covering. For example, if you're promoting a product, your press release should discuss what the product is, why there's a need for it, and why, for example, a magazine, newspaper, or radio or TV station's audience would be interested in it. The press release should position the executives within the company as experts in their field who are available to be interviewed.

If you're not familiar with how PR works, consider hiring a PR firm or consultant to assist you in generating media coverage for your online business. You can also read how-to books on the topic. Additional information about how to launch a PR effort for your business can be found online at the PR Place (www.prplace.com).

According to an article by John Hewitt (www.azstarnet.com/~poewar/writer/press.html) that appears on PRWeb.com (www.prweb.com/coach/970722a.htm), before sending out any press release, make sure you:

1. Know who to send it to, not just where. Find out who the editor or reporter is for the section you want your release to appear in.

2. Only send the release to one person per news outlet. Any problems that develop from duplicate coverage and effort will be blamed on you.

3. Don't just send press releases—call the editor or writer directly. If you want your release covered, call the person before sending the release, and call a couple of days later to make sure they received it. Just don't become a pest.

4. Know your deadlines. Magazines, even weekly ones, are often planned months in advance.

Bright Idea
Whenever you distribute a press release, also post the release somewhere on your Web site, under the heading "Corporate Information," "Company Background," or "Press Releases."

Seasonal events, such as Christmas and Easter, are great examples of this. For calendar items, know the news outlet's deadline for the section.

5. Keep it short and informative. Reporters and editors are notoriously busy. Most press releases should be kept to one page. Two is acceptable. If they want more information, they'll ask.

6. Write it in a news style. That means putting the prime information (who, where, what, and when) into the lead (first paragraph). It also means keeping the sales pitch subtle. No exclamation points!!! Many papers will directly reprint a press release, as long as it is written in a professional news style. Use short words and sentences. Make sure what you're saying is very clear.

7. Always include, at the top corner of every page, a two- or three-word description of the story, the name and phone number of key contact people (no more than two), the page number (if there is more than one page) and the release date (usually "For Immediate Release"; otherwise "Please hold until xx/xx/xx").

8. End a press release with ### typed across the center of the margin a couple lines below the end of your text. If a release is continued on another page, type "-more-" at the bottom of the page in the center.

9. Use standard 8 1/2" × 11" paper typed on one side only. Never break a paragraph across two pages. Leave plenty of margins for editors to write notes—an inch and a half all around should be fine.

Online chats

Hosting an online chat either through your own Web site or through a major online service is one way to communicate in real time to an audience. While it's inexpensive to host an online chat, if you want potential customers to attend the chat, it's important that you offer them information of value and not simply use this as a vehicle to convey your marketing or advertising message. For example, for a special guest, you might consider having an expert, celebrity, or author who will answer questions from chat participants.

Watch Out!
Spamming won't just annoy the people who receive it. It will also cause them to associate your company with cybersex, multi-level marketing schemes, or scams. This will hurt your brand and, ultimately, your sales.

Why you should avoid using spam

Let's face it, the concept of instantly sending thousands or millions of promotional e-mail messages to people on the Internet is very appealing, because the cost associated with doing this type of mailing is extremely low. The problem is, when you send someone an unsolicited e-mail message that's trying to sell him something, it's called *spam*, and most Internet users absolutely hate receiving spam because it clutters their e-mail in-box. If your online business is legitimate and offers a valuable or useful product or service, do you really want to alienate potential customers by sending them spam? Probably not!

The term *spam* refers to e-mail that's sent unsolicited to the recipient. Using e-mail as a marketing tool can, however, be a very powerful way of communicating with customers (or potential customers) who specifically request e-mail from your company. If your company sponsors an electronic mailing list through which you distribute a weekly or monthly newsletter for free, and you have people "subscribe" to this electronic publication, this is one highly effective way of using e-mail. You can also use e-mail to confirm orders, handle customer service inquiries or answer technical support-related questions.

As an online business operator, you will most likely see ads for online companies that specialize in sending spam very inexpensively to many people quickly. There are also several different software packages allowing the user to gather e-mail addresses and then send junk e-mail quickly. Again, if you're attempting to create a reputable business, this is not the marketing approach you want to take.

Some companies, such as PostMaster Direct Response (www.postmasterdirect.com), develop lists of e-mail users who specifically request information on specific topics of interest to them. You can purchase or rent these targeted e-mail lists and send these people e-mail for much less money than it would cost to send a mass mailing via the U.S. postal service.

If you choose to use some form of e-mail to communicate with your customers or potential customers, be professional. In the subject line of your message, clearly state what the content of your message is so the recipient can choose to read the message or delete it without having to spend time opening the message. Some companies choose to use misleading message subjects in order to get people to read their messages. While this may get someone to open the message, it does create a sense of resentment because the recipient was tricked. Keep in mind that some people receive dozens or even hundreds of e-mail messages per day, and they don't have time to read messages that aren't of direct interest to them.

Watch Out!
In the future, sending spam could become illegal. Moreover, many Internet Service Providers already refuse to allow their clients to send large amounts of e-mail from their accounts, and breaking these rules can result in costly penalties or having your online accounts through the ISP cancelled.

An opt-in e-mail list is one which the recipients have requested to receive in order to get information about a specific topic. One benefit of using such a list is that the audience is preselected and already somewhat interested in what you have to say. As a result, if you use an opt-in e-mail list in conjunction with a well-written e-mail message, your response rate will probably be considerably higher than the 1-percent or 2-percent response rate you can typically expect from sending a direct mail piece via the U.S. mail service.

When using e-mail as a promotional tool, be professional, be conscientious, and don't abuse the power of e-mail to harass the recipient.

Taking advantage of traditional advertising

For some online businesses, focusing exclusively on online advertising, marketing, and PR will be extremely effective. It's important to understand, however, that the really successful online businesses also use traditional advertising media to promote their Web site and generate traffic to their sites.

Traditional advertising vehicles include newspapers, magazines, radio, network television, cable television, syndicated television, billboards, in-theater advertising, direct mail, trade shows, and so on. Whether or not you choose to take advantage of any of these powerful media vehicles will depend on the audience you're trying to reach and your budget. One inexpensive way to tap the power of traditional print advertising is to run an ad in a special interest magazine or newsletter that caters to the target audience you're trying to reach. You can also use

> **"**
> Nearly 50 percent of the U.S. population, or 135 million people, will communicate via e-mail by 2001. Fifteen percent of the U.S. population (approximately 30 million adults, age 16 and over) use e-mail now.
> —Forrester Research
> **"**

classified advertising as a way to get short, text-based messages across to readers.

Millions of everyday people are Web surfers. So it makes perfect sense in some cases to promote your Web site using traditional newspaper, TV, radio, and magazine advertising. If your company already does traditional advertising, be sure to include your site's URL in the copy once your site goes online. The more prominent the URL is displayed in your print ads, the more traffic you'll ultimate generate to your site.

Just the facts

- Promotion and advertising are the keys to success for any online business.

- Aside from purchasing banner advertising space on the search engines, you can also either purchase or trade banner ad space with other sites.

- Your mission is to drive people interested in your product to your site. This means choosing a target audience and marketing to that audience.

- Advertising and marketing opportunities include trading links with other sites, taking advantage of newsgroups and mailing lists, using e-mail, hosting online chats, and distributing press releases.

- If you can afford it, also take advantage of traditional media outlets to advertise and promote your business.

GET THE SCOOP ON...
Your child's needs ▪ Your family's needs ▪
Key decisions and how to make them ▪
Preparing your child for care ▪ What to expect
the first day

Tapping the Power of Internet Search Engines and Portals

Chapter 11

There are literally millions of Web sites in existence, and more being created every day. No matter what topic you want to learn more about or what type of product or service you want to acquire, chances are you'll find it on the Internet's World Wide Web. With so many Web pages in existence, however, how do you actually find the information you're searching for? The fastest and easiest way to locate information on the Web is by using a search engine, Web directory, or information portal.

Internet search engines and portals

Initially, a search engine was nothing more than a database of Web sites that could be searched based on a keyword or search phrase. This has changed. These days, services like Yahoo!, Excite, AltaVista, The Go Network, InfoSeek, Lycos, and many others

Unofficially...
According to MRI Research, in Spring 1998 Yahoo! reached more Americans over the age of 18 (a total of 30.2 million) than many popular television and print media outlets, including *National Geographic* magazine (29.7 million), *Frasier* (NBC-TV, 29.2 million), *Time* magazine (23.5 million), *Sports Illustrated* (22.3 million), and MTV (21.7 million).

have become information portals. While they still work as basic search engines or Web directories, these services also offer a variety of other free services to surfers, ranging from personalized news, sports, and weather reports to private e-mail accounts and online chatting.

On the World Wide Web, search engines were among the first viable online businesses. Millions of Web surfers visit these sites daily in order to find information. Since Internet search engines are free to use, companies like Yahoo! sell online advertising space (banner and button ads) and sponsorships of their service. Of course, advertising on a popular search engine, Web directory, or information portal is an ideal way to reach large numbers of Internet users, and even target the audience you're trying to reach.

In addition to helping people find specific information, search engines, Web directories, and information portals are often used as a launch pad for people exploring cyberspace. Virtually all search engines and Web directories are searchable by keyword or phrase, but like the Yellow Pages, they're also divided into categories, allowing people to pinpoint links leading to topics of interest. So, even if someone might not know your online business exists, if he happens to seek out a list of sites under a topic for which your business is listed, you have a good chance of catching his attention and having him visit your site.

By visiting the powerful search engines yourself, you'll quickly discover that each is slightly different in terms of its layout and design. As an online business owner, ultimately you'll want to spend time pinpointing exactly how and where you want to be listed on each of the popular Web directories. Just like a telephone book, having your Web site (online business) listed with a search engine is totally free. All you need to do is complete an online form when visiting each search engine. (This process is described later in this chapter).

Understanding search engine lingo

Services like Yahoo!, Excite, AltaVista, and InfoSeek are considered Internet search engines. These and other services are also called Internet information portals, online services, Internet guides, and Web directories, based on the additional features and services they offer.

In everyday conversation, the terms "search engines," "Web directory," and "information portal" all refer to services like Yahoo!, AltaVista, The Go Network, InfoSeek, Excite, and so forth. But strictly speaking, there is a difference between these types of services. Yahoo!, for example, is technically a directory and not a search engine. The key difference is that search engines use "spiders" to crawl across the web. Directories are hand-assembled databases. Humans at Yahoo! determine what they list, not automated spiders…Alta Vista, Excite, HotBot, Infoseek, Lycos, and WebCrawler are the main search engines. Most others are directories.

They all offer the same basic Internet searching features, but how these features are implemented and what additional services are offered allow companies like Yahoo! to broaden their appeal and become more practical for Web surfers through the value-added services offered. (All of these are free to the user, thanks to paid advertising support from e-commerce companies like yours.)

When you visit Yahoo!'s main page (www.yahoo. com), one of the first things you'll see at the top of

Bright Idea
While descriptions of search engines are good starting points, there's no substitute for visiting the sites yourself. Try several different sites to get a feel for how they work, how one differs from another, and how you might be able to tailor your own business needs to the special features of each one.

the screen is an input prompt that allows you to enter a keyword or search phrase. Based on what you enter, Yahoo! will pinpoint and list Web sites that may be of interest to you.

A search engine is able to match up your keywords with the content of all Web sites in the service's massive database. This is done using specialized software called "robots," "spiders," or "crawlers," which scan Web sites to create a detailed index of keywords found on sites that have been registered with the search engine. The search engine's index is compared to the keyword or search phrase you entered and a listing of related Web sites is displayed, all in a matter of seconds.

The Web directory aspect of certain search engines

If you scroll lower on the Yahoo! main page, you'll discover an Internet Guide (Web directory), which begins by listing main headings. These include Arts & Humanities, Business & Economy, Computers & Internet, Education, Entertainment, Health, Recreation & Sports, Science, and Society & Culture. Below each of these headings are subheadings, which are hyperlinks that lead to still further subheadings. These headings allow a Web surfer to find information he's looking for based on a general topic, and then narrow down his search.

Online services are also sometimes referred to as Internet portals, because they provide a starting point for people to begin surfing the Web. Portals typically offer customized news and other features, allowing people to customize their online experience and also to search for information. Unfortunately, how well an engine is organized and indexed varies widely from one search engine to another, so it may require a bit of investigation to get the information you need.

MetaTags

A *MegaTag* is a search engine indexing device. The best summary I have found comes from WebPromote (www.webpromote.com), an Internet site promotion service.

> *MetaTags are a tool for helping a Web site to get indexed correctly by many of the major spider-based search engines. They are a couple of simple lines of text that go into the header of the HTML source document. Since spider-based search engines index Web sites based upon what they find in the HTML code of the site, MetaTags help to ensure that the visiting spider finds the information you want it to.*
>
> *The two tags that are the most important are the description tag and the keywords tag. The description tag gives the search engine the description that you want for your Web site. Without this tag, search engines will usually take the first few words it finds from your site and make that the description. The keywords tag tells the search engine exactly which keywords you want your site to be searchable under. Without this tag, a search engine will choose words for your site to be searchable under from the title and text of your site.*
>
> *It should be understood that MetaTags are not a turnkey solution for getting your site to the top of search engine lists. They will help to get your*

Unofficially... "Robot" or "crawler" software used by search engines will scan your site for the keywords you designate for your site. Make it easy for the search engines to determine what information, products, or services your online business offers. Incorporate MetaTags into the HTML programming of your site.

Watch Out!
When using a
search engine,
only the text
portion of vari-
ous Web sites
will be matched
to the keywords
or search phrase
you enter. Any
text that's incor-
porated into a
graphic file
within a Web
site, such as a
company logo,
won't be recog-
nized by a search
engine.

*site indexed correctly, and they increase the rele-
vancy for the keywords you chose, but they do
not guarantee top placement.*

InfoSeek, for example, is what's called a
MetaTag-enabled search engine. This means that as
a Web site creator (Webmaster), you can directly
determine your listing on InfoSeek (or any other
MetaTag-based search engine) by incorporating
MetaTags into your home page.

What a MetaTag looks like

Incorporating MetaTags into your site is optional. In
terms of generating traffic to your site that originates from the various search engines, the few minutes it takes to add MetaTags to your site will be
extremely beneficial, especially since there is
absolutely no cost involved.

The first box on the next page is a sample of
what MetaTag HTML programming looks like. It
was created using WebPromote's MetaTag Builder
for a fictional site that could be used to promote this
book.

The second box contains lines of HTML programming would be placed within the site's existing
source code and inserted into the head section
(codes between <head> and </head>). This can be
done through any ordinary text editor (for example: Microsoft Notepad) or using Web site creation
software, such as FrontPage or Visual Page.

Incorporating Meta-Tags into the core HTML
programming of your Web site will help people find
your site, which will boost traffic to it. Adding Meta-
Tags is a quick and simple process, and should be
done as standard practice when launching any Web
site.

Your Name:	Jason R. Rich
E-mail Address:	jr7777@aol.com
WebPage URL:	www.jasonrich.com
WebPage Title:	The Unofficial Guide to Starting a Business Online
Keywords:	E-commerce, Web site, book, business, e-store, virtual store, Internet marketing, IDG Books, Jason Rich, sales
Description:	*The Unofficial Guide to Starting a Business Online* is a step-by-step guide to creating and managing a successful business (e-commerce site) on the Internet. The book was written by Jason R. Rich and published by IDG Books as part of the company's best-selling *Unofficial Guide* series. The Web site offers information about this book.

Sample MetaTag HTML Programming

```
<TITLE>The Unofficial Guide to Starting a Business Online</TITLE>
<META NAME="keywords" CONTENT="e-commerce, Web site, book,
business, e-store, virtual store, Internet marketing, IDG Books, Jason
Rich, sales">
<META NAME="description" CONTENT="The Unofficial Guide to Starting
a Business Online is a step-by-step guide to creating and managing a
successful business (e-commerce site) on the Internet. The book was
written by Jason R. Rich and published by IDG Books as part of the
company's best-selling Unofficial Guides series. The Web site offers
information about this book.">
<!— MetaTags Created by: WebPromote metatag.webpromote.com/ —>
```

Unofficially...
According to
LinkExchange,
Inc., more than
85 percent of
Web surfers use
search engines
to find what
they are looking
for on the Web.

Help new customers find you

Aside from promoting your online business using traditional advertising, one of the cheapest and easiest ways to drive traffic to your Web site is to list your site with all of the popular Internet search engines. As noted earlier, listing your site with a search engine is free if you submit the listing yourself. There are, however, many services that for a small fee will register your site with hundreds or thousands of search engines, Web directories, and information portals.

When people need to find information on the Web, they typically enter a keyword or search phrase into a search engine and then visit the sites listed by the search engine as being relevant to their interests. For example, if your online business involves selling nutritional items, such as vitamins, you will first register your site with search engines. Then, when someone enters a search phrase such as "vitamins" or "nutritional supplements," for example, your site should be among those listed. In this way, someone who didn't even know your company existed would be able to find your site with ease, simply by typing a keyword or search phrase into a search engine.

Search engines: the next millennium's Yellow Pages

Information is power, and the computer users with the most information available to them are those who can quickly navigate their way around the various Internet search engines in order to find the information they need or want.

While Yahoo! was the first search engine on the Web (it was created by two Ph.D. candidates at

Stanford University in 1994), over the past few years, literally hundreds have gone online, each offering slightly different tools for navigating in cyberspace.

The following is a list of a few of the most popular and powerful search engines on the Web. As an online business operator, you'll probably want your Web site listed on each of these search engines, Web directories, and information portals.

Unofficially...
Many Web directories share the same search engine database. Thus, for example, you might see a little icon reading "Powered by InfoSeek" on a service other than InfoSeek. If your site is listed with InfoSeek, it will automatically be listed with InfoSeek's various affiliates.

Popular Search Engines

AltaVista	www.altavista.com
AOL.Com	www.aol.com
Ask Jeeves	www.askjeeves.com
Excite	www.excite.com
GoTo	www.goto.com
Hotbot	www.hotbot.com
Infoseek	www.infoseek.com
ISP Internet Yellow Pages	wwww.index.org
LookSmart	www.looksmart.com
Lycos	www.lycos.com
Magellan	magellan.excite.com
MSN	www.msn.com
NetFind	www.netfind.com
Netscape	www.netscape.com
Northern Light	www.northernlight.com
Search.Com	www.search.com
Snap	www.snap.com
The Go Network	www.go.com
WebCrawler	www.webcrawler.com
Yahoo!	www.yahoo.com

The most important search engines

Using any search engine, if you use the keyword or search phrase "search engine," you'll see listings for hundreds of other Web directories. However, over 90 percent of the Web surfing public use only the top 10 search engines, such as Yahoo!, AltaVista, Excite, AOL.Com, Hotbot, and WebCrawler. This means it's vital that you spend extra time registering your online business's URL with these popular search engines and make sure that your listing remains prominent and current.

If your online business is reachable via multiple URLs, make sure you list all of your URLs with each search engine to increase the probability that Web surfers will find you with ease. See the appendix for a detailed list of the major search engines, ranked by number of visitors.

Bright Idea
For up-to-date demographic statistics on who is using the Internet and the World Wide Web (by age, gender, household income, education, and so forth), visit Yahoo!'s "State of the Web" information at sales.yahoo. com/public/ research/ information/ salescentral. html. This data is updated monthly and reflects research from several different sources.

Registering your site with the search engines

In order for search engines to list your Web site, you must first register your site with each one individually. When visiting any search engine, look for a link that says "Suggest A URL," "Add A URL," or "How To Suggest A Site." These should lead you to more information on how to proceed.

The Web site registration process varies from one search engine to another. Moreover, the quality of their explanations and service varies. One good example of site registration is Yahoo!, which pays close attention to the placement of your site. In fact, unlike with most other search engines, an employee will visit and evaluate every Web site suggestion. In Yahoo!'s own words:

> *The Yahoo! directory is organized by subject. Most sites in it are suggested to us by users. Sites*

*are placed in categories by Yahoo!. Yahoo!'s
surfers (employees of Yahoo!) then visit and
evaluate your suggestions and decide where they
best belong. We do this to ensure that Yahoo! is
organized in the best possible way, making the
directory easy to use, intuitive, helpful, and fair
to everyone.*

*Finding an appropriate category for your site is
at the heart of this [the site registration] process.
Remember that Yahoo!'s surfers visit each site
suggested to us, and proper categorization on
your part helps us process suggestions quickly.*

When it comes to registering your site with
Yahoo!, suggest your site by going online and visiting the category you think is most appropriate.
Next, click on the "Suggest a Site" link at the bottom
of that category page. (It's just to the right of the
copyright and the "Company Information" link.)
While Yahoo! invites suggestions as to the best placement for your site in its directory, the final placement of your site is determined by Yahoo!'s surfers.

After completing the "Suggest a Site" process,
which involves completing an online form and electronically submitting the form to Yahoo!, the
amount of time it takes your site to get added to
Yahoo!'s database will vary from a few days to a few
weeks. (You can expect some lag time with any
major engine—be sure to ask for details, if they do
not offer any.)

Getting help with registration

Registering your site on the various search engines
and keeping the listing current can be a time-
consuming process. While you'll want to take the

time to personally ensure your site gets listed with at least the top ten search engines, for a relatively small flat fee, you can hire a company online that will register your URL with hundreds of search engines and Web directories.

WorldSubmit (www.worldsubmit.com) will submit your URL to up to 1,550 search engines and Web directories throughout the world. The staff of this service will analyze your site and help select the best placement on search engines such as Yahoo! Prices for this service range from $9 (for submission to 100 search engines) up to $89 (which includes URL submissions to 1,550 search engines and updated listings for six months, to ensure your listings remain timely during that period.) Upon visiting the WorldSubmit site, you'll be asked to complete an online questionnaire and include keywords pertaining to your site, a brief description of your site, and other basic information. The process takes under two minutes and all major credit cards are accepted for the service. How long it actually takes for your URL to appear in the search engines' databases will vary.

!Register-It! (www.registerit.com) is another URL registration service which is offered by Netscape. For an annual fee of $39.99, the service will register your URL with 400 of the top search engines and Web directories. One feature of this service is the "Hitometer," which helps you measure which search engines actually generate the traffic for your site. You can also determine what keywords and search phrases Web surfers are using to locate your site. For online business operators, this information is particularly useful, especially if you're considering doing paid online advertising and you want

Unofficially...
To learn how your Web site will be ranked once it's registered with the various search engines, go to www.trafficbuilding.com and read the "Five Immutable Laws of Web Marketing." Also look at "Search Engine Secrets" by AMSI (www.simple123.com/secrets01.htm).

to determine which services are already generating traffic for you.

Submit It (www.submitit.com) is a service of LinkExchange (MSN) and can also be used to register your URL with multiple search engines and Web directories quickly and easily. For a one-time fee of $59, this service will register your URL with 400 search engines. The company also offers many other services to online business operators designed to assist in promoting your site. For example, for a monthly fee of $12.99, the company offers "Premium Membership Services," which include:

1. The submission and updating of up to five different URLs with the search engines

2. Banner advertising worth $300

3. Reports that track your site's ranking on the various search engines

4. An online Web site analyzer

5. The ability to generate and maintain an e-mail-based newsletter using ListBot Gold.

Taking the time to properly register your site with the ten top search engines, Web directories, and information portals is an excellent way to begin spreading the word about your Web site. Once you've registered your site with each service, be sure to check your listing periodically to ensure it's kept up to date. After all, a huge percentage of Web surfers use one of the top ten search engines to find what they're looking for on the Web, so it's important to have your site listed with these services. The time you spend registering your site and keeping the listing up-to-date will prove to be an excellent investment when it comes to generating traffic to your site.

Moneysaver
!Register-It! offers a free trial version of its service, allowing visitors to register their URL with eleven search engines for free.

Paid advertising opportunities on search engines

Registering your URL with the major search engines is a no-brainer if you want to begin generating traffic to your site. Just because your site is listed on the popular search engines, however, doesn't mean people will automatically begin flocking to it, anxious to buy whatever product or service you're selling. Registering your URL with the search engines is certainly a quick and inexpensive way to start promoting your Web site, but it should be only one component of your overall marketing strategy.

In the previous chapter, you read about using traditional advertising and public relations methods for generating traffic to your site. The chapter also touched on online advertising and various ways you can use the Web itself to promote your online business. No matter how large or small your advertising budget is, consider taking advantage of the advertising and sponsorship opportunities available on the most popular search engines as a way of finding new customers and attracting them to your site.

Research has shown that online advertising using banner ads can dramatically increase brand name identification; it can also be effective for direct response advertising. According to Yahoo!, over 85 percent of the top 50 national advertisers use banner advertising on Yahoo! in addition to their traditional advertising methods. Meanwhile, InfoSeek reports it currently reaches 20 percent of all Internet users, with a total unduplicated monthly audience of over 11 million.

When you visit a search engine or information portal such as Yahoo!, at the service's main page you'll immediately see a banner ad. This "front page ad" is designed to target a very general mass market audience and is displayed prominently for all who visit the main page to see. In March 1999, the cost of this front page marquee ad space at Yahoo! was over $88,000 for a two-week period.

A front page ad on a search engine is probably the most expensive online advertising space you can purchase, yet if you have the budget and you're trying to reach a large number of computer-savvy people fast, purchasing this advertising space can be extremely effective.

If your product or service is designed for a niche market, however, purchasing the main banner ad space on a search engine won't necessarily be cost-effective. While you'll be reaching millions of people with your message, the message you're trying to convey will only be of interest to a small percentage of those people.

When deciding to use the various paid advertising opportunities offered by the various search engines, here are a few basic steps to follow:

1. **Carefully plan and create your online banner ad.** If you've never designed a display ad before, consider hiring a professional graphic designer or an advertising agency to assist you.

2. **Carefully design your ad.** You'll need to consider what message you want to convey and determine the very best wording, color scheme, and visuals to get your message across quickly.

3. **Define your target audience.** Are you trying to promote your overall business and attract new customers, or to get people to buy a specific product or service?

5. **Do research.** Which search engines/Internet portals you're interested in advertising on? The

Bright Idea
Because of the high number of visitors to the major search engines, placing an ad with one can be comparable to (if not superior to) placing an ad in more traditional venues. Yahoo! does not exaggerate when it claims that "being on the front page of Yahoo! is like having the largest billboard in Times Square."

Moneysaver
It's possible to target users of the search engines based on the domains from which their browser originates (*.com, .net, .edu,* or domains specific to countries), by computing platform (Windows 95/98, Mac OS, Unix, etc.), or by browser and version (Microsoft Internet Explorer 5.x or Netscape 4.x).

best way to do this is by surfing the Web and actually visiting the various services. Next, contact the advertising sales department for the search engines you're interested in and obtain a media kit containing current rates and advertising guidelines.

Before actually engaging in a discussion with a advertising sales representative, determine for yourself which areas of the search engine you're interested in advertising on in order to target the audience you're trying to reach. You'll notice that when you do a keyword search or use the Internet directory feature of a search engine, each subscreen you view usually offers at least one banner ad that's directly related to the topics you're searching for.

Each search engine offers different advertising opportunities at different price points. For example, InfoSeek and The Go Network offer run-of-site rotations that appear throughout their sites for an initial monthly advertising investment of $2,500 (as of March 1999). A $1,500 banner test package was also available.

In addition to having banner ads displayed randomly throughout the site, advertisers can target user's keyword searches.

The cost of advertising on any Web site, whether a search engine or any other type of site, is typically based on the number of views your banner ad receives. For example, through AdStore (a division of LinkExchange, store.linkexchange.com/yahoo/index.html), you can purchase inexpensive advertising on Yahoo! starting as low as $100 for 10,000 impressions (as of March 1999). The "Run of Network Advertising Program" distributes your banner randomly throughout the entire Yahoo! site.

Through AdStore, you can also take advantage
of Yahoo!'s targeted advertising opportunities by
choosing where your banner advertisement will
appear. This will help you reach a more qualified
audience. If you were to purchase an entire campaign through Yahoo!, you could choose exact locations for where your banners would appear. Using
AdStore's discounted targeted advertising opportunities for Yahoo!, you can choose which category
you'd like your banner ads to appear under, and
then have your banner randomly rotated throughout your selected category. Based upon availability,
categories include: Classifieds, Entertainment,
Finance, Maps, News, News & Media, Recreation &
Sports, and Weather.

The price of targeted advertising on Yahoo!
(when purchased from AdStore) begins at $100 for
5,000 ad views, and goes up to $1,000 for 50,000 ad
views (as of March 1999). If you plan to spend more
than $1,000 advertising on Yahoo!, contact Yahoo!'s
advertising department directly (www.yahoo.com/
info/advertising).

To learn about the advertising opportunities on
several of the most popular search engines, contact
each service directly.

■ **Yahoo!**—Contact Yahoo!'s advertising department by completing the online information
request form (www.yahoo.com/info/advertis-
ing). You can access Yahoo!'s online media kit
at adkit.yahoo.com or www.yahoo.com/docs/
advertising. As with many other search engines,
advertising rates for Yahoo! are based on the
duration (weeks or months) your banner ad will
appear and vary based on how busy the area of
Yahoo! is that you want to advertise on.

- **America Online**—Visit AOL's advertising information site at mediaspace.aol.com. This is one of the most visited Web sites in cyberspace. Advertising with America Online lets you reach both the Internet audience and America Online members with one advertising buy.

- **Netscape**—Visit Netscape's advertising information site at www.netscape.com/ads/ad_rate_card.html for information about advertising and promotion available from this site. Netscape.com is the official Web site of the Netscape Web browser software, the second-most popular browser software in the world.

- **InfoSeek**—Its advertising information site at info.infoseek.com/doc/media_kit/menu.html also includes information on advertising on The Go Network.

- **Excite**—Like Yahoo!, Excite offers small businesses the opportunity to advertise on its service, starting as low as $100. Small business operators should visit AdStore (a division of LinkExchange) at www.le-express.com/excite. For more extensive information, visit www.excite.com/info/advertising.

- **AltaVista**—AltaVista helps people find the exact piece of information they are looking for. AltaVista's specialty among the search engines is that it gives users instantaneous access to an index of 140 million pages and more than 16,000 Usenet newsgroups. The site is refreshed by constant crawls of the entire World Wide Web, with continuous purging of dead links, duplicates, and "index Spam," making AltaVista index one of the highest quality indexes on the Web. For advertising

information on AltaVista, visit www.
doubleclick.net/contact_us/advertiser_form_av.
htm.

■ **Lycos**—If you're interested in targeting specific
audiences by keywords, word phrases, domains,
operating systems, or browsers, Lycos will
deliver your advertising message. Additionally,
Lycos has 18 Web Guides to help you target
your audiences. For advertising information,
visit www.lycos.com/lycosinc/advertising.html.

■ **MSN**—This site, which is maintained by
Microsoft Corporation, caters to a general audience. MSN offers online advertising, sponsorship, e-commerce, and distribution opportunities. Advertising is available on the MSN
LinkExchange network; for information, visit
msnsales.com/default.asp.

Moneysaver
Do research to
determine the
rates for the ad
space you need.
A company like
AdAuction
(www.adauction.
com) or AdStore
(store.linkex-
change.
com) can tell
you about dis-
counted pricing
available to
small business
operators. Ads
on services such
as Yahoo! and
Excite! can be
purchased for as
little as $100.

Planning your banner ad

The majority of search engines offer what they call
"beyond the banner" advertising opportunities,
allowing advertisers to use new ways to build relationships with customers, build brands, and distribute content. This includes sponsorship of particular
online events, specific content, or areas of a service.

Every search engine and Web site you can advertise on has strict guidelines for banner ads. Typical
guidelines are:

1. 468×60 pixels for a full-size banner or 234×60
   pixels for a half-size banner. Other popular sizes
   are 100×100 and 120×120. A popular vertical
   banner size is 120×240 pixels, while a button-
   size banner is typically 120×90 or 120×60
   pixels.

2. Typically, only .GIF images are accepted.

3. The size of the graphic file containing your banner ad usually needs to be kept smaller than 15K, but the smaller the file size, the better. A 12K file for a banner graphic will load faster.

4. Consider the use of tag lines directly below a banner. Tag lines are offered at the discretion of the online service and are usually limited to 12 words or less.

5. If you're designing an animated banner, pay careful attention to file size and the length of the animation, which can typically be no longer than four to seven seconds.

6. All banners ads are subject to approval by the search engine or the site where you'll be advertising.

In terms of your banner ad's content, a few general rules apply:

66

A banner trying to generate click-through should sound a call to action, and give viewers a reason to click through. This can improve Internet advertising response rates by as much as 15 percent.
—LinkExchange

99

- Keep the message simple and uncluttered.

- Target your audience carefully.

- Consider offering something of value for free as a way to capture someone's attention. Just make sure you follow through when someone clicks on your banner in order to visit your site.

- If you're not offering something free, use some other gimmick that will encourage people to respond immediately.

When it comes to online banner ads, animation can be used to get the viewers' attention. Use simple animations that aren't distracting, but help get your message across.

Use banner ads as a way to grab an audience's attention so they want to visit your site for additional information. For example, you can pose a question as part of your banner ad, and require the viewer to click on the ad and visit your site for the answer.

Make sure you state the obvious. Iif you want someone to click on the banner and visit your site, include the message "Click Here," or use some form of graphic to make it perfectly clear what the viewer should do.

Develop several messages and approaches for your banner ads and test them to see which ones generate the best response or the most traffic. One of the great things about online advertising is that it's easy to instantaneously measure the impact the banner ad has. It may be necessary to test several messages or approaches and fine-tune your advertising until you develop an approach that works the best.

As you do further research, you'll encounter more and more specialized lingo. Refer to the glossary for a definition of several key terms.

Banner ad creation tools and services

There are many graphics creation programs available for generating attractive and professional-looking banner ads. One of the best is Paint Shop Pro 5, a graphics program developed by Jasc Software, Inc. (www.jasc.com) that's available for under $100. The software includes a second program, Animation Shop, which allows users to create animated graphics for use on the Web. A free trial version of the software can be downloaded from the company's Web site.

Creating a still or animated banner ad can be a bit tricky, especially if you have no graphic arts talent. There are, however, dozens of online agencies that will create professional-looking banners for

Bright Idea
For tips on how to create your own banner ads using a PC-based computer and Paint Shop Pro 5, point your Web browser to adnetwork. linkexchange. com/help/ howtoban.html for step-by-step directions.

you, usually within 24 and 48 hours. The cost of this service ranges from free to several hundred dollars. Using any search engine, type in the search phrase "Web banner design" to find companies that will create ad banners for your business.

Just the facts

- Registering your online business's URL with popular Internet search engines and Web directories allows Web surfers to locate your site.

- Using the search engines can be one of the least expensive and most powerful methods for generating traffic to your site.

- Take advantage of free listings for your site's URL, or invest in online banner advertising.

- Advertising on a search engine gives you the opportunity to target a general Web-surfing audience or reach people with very specific interests.

Improving and Analyzing Your Site

PART V

GET THE SCOOP ON...
Animated GIFs ▪ The pros and cons of
plug-ins ▪ Using video, Java applets,
Shockwave, and other graphic technologies
▪ Cookies ▪ Free Web site design help

Making Your Site Look and Sound Great

Chapter 12

Several times throughout this book, the importance of having a professional-looking Web site has been stressed. Creating a professional-looking site doesn't necessarily mean incorporating a lot of flashy graphic effects, audio, and other technologies, but these technologies should be used if appropriate.

Using text and simple graphics throughout your Web site will allow you to convey key points about your company and the product or service you're offering. Consider taking advantage of the fancy features described in this chapter only if they'll help your site achieve its objective—to sell your product. If design features distract visitors, confuse them, make your site too busy or complex, or take away from the messages you're attempting to convey, avoid using them! Keeping your site simple, straightforward, visually appealing, and easy to navigate will be far more beneficial than creating a site that's flashy.

Plug-ins

The most popular Web browsers, from Microsoft and Netscape, are both expandable and upgradable using plug-ins. These are add-on programs you can download, usually for free, to enhance your Web-surfing capabilities. From this chapter, you'll learn about some of the popular Web browser plug-ins. If someone has the RealPlayer plug-in, for example, she can listen to streaming audio or watch streaming video that's being broadcast from Web sites. (Streaming audio or video refers to broadcasts of audio, as if you were listening to the radio, or broadcasts of live-action video/t.v. footage over the Web.) Thus, if you decide to offer video or audio on your site, anyone with the RealPlayer plug-in will be able to hear the audio and see your video content automatically. Some of the popular plug-ins you can use on your site are discussed below.

Unofficially...
To learn more about plug-ins endorsed by Netscape for its browsers, visit home.netscape. com/plugins/ index.html.

Adobe Acrobat

Many Web surfers now have access to color printers or black and white laser printers. If you have a traditional printed product brochure that you use as a powerful sales tool, you can convert the brochure into an electronic file in the Adobe Portable Document Format (PDF) and offer it on your site to anyone with the Adobe Acrobat plug-in (www. adobe.com/prodindex/acrobat).

Using this plug-in, the visitor can quickly download the PDF file and view it on her computer screen or print it out in the exact format it was originally created in. In other words, your printed brochure can be transferred electronically to Web surfers and used as a powerful sales tool in conjunction with your Web site.

Acrobat lets you convert any document into an "adobepdf.html" file, with its original appearance preserved. You can then distribute it for viewing and printing on any system. Businesses can now expand their use of Adobe PDF—the standard for publishing documents online—to include more interactive and efficient Web-based business applications.

With Acrobat's new features, any paper or electronic document can become an Adobe PDF form that will display or print exactly as the customer intended.

Adobe PDF is the standard for electronic document distribution worldwide. PDF is a universal file format that preserves all of the fonts, formatting, colors, and graphics of any source document, regardless of the application and platform used to create it. PDF files are compact. You can convert any document to PDF, even scanned paper, using Adobe Acrobat 4.0 software.

According to Adobe, PDF also offers the following benefits:

- PDF files can be published and distributed anywhere: in print, attached to e-mail, on corporate servers, posted on Web sites, or on CD-ROM.

- More than 40 million people already have the required Adobe browser plug-in.

- Compact PDF files are smaller than their source files and download a page at a time for fast display on the Web.

- Using Acrobat 4.0 software, bookmarks, cross-document links, Web links, live forms, security options, sound, and video can be added to PDF files for enhanced online viewing.

Moneysaver
Acrobat Reader is free, it's easy to download from the Adobe Web site, and it can be freely distributed by anyone.

RealAudio/RealVideo/RealPlayer

RealNetworks (www.real.com) lets you "broadcast" audio and video over the Internet. It develops and markets software products and services to help PC users send and receive audio, video, and other multimedia services using the Web.

RealPlayer is the most popular application for playing real-time or streaming media on the Web.

In 1998, RealNetworks released a second generation of streaming media technology, RealSystem G2. It vastly improves the quality of streaming media delivery. It streams virtually any type of media, synchronizes clips to deliver true multimedia, and adds features and tools that simplify the creation of streaming content. RealProducer and RealProducer Plus make it easy to create RealSystem content.

RealPlayer G2 (the browser plug-in) has become one of the most popular Internet applications, with over 150,000 downloads per day.

World Wide Music (www.worldwidemusic.com) is one example of how Web business sites use RealNetworks. World Wide Music allows visitors to hear over 300,000 thirty-second sound samples from the more than 50,000 albums for sale on their site.

If you believe your Web site needs to broadcast audio or video content to visitors, RealNetwork has the Web's largest audience. According to the company:

- There are over 30 million unique registered RealPlayer users.

- Approximately 120,000 RealPlayers are downloaded each day; this makes RealPlayer the third-most popular download on the Internet, and among the top 20 most trafficked sites worldwide.

"
Streaming media is a method of making audio, video, and other multimedia available in real time, with no download wait, over the Internet or corporate intranets.
—RealNetworks
""

- RealPlayer is distributed with AOL's software, Microsoft's Internet Explorer 4.0 and 5.0, US Robotics' modems, and Creative Labs' sound cards.

- More than 85 percent of Internet Web Sites with streaming media use RealAudio, RealVideo, or RealFlash.

According to an article on Builder.com entitled, "Webcasting 101,"

If you want to broadcast only occasionally or send out just prerecorded files, several ISPs will rent you Webcast time (check with your local ISPs to find out if they offer such services or know a company that does). The ISP handles the technology, and you deal with the content (usually if you pay them a setup fee and additional subscription charges) .... While the encoder and player are free, setting up a streaming audio environment requires the RealAudio Server, which can get expensive. While RealNetworks recently announced a free personal server kit that allows two people to listen to your RealAudio content simultaneously, going beyond that begins at $495 for five simultaneous listeners and quickly climbs into the multi-thousand-dollar range for as few as 50 simultaneous listeners. Even worse for most Webmaster wanna-bes, you have to either run your own server or convince your Internet Service Provider (ISP) to load up the RealAudio Server for you—something many ISPs may not be willing to do unless you pay them hefty fees.

Bright Idea
To discover how to incorporate QuickTime video into your Web site, read the tutorials offered by QuickTime's creators by browsing: www.apple.com/ quicktime/ authoring/ tutorials.html.

QuickTime 4.0

The QuickTime 4.0 plug-in (www.apple.com/quicktime) lets Web surfers view over 400 different audio, video, and graphic formats conveniently. QuickTime works on both PC and Macs computers, and over half of Web sites that use video use QuickTime. Special applications include news events, educational CD-ROMs, and entertainment.

Shockwave

According to Macromedia, "Shockwave...lets you view interactive Web content like games, business presentations, entertainment, and advertisements from your Web browser." Shockwave (www.macromedia.com/shockwave) has been incorporated into thousands of Web sites, including Disney.com, IBM, and Palm Computing. Shockwave is readily available, and easy to download and distribute. Shockwave attracts visitors, engages them, and brings them back often. Macromedia, Inc., now sells improved versions of the Shockwave 7 and Flash players for users of desktop computers using Intel Pentium III processors.

Chatting within your site

Online chat rooms are a way a Web site can be transformed into a virtual community and companies can communicate, in real time, with their customers. Through a chat room, customers can also communicate with each other. Depending on the type of online-based business you're seeking to establish, adding chat capabilities to your Web site could be used as a way to encourage visitors to keep returning to your site.

The eShare Expressions Interaction Suite (www.eshare.com) from eShare Technologies, Inc., is one of several turnkey solutions for adding chat, threaded discussion forums, and online presentations to Web sites. It enables organizations to promote community, collaboration, and interaction. It can be used for virtual meetings, live training and conferencing, distance learning, moderated events, and social chat.

With the eShare Expressions Server, users can perform a number of functions through any standard Web browser, without needing to download any special software of plug-ins. Features of this chat solution are that:

Moneysaver
The interface of the eShare Expressions Interaction Suite works in any browser, and it doesn't require users to have special client software.

- Users can communicate in real time, create rooms, group "peers," and join moderated events.

- Users can post, reply, and attach files on public password-protected discussion forums.

- Users can be led from site to site on an online tour.

- Administrators can customize system settings quickly, capture valuable user account information, and profit from built-in ad banner capabilities.

Beware! Not everyone uses plug-ins

The problem with designing a Web site requiring someone to have special plug-ins is that not everyone has or wants these Web browser add-ons. Requiring visitors to have them might discourage them from spending time exploring your site and receiving whatever sales or promotional messages you're attempting to convey. Also, plug-ins tend to be used by the Web's more savvy users, not the mainstream Web surfers. Thus, if your product is

Bright Idea
Consider using hyperlinks to additional Web pages. This will allow visitors to your site to roam, explore, and gather the information they're interested in, all at their own pace.

targeted to a general audience, your Web site should be readily accessible to that audience.

The Internet is an extremely unique marketing tool. You have at your disposal the ability to communicate in many ways, using the printed word and still images (like you'd see in a newspaper or magazine, on a billboard, or within a printed product brochure). Also at your disposal are animated graphics, video, and audio (like you'd see on television or hear on the radio). Unlike any other form of media, these communication methods can be combined in whatever way you see fit to capture the attention of your visitor and sell your product.

What's more, the Internet is interactive. You're not limited to a 30- or 60-second time period to get your sales pitch across, nor are you confined to a specific size print ad to convey your messages.

It's your job to offer an online environment that provides the information your visitors are looking for using the best possible communication tools. You must decide if you can convey your message best using text, still graphics (like line art and logos), photographs, animated graphics, audio clips, video clips, or a combination of these elements.

Creating and using animated GIFs

Animated GIFs add visual appeal to your site without compromising download time or making the site overly complicated. As the name suggests, these images are animated, colorful, extremely easy to incorporate into any Web site, and available free of charge. You can also create your own animated GIFs using a software package such as Paint Shop Pro (which comes bundled with Animation Shop) from Jasc Software (www.jasc.com).

Animated GIFs can be used for many purposes, including highly functional banner ads, navigational icons, animated lines and dividers, and arrows to highlight key information. These images can also be used simply to make your site more visually appealing.

An animated GIF is created in much the same way as an animated cartoon. The artist creates a series of single frames, each of which is slightly different. When the frames are displayed quickly, one at a time, and in a specific order, an animated picture is created. The final animated GIF is one file containing a series of single GIF images. The person creating the animated GIF can determine at what rate the individual frames are displayed. One can also add special effects, like fades, to switch from one image to the next.

To see how a simple animated GIF is created, point your Web browser to www.webpedia.com/animations/resources/creating/create1.htm. If you're looking for precreated animated GIFS that can be downloaded for free, use the search phrase "Animated GIF" on any search engine.

Live Webcam broadcasting

Adding live Webcam broadcasting to your site is extremely cheap and relatively easy using special software and a QuickCam Pro ($149) digital camera from Logitech (which offers 640 × 480 resolution and 30-bit color). If you'll have a constant link to the Internet, you can send live digital images (with no sound) to your site, where visitors can view them without using any special browser plug-ins. Some online businesses have found highly creative and original ways of using this technology to add entertainment value to their site.

Watch Out!
As you create an animated GIF, the more individual frames you use to create the animation, the larger the file and the longer it takes to download. This is something you want to avoid. Thus, it's best to keep your animations simple, as long as it attracts the viewer's attention.

For example, some companies place digital cameras in their offices, so visitors can take a peek inside the company and watch people at work. The official Web site for The Walt Disney World Resort (www.disneyworld.com) uses live Webcams to allow visitors to the site to see what's happening at The Magic Kingdom, Epcot Center, and The Disney/MGM Studios at any given time.

One of the most famous examples of how Webcam technology has been used as an intricate part of a profitable online business is the JenniCAM (www.jennicam.org). According to Jenni, "Initially I bought the camera to update portions of my Web page with pictures of myself. A friend joked that it could be used to do a fishbowl cam, but of a person. The idea fascinated me, and I took off with it. Initially the JenniCAM had an audience of half a dozen of my close friends, and it spread like wildfire from there." Today, thousands of people pay $15 per year to watch Jenni performing everyday activities in her apartment, such as reading e-mail, sleeping, working, goofing off, and entertaining guests.

Many of the adult-oriented Web sites have discovered unique ways of using this technology to distribute pornographic content; however, many legitimate online businesses are also capitalizing.

Webcam technology doesn't offer streaming video. Instead, you'll be able to send single snapshots several times per minute (WebCam Now, for example, sends 12 frames per minute) over the net, in order to offer an ongoing time-lapsed series of pictures. If you're interested in incorporating this type of technology into your Web site, visit Logitech's Web site at www.logitech.com to learn more about the QuickCam hardware.

Using Java applets and other graphic technologies

Most text- and graphic-based Web pages that don't contain anything fancy are created using only *HyperText Markup Language (HTML)* programming. HTML is a page description language that determines the position of Web page elements on the actual page. In order to make the Internet more interactive and give Webmasters the opportunity to add functionality to their sites, an actual programming language for the Web, called Java, was created by Sun Microsystems.

Most Web pages that incorporate Java applications, called applets, do so to add special features to their site. While someone with no programming knowledge can create a Web site using a software package that automatically produces HTML programming based on point-and-click, drag-and-drop user interface, adding Java applets to a Web page is a bit trickier for someone who doesn't know the programming language. Many Web sites, however, offer hundreds of free, prewritten Java applets that you can download and incorporate into your site. This requires only minimal knowledge of Java, unless you choose to customize the applets you download.

To find prewritten freeware or shareware Java applets you can add to your Web page, using any search engine, enter the search phrase "Java applet." Some of the sites listed will include:

> **Chris Cobb's Obligatory Java Applets Page—** www.ccobb.org/ javalinks.asp
> **Java Boutique—**javaboutique.internet.com
> **Applets.com—**www.applets.com

Bright Idea
Check out the software packages that have been developed to make it easy to add Webcam technology to your site. Two of these packages are WebCam Now (webcamnow. com) and NetSnap (www. netsnap.com).

ET Applets—www.entanke.se
Freeware Java.Com—www.freewarejava.com
Java.Sun.Com—java.sun.com/applets/
index.html

According to SideNet (www.sidenet.com/faq.html#java),

> *The Java platform is a fundamentally new way of computing, based on the power of networks and the idea that the same software should run on many different kinds of computers, consumer gadgets, and other devices. With Java technology, you can use the same application from any kind of machine—a PC, a Macintosh computer, a network computer, or even new technologies like Internet screen phones.*

The official Web site for Sun Microsystems (java.sun.com/openstudio/guide.html), the creators of Java, is an excellent resource for learning more about this programming language and how Java can be used on your Web site. On this site you'll find informative FAQs, tutorials, downloadable applets, and hundreds of links to other relevant sites.

According to Sun's Web site,

> *Adding applets to your site is much like adding images. The page on which you wish to present the applet needs to reference the location of the applet code. Applet code filenames end with .class. You must also have the xxx.class file located in the same directory as the HTML file which is calling it.*

Programming using Java is a bit more complicated than HTML, but the capabilities of this

---

66

Java is a programming language expressly designed for use in the distributed environment of the Internet. It was designed to have the 'look and feel' of the C++ language, but it is simpler to use than C++ and enforces a completely [object-oriented] view of programming.
—Whatis.com

99

language are far greater. If you're interested in incorporating Java applets into your site, it's a good idea to familiarize yourself with this programming language first.

How do Java applets benefit your site? Some of the common Java applets for Web sites include:

- Hit counters.

- Clocks.

- Animated ticker displays (for displaying custom text messages).

- Animated LED signs.

- Text animation and special effects.

- Interactive games.

- The ability to add search capabilities to your site.

- Password protection to your site.

- The ability to collect information or take quick polls.

- A real-time calculator.

- Display of a "slide show" of images.

Should your site use cookies?

There's been a lot of hype about how companies using the Internet to conduct business are using cookies as a way to invade peoples' privacy. Much of this hype is based on a misconception about what cookies actually do and what they're capable of. In reality, a legitimate online business can use cookies to make visitors' experience on their Web site less troublesome, especially if they return to the site often.

Whatis.com (www.whatis.com) describes a *cookie* as:

Unofficially...
You don't have to fear cookies. A cookie is just text, not a program or a virus.

A special file that a Web site puts on your hard disk so that it can remember something about you at a later time. Typically, a cookie records your preferences when using a particular site. Using the Web's Hypertext Transfer Protocol (HTTP), each request for a Web page is independent of all other requests. For this reason, the Web page server has no memory of what pages it has sent to a user previously or anything about your previous visits. A cookie is a mechanism that allows the server to store its own file about a user on the user's computer. The file [may be] stored in a subdirectory of the browser directory (for example, as a subdirectory under the Netscape directory). The cookie subdirectory will contain a cookie file for each Web site you've been to that uses cookies. Cookies can be used to customize the pages sent to you based on your browser type or other information you may have provided the Web site. Web users must agree to let cookies be saved for them, but, in general, it helps Web sites to serve users better.

For someone interested in learning more about cookies, David Whalen's *The Unofficial Cookie FAQ* (www.cookiecentral.com/faq) (an electronic document not affiliated with IDG Book's *Unofficial Guides*) is a useful resource. This document states,

Cookies are a very useful tool in maintaining state variables on the Web. Since HTTP is a 'stateless' (non-persistent) protocol, it is impossible to differentiate between visits to a Web site, unless the server can somehow 'mark' a visitor. This is done by storing a piece of information in the visitor's browser. Cookies can store database information, custom page settings, or just about

*anything that would make a site customizable.
An analogy I like to use is that cookies are very
much like a laundry 'claim-check' of sorts. You
drop something off, and get a ticket. When you
return with the ticket, you get that same something back. A cookie is simply an HTTP header
that consists of a text-only string that gets
entered into the memory of a browser. This
string contains the domain, path, lifetime, and
value of a variable that a Web site sets. If the
lifetime of this variable is longer than the time
the user spends at that site, then this string is
saved to file for future reference.*

*There are many reasons a given site would wish
to use cookies. These range from the ability to
personalize information (like on My Yahoo or
Excite), or to help with on-line sales/services
(like on Amazon Books or Microsoft), or simply
for the purposes of tracking popular links or
demographics (like DoubleClick). Cookies also
provide programmers with a quick and convenient means of keeping site content fresh and
relevant to the user's interests.*

Watch Out!
Many Web surfers
don't truly
understand what
cookies are all
about. As a
result, they have
set their Web
browser software
to ignore cookies
and avoid
accepting them.
When a user
does this, any
uses your Web
site has involv-
ing cookies won't
work.

One of the most popular features of Amazon.
com (www.amazon.com) is the "1-Click Ordering"
feature. After you enter your personal information
once (such as name, address, phone number, e-mail
address, and credit card information), you can then
return to the site anytime and Amazon.com knows
exactly who you are, your buying history on the site,
and what your preferences are. Now, when you find
a book you want to order, you simply click the
mouse on the 1-Click Ordering icon, and that book
you ordered will be automatically shipped. There's

Bright Idea
Based on the type of online business you're looking to establish, if you're planning to have customers return to your site often or place multiple orders over time, using cookies is one way to make their visits to your site easier and make ordering more convenient.

no need for visitors to keep having to fill out electronic order forms each time they place an order.

Many of the search engines/information portals also use cookies to allow visitors to customize their main page. Once someone fills out the online questionnaire for My Yahoo!, for example, each subsequent time they visit Yahoo!, the service will display customized news, weather, stock market and sports reports, entertainment news and/or local lottery numbers, and display only personalized information specifically requested by the visitor.

Paying attention to download times

One of the best ways to determine which Internet technologies and features you want to incorporate into your Web site is to spend time surfing the Net and see how other companies are using these technologies to their advantage. Adding these technologies may make your site look absolutely fantastic, but the majority of Web surfers who will visit your site are probably connected to the Internet using a dial-up 28.8K or 56K baud rate. So, the more "cool" stuff you add to your site, the longer it will take for your site to download.

When it comes to e-commerce and keeping people's attention on the Web, long download times are an absolute no-no! If someone has to wait between 30 seconds and 2 minutes for a Web page to load, chances are she won't have the patience to wait and will surf elsewhere. As you design your site, assume that the majority of people visiting will be connected to the Web via a 56K connection, and then plan what types of graphics and other glitzy effects you want to offer based on how long each takes to download. Optimize your site to achieve the fastest possible downloading time.

If your site features a lot of GIF or JPEG graphic images, use a service like GIF Wizard (uswest.gifwizard.com) to determine which of your graphic files can be compressed in order to speed up the load time of your overall Web pages. GIF Wizard is software that can identify which GIFs and JPEGs need compression and by how much. While there is a fee for using this service, it can be used to greatly improve the functionality and download time of your site.

GIF Wizard can reduce the size of your GIF, JPEG, and GIF animations up to 90 percent so your Web site downloads faster. Use GIF Wizard to compress images from your Web site or directly off your hard drive for maximum productivity. To maintain the quality of your Web site, you can use GIF Wizard SiteScan Analysis to automatically search your Web site for broken links and bloated graphics.

An article entitled *GIF vs. JPEG* by John Wurtzel that appears on Hotwired.com suggests basing your decision on which graphic format to use on the type of image you're looking to add to your site.

> *One of your primary considerations is the type of image you're working with. Photographs and graphics with lots of color fields, and particularly colors that blend and fade into one another, are best served by JPEG. If, on the other hand, your image has flat color fields, it will compress well in the GIF format.*

The best way to determine the download time of your site is to connect to the Internet at various baud rates, grab a stopwatch, and from a search engine, time exactly how long it takes for your site to download once you enter the URL into your

Unofficially...
If a larger graphic (such as a product shot) is absolutely necessary, consider using a small thumbnail image on your main Web pages and let the visitor click on the image if he wants to see a slower-loading but larger image.

browser software. In between tests, be sure to clear your "Internet Temporary Files" subdirectory on your hard drive, so that your later download times won't be misleadingly fast. To do this using Microsoft Explorer 5.x, for example, click on the "Tools" pull-down menu, then click on the "Delete Temporary Files" icon found under the "Temporary Internet Files" heading.

Take note of what graphic images or aspects of your site take the longest to load, and see what can be done to speed things up. You might consider reducing the size of your graphic images, reducing the number of animations on each page, and deleting all unnecessary graphics.

Giving visitors something of value

The purpose of any online-based business is to sell products directly over the Web. The goal of a business is, of course, to make money. As you've probably figured out by now, the Internet is like no other sales tool/advertising medium in existence, because of its interactive and information-on-demand nature.

By offering something Web surfers are interested in, you'll most likely be able to generate traffic to your site; the trick, however, is to keep them there long enough so you can sell them your product. Using the various Web technologies described in this chapter can help you create a Web site that's visually appealing, highly engaging, interactive, and exciting. While the look, layout/design, and user interface of your site are all important, the other key ingredient of a successful site is providing information that your visitors want.

Only by providing information that's unique, informative, timely, and considered valuable to your visitors will they be encouraged to stay on your site, explore it, and then return to it often. Thus, it's important to regularly update the content and even the look of your site. As you determine ways to keep the content of your site fresh, keep trying to make your site more of a valuable information resource, where someone can go for accurate and timely information about your product.

Depending on the type of online business you'll be creating, consider offering something of value on your site for free. Many e-commerce sites that sell software packages, for example, offer free 30-day trial versions of their software. Companies that are selling products online but ship them to customers via a traditional courier sometimes offer free shipping or some type of value-added incentive for shopping online. Using your Web site to offer something that the visitor to your site perceives as valuable (whether it's information or something tangible) will help keep her attention and help you build consumer confidence.

Combining valuable and informative content with a sales pitch for your product and the ability to place orders securely online are important elements of a successful e-commerce site. Using the various Internet technologies described in this chapter to help you convey your information can help you transform a basic Web site into a powerful marketing and sales tool.

Free online Web site design help

Making use of browser plug-ins, Java applets, or other special features within your site isn't always as easy as one would hope, especially if you're not an HTML or Java programmer. There are, however,

Bright Idea
In order to make your customers more comfortable shopping online from your site, it's an excellent strategy to offer a 30-day trail. This means they can return the product, with no questions asked, within 30 days for a full refund. This is one way to build credibility among new customers because you're taking some of the risk out of making a purchase.

many Web sites designed to offer free Web page design/programming advice, tutorials, and other resources you'll find extremely useful.

Builder.com (www.builder.com), for example, offers a wide range of useful articles, design tips, and tutorials that will walk you through the entire Web page creation process. The MSDN Online Workshop, sponsored by Microsoft, offers all sorts of useful information for users of Microsoft Front-Page 98 and FrontPage 2000. The Pixel Pen (home.earthlink.net/~thomasareed/pixelpen) offers very basic, step-by-step information for designing and publishing a Web site.

There are also technical support Web pages for virtually every Web site creation software package available (see your software manual for details). Many ISPs and services that offer complete e-commerce solutions also offer extensive online support and free online tutorials.

Bright Idea
Throughout this book, hundreds of URLs are listed where you can go for additional information about specific topics. As part of your research as you gear up to launch an online business, spend time visiting these and other sites to learn about the e-commerce industry and the capabilities of your Web site.

Think before you act

Before you spend countless hours (and dollars) adding a bunch of really cool features to your Web site in order to improve its "look," consider the following:

- Who is your target audience? Unless you're catering to the relatively small group of highly computer-literate, Internet-savvy Web surfers, think twice about incorporating technology into your site that might be difficult for average visitors to figure out. Also be careful of technologies the average user might not have the necessary browser plug-ins to use.

- Does the Web technology you plan to incorporate into your site help sell your product? Does it serve a definite purpose, or is it there just make your site look flashy?

■ Does the Web technology or graphics incorporated into your site slow down downloading time dramatically? What is the average download time of your site for someone surfing the Web at 28.8K or 56K?

■ What can be done to better optimize your site and improve download times? When it comes to surfing the Web, speed is critical!

As you plan and ultimately create your site, stay focused on conveying your message and achieving your goal of generating business and orders. While it's vital that your site have a professional appearance, don't get caught up in all of the exciting technologies at your disposal and incorporate them into your site simply to add flash. Only use the technologies you need to achieve your ultimate goals. Often the simplest Web sites work the best for selling products, providing information to (potential) customers, and generating online business.

Just the facts

■ Use fancy features described in this chapter only if they'll help your site achieve its objective—to sell your product.

■ The most popular Web browsers, from Microsoft and Netscape, are both expandable and upgradable using plug-ins. These are add-on programs you can download, usually for free, to enhance your Web-surfing capabilities.

■ Animated GIFs can be used for banner ads, navigational icons, animated lines and dividers, and arrows to highlight key information.

- Java was created by Sun Microsystems. Using Java, special applets can be created and used within your site.

- Long download times cause you to lose people's attention on the Web. Keep it under 30 seconds, or they'll surf elsewhere.

- By offering something Web surfers are interested in, you'll most likely be able to generate traffic to your site.

GET THE SCOOP ON...
Final steps ▪ How visitors see your site ▪
Soliciting feedback ▪ Updating your site

Chapter 13

Analyzing Your Site

Okay, you're nearing the end of the planning and Web site creation phase, and you're preparing to open for business by going online. At this point, you should be preparing to launch your promotional and marketing efforts for your site, keeping in mind that these efforts may take several weeks to kick in.

Before going online, however, it's important to review your site carefully to determine that everything is how it should be and that it conveys a highly professional image. Visitors to your site should find all of the content informative, easy to find, and valuable. At the same time, the site should help to build your company, product, or service's brand and overall image, and it should make visitors feel comfortable with making a purchase online (if your online business is set up for e-commerce).

The following last-minute checklist should be used to make sure you've dealt appropriately with many of the details regarding the creation of your site. The actions outlined in this list should be taken before opening your site to the public.

Unofficially...
A *dead link* is a hyperlink that is no longer active. When someone is surfing the Web and they try to activate a dead link, they will receive an error message because the Web site or Web page at the other end of that link is no longer online or its URL has been changed.

The Web site checklist

Take the following actions before putting your site online.

☐ Use a spell checker and have the site proofread by multiple people who have a flair for writing to ensure that the entire site contains no spelling, punctuation, or grammatical errors.

☐ Review the actual content of your site to ensure that all information is factually correct. This includes checking product numbers, making sure that all photos and artwork correspond to the proper product descriptions, and verifying that all prices are listed correctly.

☐ Check all links within your site to ensure they lead visitors to the appropriate locations. It's extremely unprofessional for your site to have "dead" links—that is, links to sites that are no longer running. If your visitor clicks on a dead link, he'll be stuck having to wait while the site is being looked for, then getting an annoying error message.

☐ Review the online order forms/shopping cart features of your site to be certain you'll be obtaining all the information you need from customers to process their orders.

☐ Make sure your company's phone number, fax number, mailing address, and e-mail address appear prominently within the site, and that all of this information is listed correctly.

☐ Using several different 28.8K and 56K dial-up Internet connections, visit your site several times, and check the download time for each page. If download times are long, determine ways to reduce them whenever possible (using

GIF/JPEG file compression utilities, for example.) According to the Web Site Journal (www.websitejournal.com), Web pages that take over 20 seconds to download lose over 50 percent of their potential visitors.

☐ Try accessing your site using different versions of the popular Internet browser programs. It's critical that your site be accessible by people using all versions of Microsoft Internet Explorer, Netscape Navigator, the AOL Web browser, and the WebTV browser. The site should look consistent using all of these browser programs. Make sure you've used a Web-safe color pallet and that all colors and graphics appear as they should using each browser program.

☐ Pretend you're a shopper and place a number of sample orders. For example, place an order for a single product, then for multiple products. Enter a separate "ship to" and "bill to" address for each. Experiment with all of the various options, in different combinations, to ensure everything works properly.

☐ Make sure the text on your site is written in easy-to-understand language, and will appeal to people with extremely short attention spans. Be sure to limit the length of your text. Keep word counts below 800 words per page.

☐ Find a group of people not directly involved with the creation of the Web site to test it out before it actually goes online. These people should not necessarily be highly computer literate; you want to make sure they find it easy to navigate through the site. Pay careful attention to the feedback these people offer. Be sure you

Watch Out!
Be sure to use plenty of white space, graphics, and different type sizes to create a visually appealing page on your Web site. The actual text should be displayed in an easy-to-read font and a good-size typestyle (no smaller than 10-point type for the main text).

communicate to your testers exactly what the purpose of your site is and what it's supposed to offer. This will help them determine if what you've created lives up to the overall objective of the site.

☐ Ask your site's testers specific questions about the site's content, the ease of navigation, the layout and design of the site, and the look of the site (such as the text and background colors, or the fonts and typestyles used). Do they feel anything is missing from the site? Ask specific questions in order to generate feedback that will be useful for improving the site before it actually goes online.

☐ Make sure your site has a "Search" feature, allowing a visitor to find the information she's looking for quickly by entering a keyword, search phrase, product name, or product number.

☐ Give your testers specific assignments while they're online and measure how long it takes them to accomplish those assignments. For example, ask them to find a specific product on your site, place an order for that product, and then request it to be shipped as a gift to someone else. Are average Web surfers able to do this with ease?

☐ Obviously, once your site is ready to go online, register it with all of the major search engines. Nearly 85 percent of the visitors to most Web sites find their destinations using a search engine.

Make sure you have your site's testers document (in writing) all of the problems they encounter. This will help you fix the problems quickly. Also, provide them with a questionnaire that addresses specific issues you're concerned with.

If you find your testers are having problems placing orders or finding specific information on your site, or if they seem to be losing interest in your site quickly, consider revamping before going online. Remember that old saying, "You only get one chance to make a first impression." If you go online and the people who visit your site early on aren't impressed, don't count on them ever returning. Don't be so anxious to go online that you put off fixing the major problems with your site and addressing the criticisms your testers offer.

Determining how your site is perceived

The concept of making your site look professional and easy to navigate through has been repeated several times throughout this book, for one major reason—it's extremely important! Prior to actually designing your Web site, you should have determined what type of image you want to portray, and you should have taken steps to ensure that your site will appeal specifically to your target audience.

Now that the site is actually ready to go online, using feedback from your testers, make sure the site actually lives up to your goals. When someone visits your site, will they believe they're dealing with a highly professional and reputable company? Will they feel comfortable placing orders online? Does your site offer them information they want and are looking for?

In addition to using testers, there are many Web site traffic tracking services and software packages you can use to determine exactly who is visiting your site, where they came from, what they did while

Bright Idea
One way to find potential "testers" for your site is to contact some existing customers and offer them an incentive to visit your site. Consider offering them a substantial discount on their online purchases, holding a contest with a prize, or giving them something of value for their time and honest feedback.

surfing your site, and so forth. WebTrends Corporation (www.webtrends.com), for example, is one of many companies offering software packages designed to track Web site traffic information.

Other products and services for analyzing Web traffic are available from Millard Brown Interactive (www.mbinteractive.com). The company's WebSET product, for example, provides Web site publishers and marketers with crucial information about their Web site's users. Information to users of this software include who the site's visitors are, what motivates them to visit your Web site, what the source of awareness about your site was, and whether your Web site is satisfying consumer expectations and requirements. This software will also help you determine how effective your site is at driving repeat visits.

Knowing this information will help you better tailor the content to your audience.

Business development refers to determining who is visiting your site and what content they're accessing. The article on Builder.com suggests,

> *Gathering this information lets you develop, expand, and refine your content. If you discover that your audience is very different from what you originally anticipated, you can adjust your site's content, design, style, product line, and features to recapture the audience you originally sought or to satisfy the audience you've actually attracted. You can convince potential advertisers that your users are people who will be willing and able to buy their products. The more information you can supply—raw data, specific trends, and detailed facts—the more you can advertise to vertical markets.*

66
The three most common motivations for analyzing Web traffic are business development, increasing marketing and advertising sales, and technical resource and capacity planning.
—"Why Collect Statistics?" published on Builder.com (www.builder.com)
99

If you'll be selling advertising space on your site, you must be able to provide the advertiser with statistics about how much traffic each page of your site receives, when the peak times are, and who the primary audience is. If your site becomes very busy, it's important to track traffic to ensure that your servers (or the ISP you're using) can handle the traffic and that visitors can access your site whenever they choose—even during peak periods. Having insufficient bandwidth or capacity will result in the loss of customers.

There are also services to help you check your site for errors. For example, The Web Site Garage (www.websitegarage.com) offers a selection of utilities to help improve your site by reducing the file sizes of graphic images, locating dead links, analyzing download times, and so forth.

Soliciting comments and feedback from visitors

Even after your site goes online, it is and will always be a work in progress. Since you and anyone working for you will be extremely close to your business emotionally, it's easy for you to lose track of what's really happening on your site in terms of how people perceive your online-based business.

It's important to constantly seek out feedback from people not directly associated with the operation of your business—ideally, members of your target market. Actively soliciting comments, ideas, and suggestions relating to your site (and offering a reward for people who share their thoughts) is one way to conduct market research that will provide valuable insight into what people really think of your site. On your site, develop a short survey asking

Bright Idea
If you receive positive feedback from customers, post it directly on your site for others to read, but don't attribute it without permission. Some people are very touchy about having their praise for a product posted. Many companies use just the first name and city/state of their customer when quoting them.

questions such as what visitors like about the site, what problems they experienced while exploring the site, and what could be added to improve the site. In exchange for this feedback, offer free shipping, a discount on the visitor's next order, or something else of value.

Another more obvious approach is to focus on the people's actions. Examine what parts of your site are visited the most and which areas of your site are receiving less traffic. If you receive complaints that a product offered on your site was misrepresented, for example, consider rewriting the product description in order to make it more accurate.

It is common for someone to call a business on the phone to place an order, mentioning they first visited the business Web site. If this happens to you, while taking the phone order, ask why the person chose to call instead of placing her order online. Listen carefully to her response, and don't be afraid to ask a follow-up question, if necessary. Your goal is to find out if the Web visitors trust your site enough to place orders directly on it, and if not, why not.

Finally, learn from other people's mistakes. As you surf the Web looking at other sites, take detailed notes when you visit a site that simply doesn't work, and be sure to do things differently on your site.

Keeping your site's content fresh

Repeat business is one of the ways you'll generate long-term revenue. Thus, in addition to offering top-notch customer service, providing personalized attention to customers when it's needed, and making visitors to your site feel welcome, it's important to encourage them to return to your site often. One of the best ways to keep people coming back is to constantly update the content of your site. Depending on the type of business you're operating, this may mean including information on new products, posting news-related announcements about your industry, holding weekly contests, and so forth. In addition, consider giving your site a major design overhaul at least once or twice a year.

No matter how successful your online-based business becomes, always be thinking about new features, services, types of information, or content you can add that will increase the overall value of the site, make it easier to use, and more enjoyable for the visitors.

If you visit any retail store or department store, you'll notice that displays change regularly. This is to ensure that customers keep coming back to see what's new. Changing the look and content of your site will have the same impact on customers, encouraging them to return.

Watch Out!
One of the worst long-term mistakes you can make as an online business operator is to simply leave your Web site's content the same. Look for opportunities to change or update your site in creative ways. If it's appropriate, offer special content, sales, or promotions focused around upcoming holidays.

Just the facts

- Visitors to your site should find the content informative, easy to find, and intuitive, and they should feel comfortable making a purchase online.

- Before going online, review the checklist offered in this chapter to make sure your site is 100 percent error-free and user-friendly.

- Try accessing your site using different popular browser programs. Your site must be accessible by people using all versions of Microsoft Internet Explorer, Netscape Navigator, the AOL Web browser, and the WebTV browser.

- Find a group of people not directly involved with the creation of your Web site to test it before it goes online.

- Constantly seek out feedback from people not directly associated with the operation of your business—ideally, members of your target market.

The Experts Speak

GET THE SCOOP ON...
Interviews with experts and pioneers
▪ Firsthand experiences ▪ Tips for succeed-
ing online ▪ How to avoid common mistakes

The Experts Share Their E-Commerce Knowledge and Experience (I)

Chapter 14

Many companies have lost a fortune attempting to launch some type of online business. As you should have learned already from this book and by conducting your own research, there are many potential pitfalls in the e-commerce industry. A failed venture could be a result of a lack of planning, poor funding, bad management, an inadequate business plan, unrealistic expectations, or a lack of understanding of how e-commerce actually works.

Instead of trying to reinvent the wheel as you attempt to launch your own online business venture, this chapter and the next two offer you the opportunity to tap into the knowledge of several experts in various aspects of e-commerce. Many of these people are pioneers in their field, and all have achieved success catering to companies involved with

Bright Idea
While you don't necessarily want to follow every piece of advice given in this chapter, you can profit from the experience of others and decide how to apply what they've learned to your own needs and plans.

e-commerce. Each of the people interviewed in this chapter share their advice and firsthand knowledge of how e-commerce works and how you, too, can benefit from the products or services their companies offer.

As you read this chapter, hopefully some of the advice will seem obvious to you. You've become knowledgeable about e-commerce, which means you're well on your way to being prepared to launch your own online venture.

Obviously there are no set rules when it comes to e-commerce, and there are many ways of operating highly successful online businesses that are totally different from what the people interviewed in this chapter describe. There are also countless other products and services not mentioned in these interviews (or in this book, for that matter) that can be useful tools for helping you launch a successful online business.

Whether or not you choose to follow the precise advice of these experts is, of course, up to you. However, since all of these people are involved with products or services that have helped many start-up online businesses succeed, it's in your best interest at least to consider what these experts have to say before attempting to launch your own e-commerce venture.

Each person interviewed in this chapter focuses on one or two aspects of e-commerce as a whole and offers tips on how to best use their products or services.

Sandy Bendremer
Cofounder, Galaxy Internet Services
Topic: Choosing an ISP to host your site

Neil Cohen
Senior Vice President of Business Affairs
AdAuction.com
Topics: Buying online advertising and pro-
moting your online
business

Christopher Hadden and Todd Matzke
Webmaster and Web Program Coordinator,
Jasc Software, Inc.
Topic: Creating and using Web graphics to
enhance your site

This chapter and the next focus on offering
advice from experts who are directly involved with
helping other businesses get online. Chapter 16,
"Successful E-Commerce Entrepreneurs Speak
Out," features in-depth interviews with people, just
like you, who have already launched their own
online ventures and have achieved success. From
the people interviewed in that chapter, you'll discover the trials and tribulations they faced while
planning and launching their online-based businesses and get a more realistic idea of what it takes
to manage the day-to-day operations of an online
business venture.

Sandy Bendremer—ISPs and Web-host providers

Sandy Bendremer is the cofounder of Galaxy
Internet Services (www.gis.net), a fast-growing
Internet Service Provider and full-service Web-hosting service based in Cambridge, Mass. The company
was founded in 1995. Galaxy Internet Services offers
dial-up Internet access to individuals and small to
medium-size companies, and offers Web-hosting

and colocation services to companies of all sizes located throughout the country. The company's Web servers are monitored 24 hours a day, every day.

Galaxy Internet Services also offers full Web site development and programming services and a full range of technical support. One of the company's latest offerings is a set of online development tools people with little or no programming experience can use to quickly develop a business Web site.

Jason Rich: "What's the difference between an ISP and a Web-hosting service?"

Sandy Bendremer: "An Internet Service Provider or ISP typically offers Internet access as well as Web-hosting services. There are, however, companies that establish themselves exclusively as Web-hosting companies. These companies purchase connectivity from an ISP and then sell their Web-hosting services to clients. An ISP requires a far more substantial technological infrastructure to support dial-up Web access, leased-line access, and other methods of connecting to the Internet."

Rich: "When looking for an ISP/Web-hosting service, what should someone consider?"

Bendremer: "Look at the entire package being offered, in terms of how it can accommodate the needs of your online-based business. Typically, Web-hosting services are offered as package deals. Look at things like the amount of storage space on the Web server being provided, what type of technical support the company can and will provide, and what additional services are offered that you may require. Additional services may include consulting and/or Web site development tools.

"In terms of storage space on a Web server, very few sites are larger than five or ten megabytes. If

Moneysaver
While it's fine to look for the cheapest ISP and hosting sites, be sure that the one you choose can offer you all the features you want at the price you want. Having a low basic fee won't help you if the fee covers little and add-on services are expensive.

you're creating an e-commerce site, you'll also want to make sure the ISP/Web hosting service offers shopping carts, secure online credit card processing, the ability to handle inquiry forms, and CGI programs that can be incorporated into your site to add functionality."

Rich: "What are CGI programs and how are they used?"

Bendremer: "CGI programs reside on the Web server and can be used to extend the functionality of Web sites hosted on that server. These programs allow you to do things like secure credit card processing transactions, accepting and processing online-based forms completed by visitors to your site, and Web site hit counters. One of the more complex CGI programs involves shopping cart applications, which are important to e-commerce sites."

Rich: "After asking what services are offered by an ISP/Web-hosting service, what should a perspective client do next?"

Bendremer: "Actually visit other sites hosted by the ISP/Web hosting service. Make sure your business fits into the business model the ISP/Web hosting service is capable of servicing."

Rich: "What should it cost to get to sign up with an ISP/Web-hosting service and get a site online?"

Bendremer: "Web hosting is certainly the commodity of the 1990s. The costs can be as low as $10 per month and go up into the thousands. You need to look at the capabilities of the provider and how your business is going to operate within those capabilities, particularly if you have a high-volume Web site that will be transferring a lot of data via the

Bright Idea
Look for multiple links. If a service has multiple links to an Internet back-bone, this usu-ally indicates that the service has good band-width and back-up systems in place should a server go down.

Internet. Most of the time, when you see a price quoted for Web-hosting services, you'll see an aster-isk indicating the price is based on a predefined amount of server storage space and the amount of data you can transfer. The main costs to the Web-hosting service involve storing your data and deliv-ering it out over the Internet. The ISP/Web hosting service's bandwidth is also important. You want to ensure that the service has adequate bandwidth to manage the traffic that will be coming to your site once it's online."

Rich: "If you'll also be hiring a Web-hosting service to help create your site, what else should some-one look for?"

Bendremer: "The service should be able to develop Web pages from scratch using HTML. You also want Web page developers who have artistic abilities to ensure your site will look professional and be visu-ally appealing. The site's developer should be fully able to program back-end capabilities into your site, and be able to create shopping cart applications and links to databases as needed. This last level of service is usually the most expensive."

Rich: "What's actually required to be able to handle secure financial transactions, such as credit card processing, online?"

Bendremer: "First, a secure Web server is required. Finding an ISP/Web-hosting service that offers this technology should be very simple. In addition to being able to receive data securely from customers, make sure the ISP/Web hosting service you choose is able to keep that information totally secure once it's actually received. SSL is the standard security protocol. The people visiting your site also need to be using secure Web browser software that supports

SSL, such as the browsers available from Microsoft and Netscape."

Rich: "How can someone ensure she'll receive the technical support services she needs from his ISP/Web-hosting service?"

Bendremer: "You want to make sure the technical support staff will be accessible. The biggest complaint people have with smaller Web-hosting services is the lack of support that's offered. You need to be able to get problems fixed and your questions answered twenty-four hours a day, seven days a week. The other problem people run into is that their ISP/Web-hosting service charges a low monthly fee for the basic service, but then nickel-and-dime you if you need support or need simple things done to your site in terms of maintenance or updating. These additional fees can add up quickly and make it very difficult to develop and maintain your Internet presence the way you want to.

"Also, if you call a technical support phone number and you're put on hold for ten to fifteen minutes or longer, you should wonder if the company is adequately staffed. You also want to ensure that the people who ultimately do answer the phone will have the technical expertise to actually solve your problem or answer your questions. Before signing up with a service, ask about what type of secondary level of technical support is offered. If you call the technical support phone number and the person who answers the phone can't answer your question or solve your problem, you need to know what happens next. Does the company have the resources to help you, and will they expend those resources as needed?"

Rich: "What questions or problems will an ISP/Web-hosting service not address?"

Bendremer: "Most Web-hosting services won't address questions involving Web site development and programming, unless you're specifically paying them for this type of additional service, which is often billed by the hour."

Watch Out!
You don't want your site to be too slow, so keep an eye on your Web-hosting service. If they are hosting many other companies that require bandwidth, your site may lose speed.

Rich: "What are some of the biggest problems people run into if they choose the wrong ISP/Web-hosting service?"

Bendremer: "People often choose a service based on cost, not based on their actual needs. One common problem is the service doesn't have enough bandwidth to accommodate the number of visitors to a site or can't transfer the amount of data needed. This means people can't access your site or can't get the information they need from it. If the Web hosting service you choose is hosting too many other companies that require bandwidth, the speed of your site may suffer. I recommend asking for a list of other Web sites the ISP/Web hosting service hosts, and try to access those sites repeatedly during various times of the day and night, particularly during peak times. If you can access the various sites using different connections to the net, it will help you make a better assessment if you check from a lot of different places."

Rich: "There are local companies as well as much larger national companies offering Web-hosting services. Does it matter which one someone hires to host their site?"

Bendremer: "Most of the time, it really doesn't matter, as long as the company you hire to host your site offers the services and technical features you need to operate your online-based business or e-commerce site. What really matters is how the service you choose is actually connected to the Internet's backbone. Your host service doesn't have to be a 'tier one' Internet provider as long as they're well-connected to a 'tier one' backbone. Most ISPs and Web-hosting services can support any type of Web content, such as streaming audio and video, but if your site requires a high level of resources, make sure the service you choose has the necessary server capacity in place before signing up with them. Look at who the service's other customers are. Are they in the same league as you?

"The barrier to entry for a basic Web-hosting service is very low, so make sure the company you choose has a good reputation and will be around for years to come. Many of these smaller services can and sometimes do disappear overnight, because they can't compete in this highly competitive Web-hosting industry. When dealing with any business you're going to depend on, check references, do research, and ask questions. Never sign a long-term contract or prepay for any hosting services unless there's a real cost advantage. Especially if you're dealing with a small hosting service, think twice about prepaying for services, no matter what the cost savings."

Rich: "As a start-up company, does it make sense to develop a site from scratch by hiring programmers who know HTML and Java, or it is okay to rely on a commercial software package, such as Microsoft FrontPage, to create and help manage a site?"

Bendremer: "That all depends on your budget, experience level, and what you're trying to accomplish. Using an off-the-shelf tool allows you to quickly and easily build a highly functional Web site. If you start to do things beyond what straight HTML is capable of, however, you may need to hire a programmer to create the online applications or Web site features you need and want. This, of course, requires more of a financial investment. Building complex interactive forms or e-commerce features into your site will really start to tax the capabilities of most off-the-shelf programs, especially the cheaper ones."

Bright Idea
Think of your Web site planning like putting on a play or planning a movie. Map out or sketch each "scene" (page), imagine what each one will have and how they will interrelate, and be sure that each one contributes to the overall "picture" (entire Web page design).

Rich: "What are some of the mistakes you've seen people make when creating their Web site and getting it online?"

Bendremer: "Many people launch a Web site, online business, or e-commerce site without having realistic expectations about what's involved in actually creating and managing the site, as well as what they can expect from it once it's online. I recommend speaking with as many people as possible who have experienced the process of creating a Web site and putting it online before going through this experience yourself.

"The biggest disasters happen when you start rushing into things without proper planning and research. Before creating and programming a Web site, for example, spend time designing it on paper, perhaps using storyboards. Know exactly what you want the site to do, what content you want to make available, and how you want to present the content. Do this planning before actually starting to develop and/or program the site. You want to take an organized approach to this process in order to save yourself time, money, and frustration. I suggest looking at many other Web sites and tapping them for ideas—without stealing copyrighted materials, of course. Once you define exactly what you want, a programmer or professional Web page designer will be able to create it much easier and faster."

Rich: "What other potential pitfalls should someone watch out for when creating a Web site and putting it online?"

Bendremer: "It's very easy to create a basic Web site that looks nice and conveys information. It's much more difficult to create a truly interactive site that's useful and provides a service to your customers. If you surf the Web, only one in one hundred sites will truly offer an engaging and interactive experience that allows the visitor to do exactly what he or she needs to do. Make sure your expectations for your site are realistic. Don't expect miraculous results the first days or weeks you're online. Look at Web site design as a long, ongoing, and somewhat tedious process. Make sure your site isn't so blatantly commercial that people become offended or annoyed to the point they want to leave."

Rich: "What types of features should companies try to incorporate into their Web site?"

Bendremer: "Once you're familiar with what the Internet can do, pinpoint existing business processes that might traditionally be done over the phone or in person with your customers, and develop ways these processes can be done online in a way that helps the customer. For example, if your business currently accepts the majority of its orders from people who call your toll-free phone number, offering online ordering capabilities not only speeds up the ordering process for consumers, but in the long run will save your company money and resources.

"If you can give online customers access to your product databases and other information, that, too, can be exceptionally helpful. Amazon.com, for example, not only gives users the ability to search through a database of hundreds of thousands of book titles and order any of those books; the system will also automatically make additional book recommendations based on criteria the user selects, whether a particular subject matter or author. Amazon.com will also e-mail users when additional books in their area of interest become available, and that's something more traditional retail bookstores won't do."

> **66**
>
> "It is thrifty to prepare today for the wants of aIf only ten percent of the people will appreciate a special feature of your site, and ninety percent of the people will be annoyed that they can't take advantage of that feature, does it really make sense to offer it?
> —Sandy Bendremer-tomorrow."
>
> **99**

Rich: "There are so many new Web technologies available, such as streaming audio and video. Which of these technologies should a start-up online business consider incorporating into its site?"

Bendremer: "I recommend catering your Web site to the lowest common denominator of users. At this point, most people don't have the required Web browser plug-ins or technology to accept streaming audio or video …. Look at what features the popular Web browsers, such as Microsoft Explorer and Netscape Navigator, can deliver natively, without add-ons, and design your site around those features.

"I also strongly recommend against developing a site where the download times are too significant to keep the visitor's attention. Internet surfers have the shortest attention span imaginable. If someone gets tired of waiting, the Back or Home icon on their browser is always only a millisecond away. Always test your site using a standard dial-up Internet connection to see how the rest of the world will see your site. In my opinion, a 30-second waiting time for a page to download is too long for most sites."

Rich: "What are some of the other considerations a start-up business should think about when choosing a Web-hosting service?"

Bendremer: "If you'll be operating a high volume site requiring very specific types of services, one option is to purchase your own Web server, which has become pretty cheap these days, and locate your service with your provider. This is called 'colocation.' The provider will sell you space on an equipment rack and will maintain your server for you. The benefit is that you won't have to adhere to any restrictions imposed by the Web-hosting service regarding the use of their servers. If you're using colocation services, you'll typically be billed based on the amount of bandwidth your site requires. This has become a very common practice, even among very large Fortune 500 companies with an Internet presence who aren't themselves Internet Service Providers."

Rich: "Is it necessary to choose an ISP/Web-hosting service that's geographically located near your company?"

Bendremer: "Unless you're using colocation services where you might need hands-on access to your Web server hardware, there's absolutely no need to be in the same geographic area as your Web-hosting service. All of your Web site maintenance and programming can be done on your own computer, located anywhere, and transferred to your Web server using a standard Internet connection."

Neil Cohen—ad sales services

Once your e-commerce site is online, you'll need to promote it to the public (or your target niche market) in order to generate traffic. As we've discussed,

Moneysaver
Using an ad
sales or auction
service makes
buying online
advertising more
affordable to
start-up busi-
nesses and com-
panies looking to
stretch their
advertising
and marketing
dollars.

one way to generate traffic to your site and create awareness of your company is through advertising. AdAuction.Com (www.adauction.com) is an online service that auctions unsold online advertising space on premium, branded Web sites, search engines, and information portals.

In addition to offering unsold online advertising, AdAuction.com recently began dealing with traditional print magazines, auctioning their unsold advertising space. The company also plans to eventually offer unsold television ad time and billboard advertising space at discounted rates.

AdAuction.com provides business-to-business e-commerce service for buying and selling media on over 150 top-branded Web publishers, including Yahoo!, Netscape, E-Trade, Bloomberg Web Networks, HotBot, E! Online, Biztravel.com, and The Monster Board. The company was founded in September 1997 and is based in San Francisco.

Neil Cohen is the senior vice president of business affairs for AdAuction.com. In this interview, he offers advice on how to make full use of your business's advertising and promotional budget.

Rich: "What exactly is AdAuction.com?"

Neil Cohen: "We are an online service for the media-buying community at large. We democratize media buying for the masses, including people with small to medium-size businesses who couldn't traditionally afford advertising on such services as Yahoo! For somebody who is starting any type of business and using online advertising or traditional magazine print advertising, we offer an attractive and money-saving opportunity. We offer a way to purchase 'opportunistic' media, which is inventory that is perishable. We sell that previously unsold ad space before it expires. We sell this advertising space at a discounted rate, sometimes as low as thirty to forty cents on the dollar. We also sell the ad space in smaller chunks; then it can be purchased directly. This is very appealing to small advertisers."

Rich: "What are the steps someone should take to begin promoting her business?"

Cohen: "The first step is to develop a focused marketing program, no matter what your budget is. You need to develop a core focused message and understand exactly what you want or need to accomplish with your advertising. Next, it's necessary to define your brand and audience and make sure your message is suitable for what you're trying to do. This is pretty much stuff you'd learn in a college-level marketing course. Also, just because various opportunities are available, such as online advertising, print advertising, or direct mail, you need to determine if these are the right marketing tools for your business. Your goal is to reach your target market, and that's what will make your business successful."

Rich: "Once someone determines online advertising is suitable for their business, what's next?"

Cohen: "Choose the media properties that will allow you to best reach your target audience based on your budget. Based on what you determine, you need to develop a media plan, again based on your budget and goals. Ask yourself who you are and what you stand for as a brand. Next, create ads that will communicate that message, and then choose the best places to showcase your ads based upon who you're trying to reach. If you're not using an advertising agency, it'll require research on your part to fine-tune your advertising message and find ways to get your message out to the right audience.

Bright Idea
Remember that the goal of all your advertising is to drive traffic to your site and boost sales. Everything else, no matter how fun or interesting, is just a means to this goal.

If you don't have a big budget, you want to focus your advertising, leverage it, and make it do as much work as it can."

Rich: "How can people best use a company like AdAuction.com if they have a tight budget?"

Cohen: "Using our service as a tool, anyone can find a few media properties that they think will work well with their branding message or advertising program, and be able to buy into that property without having to pay full 'rate card' rates. Thus, anyone can extend the strength of their media dollars. So, instead of being able to afford a one-month campaign on Yahoo!, for example, you might be able to use our service and afford a three- or four-month campaign on Yahoo! It's important, however, for you to have a good understanding of what exactly you're buying and buy into media that will help you reach your target audience."

Rich: "There are a lot of advertising-related terms people need to know in order to purchase advertising space intelligently. What's the best way to learn this lingo and avoid getting ripped off or buying the wrong thing?"

Cohen: "Numerous sites on the Web offer educational resources for buying media. At AdAuction.com, for example, we offer an online resource center that offers some basic tutorials on buying and using advertising. I suggest people do research and learn the key terms they'll need to know, and become familiar with advertising strategies that are effective. If you've never bought media before, it's important to do your homework first and know what you're buying. On our site, we offer information about everything we sell. You can compare rate-card rates with our auction rates, for example.

It's also important to understand basic demographic information and advertising terms."

Rich: "What are the potential pitfalls to watch out for when buying online advertising?"

Cohen: "There are many. The biggest mistake I see people making is that they take the 'ready, fire, aim' approach. They start buy advertising before they truly understand what they're trying to accomplish. Don't rush into online advertising simply because you see everyone else doing it. The second biggest misconception about online advertising involves click-through rates. The number of people who will see your banner ad will be much, much higher than the percentage of people who actually click on that ad in order to visit your site. Advertising online does *not* guarantee high traffic to your site. The average click-through rate in the industry is about 0.65 percent. This means that for every 100 impressions or people who see your banner ad, less than one person will click through and visit your site.

"The Internet has been painted as this incredible direct marketing tool, and it can live up to that hype, but only if you're launching a sophisticated, high-budget online advertising and marketing campaign. It takes a lot of work, knowledge, and experience to put together a highly successful online marketing and advertising campaign. As a beginner, don't expect to pay for a few banner ads and have thousands of people flocking to your site in order to buy your products or services. Online advertising should be used as a branding tool as well as a method of generating traffic for your site. As a Web surfer yourself, think about how many banner ads you've seen compared to how many you've clicked on to visit a company's site. Based on the number of

Unofficially...
As you may have noted in earlier chapters, the estimated click-through rate for banner ads varies from one study to another. Be sure to check into the expected rates that apply to your particular product or field, and use the studies as guides, not sure-fire rules.

ads you've responded to, or clicked on, how many actual orders have you placed that started with clicking on a banner ad?

"In a nutshell, make sure you have realistic expectations based on your advertising purchases and implementation."

Rich: "Should someone hire an advertising agency or graphic artist to create her actual advertising (such as banner ads)?"

Cohen: "I suggest that anyone interested in using banner ads should start off by seeking professional help to do it. There are many agencies that have studied how to design and use banner ads most effectively. Anyone can take a hit-or-miss approach, but you're better off tapping the knowledge of someone who already knows what works and doesn't work, so you don't lose money trying to obtain this knowledge firsthand. If you're going to spend twenty-thousand dollars to thirty-thousand dollars or more on advertising, it makes sense to spend a few thousand dollars to hire an agency that will help you design ads that will work and then place those ads in places that will optimize your dollar spending."

Rich: "Are there other mistakes people should avoid making when it comes to online advertising?"

Cohen: "Avoid banner burnout. If you don't change your advertising creatively, people will start ignoring your ad because it's not fresh and doesn't grab their attention. Unfortunately, there is no preset dollar figure I can suggest as the ideal advertising budget for a start-up business. Some people recommend spending five percent of your annual projected gross; however, I believe this varies a lot based on what your company is offering and who you're offering it to.

"I think every successful marketing and advertising effort requires taking some risk. As a start-up company ourselves, AdAuction.com spent over $2 million on advertising during our first year. We believed it was important to quickly establish ourselves as a leading brand and establish a reputation as a company with substantial resources. Obviously, starting small is okay. Using AdAuction.com, anyone can start with a $500 media buy and see what kind of response they get. If the response is good, their next media buy might be for $1,000, for example. If you're a company targeting a niche market and you advertise on a niche-oriented site, you should be able to generate respectable results starting with a small advertising budget."

Rich: "What other advertising advice can you offer?"

Cohen: "Don't overbuy ad space on any particular Web site, especially one that targets a niche market. If the site you advertise on only has 10,000 unique users, you don't want to buy one million impressions on that site, because you'll be overreaching that audience. They'll be seeing your ad too many times, and you're paying for that. Make sure you're buying your advertising at an appropriate level without overexposing yourself."

Rich: "Does advertising on a search engine or information portals make sense for a small, start-up online business?"

Cohen: "Personally, I would recommend taking a targeted advertising approach, not a broad-based approach. If I had a small budget, I would focus on

Moneysaver
Don't overbuy.
When you over-
expose your
banner, your
marginal sales
will plummet,
and you'll just be
wasting money.

reaching the most qualified audience possible. If you can afford to focus your advertising on the search engines in order to reach a particular demographic, advertising on a search engine or portal could work very well. Otherwise, I'd look specifically at other niche-oriented sites."

Rich: "Do you have any other words of advice for online entrepreneurs?"

Cohen: "Even the smallest of businesses can become a significant entity through smart marketing. For people who are savvy and comfortable doing their own media buying, AdAuction.com offers a great opportunity for a small company to pick up brand-name media. Brand is a very important thing in business. It is who you are in the business world, what your customers and potential customers believe you are, and where you're seen and who your company is seen with.

"If your business advertises on the same sites as other well-known and established businesses, it says a lot about the company you keep and changes for the better how others will perceive you. For example, if you determine your online advertising should include PC World Online, your ads will appear with other ads from companies like Ford, AT&T, and Visa. I call this the halo effect, because being seen with these well-known and high-profile advertisers on a branded and respected Web site helps to enhance your brand."

Christopher Hadden and Todd Matzke—Web graphic design programs

If you're interested in creating original graphics or editing existing graphics for your Web site, there are many software-based tools available. One of the most popular, inexpensive, and easy-to-use tools is Paint Shop Pro 5.x for the PC (MSRP: $69) from Jasc Software, Inc. (www.jasc.com).

Using this software, you can design and produce eye-catching Web graphics. It's possible to efficiently create and add outstanding visual impact to any type of Web site and quickly import, enhance, and export a wide range of pictures with virtually any digital imaging device. Paint Shop Pro 5.x allows users to open, convert, and save over 40 different types of graphic file formats.

When it comes to designing Web graphics, Paint Shop Pro 5.x offers a collection of image effects and comes bundled with a powerful animation program that can be used to create, edit, and optimize animated GIF files to add motion to your site.

A free, 30-day evaluation version of Paint Shop Pro 5.x (along with Animation Shop) is available directly from the company's Web site.

In this interview, Christopher Hadden and Todd Matzke of Jasc Software, Inc., discuss how Paint Shop Pro 5.x can be used by Web page designers to add visual impact to their online business or e-commerce site. The two also share Web site design tips.

Rich: **"Many of the graphic design programs available are created for professional graphic artists and are difficult to use, even for people proficient in the use of Windows. How do products like Paint Shop Pro 5.x differ?"**

Christopher Hadden: "The majority of graphic design packages are geared toward high-end professionals. Ours, however, was designed to be easy to use by everyday people. As we developed each version of the software, we took to heart all of the suggestions made by our users. Our software also offers versatility. People can load virtually any type of graphic file into our software, modify it if they choose, and then save it in the format that best suits their need. All of the graphics that appear on Jasc Software's Web site were created using Paint Shop Pro."

Rich: "What is the best way for someone to learn how to use a graphics software package, such as Paint Shop Pro?"

Moneysaver
There are a series of free tutorials available online that teach people how to create animated banners or edit their digital photos, for example, using Paint Shop Pro.

Todd Matzke: "In my opinion, just load the software into your computer and start using it. Experiment! Anyone who is familiar with using programs in the Windows environment will be able to learn the basics of Paint Shop Pro in under an hour, especially if they take the time to read the software's manual or the book *Creating Paint Shop Pro Web Graphics* by Andy Shafran [$44.99, Muska & Lipman]. *Teach Yourself Paint Shop Pro in 24 Hours* by T. Michael Clark [$15.99, Macmillan] is another excellent resource for beginners."

Rich: "What should people consider when creating a Web graphic?"

Matzke: "If a graphic file will be used on the Web, the size of the file is important, because that affects how quickly it can be downloaded. When using our software, create your graphic using sixteen-million colors, and then decrease the color depth of the image as needed to shrink the file size. This Web optimization process can be done in seconds using a command that's built into the software."

Hadden: "Paint Shop Pro also allows you to create graphics using layers. If you have a white sheet of paper and you draw on it, that's the basic image. Using layers is like placing clear sheets of plastic over that image and drawing additional detail on each sheet of plastic. Nothing is changing with the core image, but by adding layers, you can add detail or effects to the original image. You can then delete layers you don't like or add new layers without having to recreate your original image from scratch as you're designing it.

"When developing GIF images, make sure you use a Web-browser-safe color pallet to ensure the image will appear the way you want it to, no matter which browser software someone is using to view your Web page. Our software will allow you to use a browser-safe color pallet and then resize an image, making it larger or smaller, without distorting it. It's best, however, to change the size of an image when it's still displayed in the sixteen-million color mode."

Rich: "To create a Web site, what software packages should someone invest in if he's not a proficient HTML programmer?"

Hadden: "Paint Shop Pro and Animation Shop can be used to create and add all of the graphic elements to your site. The actual site itself can be created using any HTML-authoring package or Web site creation software, such as Microsoft FrontPage 2000."

Rich: "When someone is designing a Web site, what's the best way to use graphics?"

Hadden: "In terms of designing a Web site, there are countless personal styles you can use to create the overall design and look of your site. This is a highly visual medium, so it's important to use at least some graphics to make the text more visually appealing to the site's visitors. There's a balance between making your Web pages aesthetically pleasing and using too many graphics, to the point it

Watch Out!
Make sure the Web site creation software you choose also offers FTP capabilities, so you can upload your site to a Web server and then manage or update your site without having to use additional software.

takes too long to load. Your graphics should never take away from what you're trying to communicate with your Web pages. A gaudy background image, for example, can make your text difficult to read and take away from the professional look of the site. Using too many animated GIFs can also be a mistake, because these graphics can be distracting. As a general rule, use graphics to support what your site's goals are and nothing more."

Rich: "Do you recommend that people create their own customized graphics, or download them from other sites?"

Matzke: "Many Web sites offer free libraries of downloadable graphic images anyone can incorporate into their sites. I do not, however, recommend simply surfing the Web and downloading whatever graphics you like and using them on your site. Unless the graphic image is specifically placed in the public domain by its creator, consider it a copyrighted image. Violating copyrights by using graphics owned by someone else can get you into legal problems. Creating your own graphics may take a bit of extra time, but it will give your site a more unique look. Once you've created your own graphics, make sure you add a copyright message on your site to help ensure others won't steal your graphics and add them to their sites."

Just the facts

- Web-hosting services are offered as package deals. Look at the amount of storage space on the Web server being provided, what type of technical support the company provides, and what additional services, including consulting and Web site development tools, are offered.

■ When choosing an ISP, make sure the technical support staff will be accessible. The biggest complaint people have with smaller Web-hosting services is the lack of support.

■ Using an ad sales or auction service makes buying online advertising more affordable to start-up businesses and companies looking to stretch their advertising and marketing dollars.

■ When developing GIF images, make sure you use a Web browser-safe color pallet to ensure the image will appear the way you want it to, no matter which browser software someone is using to view your Web page.

Chapter 15

GET THE SCOOP ON...
Additional e-commerce interviews ▪
Multiactive software tips
▪ Trends for the future ▪ Insider advice

The Experts Share Their E-Commerce Knowledge and Experience (II)

A s in the previous chapter, here we interview experts in the field of providing services for the online business manager. Our experts here are:

Brent Halverson
President, Multiactive Software
Topic: Using specialized software to create and manage your site

Brian Jamison
President, Jamison/Gold
Topic: Developing the creative content for your Web site

Tim Brady and Paul Graham
Vice President of Production and Executive Producer; Producer—
Yahoo! Store
Topics: Using a turnkey service to create, manage, and host your e-commerce site

Brent Halverson—software to create and manage your site

Multiactive Software, Inc. (www.multiactive.com) has two flagship software titles, Maximizer and ecBuilder Pro. The first is a contact management program for managing databases of contact names, addresses, phone numbers, schedules, and other related information. Maximizer and Symantec's ACT! software created the "contact management software" category.

The ecBuilder Pro software package (priced at about $100 for the core product and $500 for the professional edition) was later released. Designed for small business, this program allows you, without any programming knowledge, to create a fully functional Web site capable of handling a wide range of e-commerce applications, including shopping carts and secure credit card transactions. The software comes bundled with 30 Web site design templates and a wide range of easy-to-use wizards, allowing you to create professional-looking Web pages simply by adding your own text and graphics to the precreated templates.

While ecBuilder Pro won't meet the needs of all businesses, it is useful for small, start-up companies operated by people with little or no programming experience who want to develop a Web site and go online in a relatively short time period.

Jason Rich: "Who was ecBuilder designed for?"

Brent Halverson: "There are high-end software packages designed to help people create and manage e-commerce-capable Web sites, but they're expensive and cater to people with at least some programming knowledge. Our goal was to offer a software package for small business start-ups that was both easy to use and inexpensive. This software can be used to create e-commerce Web sites for a wide range of uses .... Our software is being used by existing small companies that want to create an Internet presence in order to reach a larger online audience, as well as people who want to start their own side business."

Rich: "Once someone begins using a software package, such as ecBuilder, what are the steps for actually getting a business online?"

Halverson: "It's important to create or gather together an assortment of pictures of your products and the text you'll incorporate into your site in order to promote or sell your products or services. You'll also want to obtain electronic images of your company logo and other related graphics. You can then use the precreated templates and wizards built into our software to create a basic Web site for yourself. Next, you'll need to sign up with an Internet Service Provider who will host your site once it's created. One of the great things about ecBuilder is that it's compatible with all ISPs and doesn't require any special server-based software [CGI programs] in order for you to implement secure order processing, hit counters, or shopping cart applications into your site."

Rich: "Is creating a Web site and launching an online business as easy as it's made out to be?"

Halverson: "Creating a Web site can be done quickly and easily. However, this is only the starting point and won't guarantee a successful business. Simply putting a Web site online doesn't mean hundreds or thousands of people will come flocking to your site right away. Promoting your site is critical. You have to find innovative ways to get your domain name in

Bright Idea
Software like ecBuilder can be used effectively for businesses which sell services online—not just products.

front of everybody you possibly can, starting with your existing customers, if you have any. All of your traditional printed materials, such as your company letterhead, business cards, and print advertising, should include your Web site's URL. The domain name you choose should also be easy to remember.

"Our software has a feature that will allow you to get your site listed on the major search engines and information portals. Listing your company with the search engines and information portals is an excellent way to start promoting your business online, and it's totally free."

Rich: "How much time will someone need to dedicate to actually creating their site?"

Timesaver
It's often a good idea to make use of templates. They will give you a quick and easy framework within which to set up your business's page. As you become more established and have more time to invest, you can begin developing more distinctive elements for your site.

Halverson: "Creating a basic e-commerce Web site with [a product like] ecBuilder is very easy. The Web site development and management process, however, is an ongoing process that involves continual fine-tuning. I recommend people start off using one of our software's predefined templates to get started, and once their site begins to expand and evolve, that's when they can start deviating from the template to add their own functionality. Step One is to get your basic site up, and that's what our software does best. Start off simply and then add the complex features as you go. Adding functionality, like shopping cart capabilities and hit counters, can be done using the software's wizards."

Rich: "What sets ecBuilder apart from other packages, like Microsoft's FrontPage 2000?"

Halverson: "Those products allow you to create a basic Web site quickly, but they don't offer the e-commerce components which online businesses need in order to accept orders online. It's possible to create an e-commerce application using

FrontPage 2000, but you will probably need to do some of your own programming and rely on your ISP to provide the CGI scripts needed for certain e-commerce applications. I use the analogy that a software package like FrontPage 2000 will allow you to create an electronic brochure, while a software package such as ecBuilder will allow you to create a totally interactive electronic store or e-commerce site."

Rich: "What types of online businesses have you seen people develop using your software?"

Halverson: "We've seen bed and breakfasts use our software to promote their business. Real estate agents have used ecBuilder to showcase homes for sale and accept electronic inquiries about properties. We've also seen people create online businesses that sell everything from baseball cards to antiques to vitamins. In the UK, we have a user of our software selling Viagra online. The possibilities are truly limitless."

Rich: "When developing a site, what are the key features that need to be added?"

Halverson: "I think pictures of your product are critical. You might also consider adding audio or video, if it will help convey information about whatever it is you're selling. One of the biggest mistakes I've seen people make when creating and then launching an online business is trying to do too much too soon. Once you get your basic site online, start to tweak it and accept whatever feedback you can get from the visitors to your site.

"Just because you read an article about the success of Amazon.com, don't expect your small online business to instantly grow. Developing a successful online business takes a lot of hard work and time.

If you put in the effort and make the necessary financial commitment, there could be a huge reward and payback. I believe the Internet is going to get bigger and bigger, and with more people coming online, the opportunity to sell products and services using the World Wide Web will grow dramatically in the near future."

Rich: "Is it necessary to hire a professional graphic artist to help create a great-looking Web site?"

Halverson: "The templates built into our software were created by professional designers, so if you start off using those, you shouldn't need to hire a graphic artist to design your site. If, however, you're looking to create a unique design or you see your business growing quickly and want to try new things from a graphical standpoint, that's when you might want to make the investment of hiring graphic designers. But hiring a graphic artist costs money. Until you know your online-based business idea is going to be successful, I don't believe it's necessary to use the services of a graphic artist, unless you're simply not comfortable or pleased with the results you create on your own using our design templates."

Brian Jamison—services for larger companies

Jamison/Gold Interactive Agency (www.jamisongold.com) provides services to medium- and large-size companies wishing to create or enhance their online presence. The company handles Web site design, developing a company's online corporate identity, Web site management, promotions, e-commerce, research and development, database integration, and reporting. Most of its clients are Fortune 500 companies, including Sony, Nissan

Moneysaver
If you have the budget available to you, by all means consider making use of a graphic artist. But don't treat it as a necessity. You may well be able to handle the graphics yourself, producing an uncluttered and attractive site at a much lower expense.

Motors, DreamWorks Interactive, Columbia-TriStar Pictures, Media One Express, and Energizer.

If you're first launching an online-based business and don't have a huge amount of start-up capital, hiring an agency like Jamison/Gold is probably out of your budget. The agency's founder and president, Brian Jamison, however, does have plenty of advice for people first entering the online business field.

Rich: "What can someone do to create and promote their online business if they can't afford to hire a full-service agency like Jamison/Gold?"

Brian Jamison: "There are a number of alternatives to hiring a large agency like ours to help you develop, launch, and manage an online business. I've seen a number of turnkey solutions available that cost only a few hundred dollars and offer the tools you'll need to get started. These inexpensive tools may not be able to handle the requirements of a large online business, but they're suitable for smaller start-ups. For a start-up company, I'd recommend starting off small using one of these inexpensive turnkey solutions and then working your way up as your business grows."

Rich: "Once someone has an idea for his online business, what steps should he follow to get his idea off the ground?"

Jamison: "First, decide how you're going to make your money and how your Web site will help you do this. You can sell advertising on a Web site to generate revenue, sell access to your Web site in the form of memberships, sell products or services from a Web site, or use a Web site as a lead generation tool …. Next, assemble the tools you'll need to create your Web site.

> **❝**
> Instead of using one of the cheap off-the-shelf software products that usually offer limited capabilities, I'd recommend learning HTML programming yourself or hiring someone who is capable of programming a Web site to meet the exact specifications you need to make your business idea successful.
> —Brian Jamison
> **❞**

"It's important to carefully define your needs before you begin gathering and using the tools, software, and services you'll need to develop your site and go online. Various Web site creation software packages and turnkey solution services all have different features and offer different services. Once you know what you want to do and pinpoint the software or tools you'll need to do it, that's when you should purchase your computer hardware, because you want the software to dictate your hardware requirements, especially if you plan on operating your own server.

"It'll also be necessary to determine if you want to operate your site from your own in-house server, if you want to colocate it, or if you want to use a server owned and operated by a Web-hosting service. Each of these options offer different pluses and minuses in terms of benefits and costs. Once all of the pieces are put together, the next steps are to actually create the site and promote it heavily. After you find ways of promoting your site that seem to be working, you should pour everything you've got into it."

Rich: "What is the biggest misconception people have about starting an online business?"

Jamison: "People spend a lot of time and money developing their site and getting it online, but they often don't realize that once all of this work is done, their job is just starting. Once your business is online, you have to attract people to your site and generate traffic. Unfortunately, there are no formulas to follow when it comes to promoting an online business. It all depends on what you're selling, who your target audience is, and what your budget is."

Rich: "**If someone already has a successful traditional business but wants to create an online presence for that business, should they hire a full-service agency, like Jamison/Gold?**"

Jamison: "This decision should be made based on the size of the company. It would probably make more sense for a small company to develop their own Web site. For a medium- or large-size company that has a reputation or image to uphold, they can't afford to make mistakes. It may make more sense for larger and established companies to contract out their Web site development and maintenance work.

"There are many small agencies that cater to the needs of small businesses in terms of helping them get online. Without question, a large company should hire a firm like ours to help them create and manage their Internet presence. It doesn't have to cost a million dollars to create a professional-looking and highly functional Web site. You do, however, need to take your Web site seriously and put as much or more effort and resources into creating your site as you would for any other form of communication."

Rich: "**If someone is starting a small start-up online business, should he visit the large and successful online sites to see how things are being done?**"

Jamison: "In many ways, what a huge corporation does online is a totally different ballgame from what a small business can do. A small business operator, however, can learn a lot about how things are done and what should be done by any online business or e-commerce site. Anyone can look at a large and successful site and learn a lot about how they

Bright Idea
Take your Web site seriously. The first impression you make with a customer, whether it's online, in person, over the phone, or by mail, is what makes the difference.

approached navigation or how they branded the site, for example. I have discovered that the majority of smaller online businesses don't have a very good sense of branding, and I believe that's a mistake. It's very easy for someone to get lost while surfing the Web. I believe it's important to put a lot of thought into how you want to organize and brand your site."

Rich: "What are some of the pitfalls you've seen people run into as they attempt to establish themselves online?"

Jamison: "People get overwhelmed by choices as they begin to learn about all of the options available to them when it comes to designing, creating, and managing a Web site. People have to choose which technologies to go with, what development tools to use, and what services are required from an ISP. One reason why companies turn to a full-service agency like ours is because we help them cut through all of that and make the right decisions.

"Another roadblock people run into is that they don't have the technical resources available to do whatever it is they want to do on the Web. People talk about Amazon.com as being the ultimate e-commerce site. It's not possible to do 1-Click ordering, for example, with off-the-shelf Web site development software a small start-up online business operator might purchase. People who shop at small online businesses have slightly different expectations and motivations than if they go to a major site, such as Amazon.com.

"Another problem I see people make is that they create a Web site that takes too long to download using a typical dial-up Internet connection. If you are channel-surfing while watching TV, would you wait one or two minutes for the programming to come on, or would you skip directly to a channel that appeared instantly? The same is true for the Internet. People hate to wait."

Rich: "Is there a super cheap and easy way for someone to develop and operate an e-commerce site?"

Jamison: "I believe that you'll get out of your business only what you put into it. If you don't put in the time and effort to create, maintain, and promote your site, people won't visit it. This isn't a case where if you build it, they will come. The biggest investment a successful online business needs to make is in time, not necessarily money."

Rich: "What are some of the trends you've noticed that will impact how business is conducted online?"

Jamison: "In 1995, a new Internet technology was being introduced virtually every week. In 1996, a new technology was introduced every month. As 1997 rolled around, it was every three or six months that a major new development was introduced in terms of Internet technology. In 1998, there was only one or two major technological advancements.

"I believe that in 2000, the biggest new technology that will impact the World Wide Web is broadband via cable modems or other types of high-speed modems. This will give people the ability to download a lot more information immediately, at extremely high speeds. Broadband won't replace television or radio, but it will allow for far more interesting and engaging experiences to Web surfers using streaming audio and video.

"Flash technology from Macromedia is another technology that I'm looking closely at because you can send graphically rich content using very small file sizes, which means fast downloading times.

Watch Out!
While it's helpful to keep an eye on new Web technologies, exercise caution when incorporating them into your site. There is always a lag from the time a new technology is introduced to its widespread use. You don't want to invest a lot of money in features that only a fraction of your visitors can take advantage of.

Right now, regular consumers typically use 28.8K or 56K modems to surf the Internet, so developing your site to cater to an audience of Web surfers using broadband is premature, at least at present."

Rich: "What other Web site design advice can you offer?"

Jamison: "Error on the side of simplicity when developing your site. Pick up any graphic design how-to book for an explanation of basic graphic design rules. Also, keep the number of choices visitors to your site can make to a minimum. The Internet is a wide-open playing field. There's a revolution going on and not being part of the Internet is a big mistake. Many people believe that all companies, big and small, are playing on a level playing field when it comes to doing business on the Internet.

"While I don't believe this is true, I do strongly believe that smaller online businesses have a much greater chance of being successful and competitive than traditional small businesses do. This is the most level playing field business has ever had. There is every opportunity for a small business that's based on a good idea and that's managed properly to hit a home run and become wildly successful. People need to be realistic in their expectations, however. I think just about any type of business can work online, but for small businesses, I think the best chance for success lies in catering to a niche audience with a specific product or service that the large companies can't touch or won't touch."

Tim Brady and Paul Graham—turnkey services

Until recently, establishing an online-based business required a significant financial investment and a high level of technical expertise. Thanks to turnkey services like Yahoo! Store (store.yahoo.com), virtually anyone with a good idea for an online venture can establish themselves online inexpensively and relatively quickly.

Unlike software packages like ecBuilder Pro, Microsoft FrontPage, or Symantec's Visual Page, the Web development tools developed by Yahoo! Store exist totally online and do not require programming skills to use. All you'll need is a computer and Internet access.

Yahoo! Store is considered a complete turnkey solution. For a flat monthly fee, most features you'll need to operate an online business are provided (not included are your business idea, product or service to sell, domain name, and credit card merchant account).

Yahoo! Store's start-up costs are minimal, and there are no long-term contracts or major financial commitments. You've no doubt noticed that I've referred to Yahoo! Store's service repeatedly in this book. There's an important reason for this: It really is a top-quality service, offered by a highly reputable company, that gives start-up online business operators good chances for success. This service takes away much of the hassle and confusion from establishing and maintaining any type of online business.

In Chapter 16, "Successful E-Commerce Entrepreneurs Speak Out," you'll be reading interviews with individuals who have created viable online business ventures. Several of these business operators use Yahoo! Store. In the following interview, Yahoo's Tim Brady, vice president of production and executive producer, and Paul Graham, producer, talk about what it takes to launch a successful online venture using the Yahoo! Store service and

Moneysaver
A turnkey is useful if you don't want to deal with an Internet Service Provider, higher-priced Web site development and maintenance software, and services to handle Web site reporting tasks.

discuss why they believe their service is superior to what their competition offers. Whether or not you ultimately decide to sign up with Yahoo! Store, the information offered in this interview will be useful to any soon-to-be online business operator.

Rich: "How would you describe Yahoo! Store?"

Paul Graham: "Our service is targeted to anyone who wants to sell products or services online. It's been described as the ultimate beginner's tool, because it's so easy to use. We also have many big-name merchants who use it. We classify Yahoo! Store as a powerful e-commerce tool for non-technical users."

Rich: "Based on your experience, what types of business ideas work best as online stores or e-commerce sites?"

Graham: "The things that work particularly well with Yahoo! Store are the same things that work well online. This includes, but is not at all limited to, virtually anything you could sell through traditional mail-order catalogs. Sometimes people say you can't sell clothing online because the customer needs to touch them. In reality, clothing is one of the most popular things sold via mail order. When someone sells clothing online, they're using an electronic catalog page instead of a paper one.

"Specific things that we've found that sell well online include anything that involves refills, such as toner cartridges or prescription medications, because someone can go online, quickly place their order, and have it shipped directly to their home or office. For me personally, I typically buy the same style of pants from The Gap, so shopping online from The Gap Online offers me time-saving convenience. Any type of gift items sell particularly well online. The reason for this is because people wait until the last minute to shop for gifts, and shopping online allows someone to have their gifts drop-shipped, so they don't have to worry about wrapping, shipping, or trekking to the mall to make their purchase.

"We've also discovered that computer equipment and software products sell well online. I believe that the online market for software will expand dramatically in the future."

Rich: "Since Yahoo! Store initially launched, what is the most outrageous product you've seen successfully sold online?"

Graham: "One of the most successful stores we've seen that uses our service sells nothing but refrigerator magnets. Their Web site is www.fridgedoor. com. When I heard about this site, I thought to myself they'd need a lot of luck to make this venture successful, but it turned out to be a brilliant online business idea. We've discovered that the merchants who cater to real niche markets tend to do well. In a traditional retail environment, niche merchants tend to fail, because their potential market for their products or services is limited by the population of their neighborhood. Online merchants, however, can target [the tens of millions of Web surfers] in order to find people interested in their specialty products or services."

Rich: "If someone has an idea for an online business, why should they consider using Yahoo! Store?"

Graham: "Generally speaking, they should choose a solution that's not technically demanding. Once you get into Web development tools that require technical expertise and programming knowledge, life can get pretty unpleasant if you don't know

Unofficially...
Personal products (such as lingerie) tend to sell well online, because people can shop in the privacy of their own homes.

exactly what you're doing. People should seek out a service that is easy to use. More specifically, Yahoo! Store offers many more services than our competition, allowing people to create far more professional-looking Web sites with much less hassle. Through the power of Yahoo!, we're also able to help our merchants generate more traffic to their site and then manage and track that traffic using tools that are far more powerful and versatile than what our competition offers. There's probably a reason why we have far more users than any of our competitors."

Rich: "Realistically, what is the learning curve for using Yahoo! Store to create an online presence for a business?"

Graham: "First, using our tools, it's actually difficult to create a site that looks unprofessional or bad. We can't keep people from making common yet stupid mistakes, like having typos in their text. But even if you just use our basic tools, you'll wind up with something that looks professional and better than ninety-five percent of all other e-commerce sites. How long it takes to create your site will depend on how long it takes to gather up your pictures and other art assets, write your copy, and post it all online. We've seen people create excellent thirty- to forty-item stores in the course of an afternoon. Of course, it takes time on an ongoing basis to maintain and perfect the online store's content."

Rich: "What are the key ingredients every online store should have?"

Graham: "First, avoid a 'splash' page. You don't want to waste a Web page or someone's time, simply displaying your company logo and requiring someone to click their mouse before you give customers what they want. Your front page should communicate a strong sense of professionalism. People will decide almost immediately if they'd consider doing business with you based on how your front page looks. From your front page, it should be very easy for your customers to find information about the products or services they're looking for. The front page should clearly explain what you do and provide links to additional information about your company and products.

"Your site should be comprised of individual product pages, which describe each of your products or services in detail, and show images of your products. Instead of using full-size images, I recommend using thumbnail images [30x30 pixels, for example] that people can then click on if they're interested in seeing a larger image that takes longer to download. If you have more than ten or fifteen products, your product pages should be divided into categories to make someone's shopping experience more intuitive. We've found that online shoppers appreciate greater amounts of text when used to describe products or services in detail. People want to learn as much as possible about what they're buying."

Rich: "In terms of credit card and online order processing or shopping cart applications, how much knowledge does someone need to add these features to their site?"

Graham: "Adding these features is very easy using Yahoo! Store. You're going to need a merchant account if you want to accept credit cards on your site. Yahoo!, however, has partnerships with merchant account providers, including Bank One (store.yahoo.com/vw/merchant.html). You can

Watch Out!
Avoid a "splash page." It wastes your customer's time. Make your front page one that includes useful information for the Web visitor.

apply for a merchant account online and have it linked directly to your Yahoo! Store online-based business automatically. Yahoo! Store merchants can automatically participate in the Yahoo! Shopping area of the Yahoo! search engine/information portal and share a joint shopping cart application, which will help drive crossover traffic to your site."

Rich: "As someone starts actually designing their Web site, what tips can you offer?"

Graham: "The most important design tip I can offer is that your site needs to look professional. This comes down to how you actually use GIF images within your site. There are really only two things on a Web page—text and images. The look of text is pretty generic, so it's how you lay out the text and combine it with images that will make your site stand out. You need to use images carefully, however, because it's the artwork and images you add that can really slow down the download time of your pages. Good Web design comes down to the careful use of images. I recommend using images that are small in size, but punchy. The Yahoo! Store tools are fine-tuned to optimize GIF file sizes and make adding pictures or images to your site easy. An ideal product page on your site, for example, shouldn't be larger than 30K, which means it'll download in about ten seconds over a typical modem."

Rich: "You mentioned earlier that Yahoo! Store is the ideal Web site development tool for beginners interested in developing an e-commerce site or online store. Are there any limitations regarding what can and can't be done using your service?"

Graham: "The only thing we don't allow Yahoo! Store merchants to do is write their own CGI scripts

and install them on our server. If absolutely necessary, someone could establish a secondary site on
another server and link to that server, but we
haven't found cases where this is actually necessary."

**Rich: "What are some of the pitfalls you've seen
online merchants run into when they first get
started?"**

Graham: "The first mistake people make is choosing
to sell something that people have no interest in
buying. This is usually a result of poor research on
the merchant's part. There's no way any technology
can make people want to buy something they have
no interest in. One way to test an online business
idea is to ask yourself, 'Do you think your store
would be successful if it were a traditional retail
store located right next door to a Wal-Mart?' If
you're selling the same stuff as Wal-Mart, your
store's chances for success are slim, because on the
Web, everyone is right next door to everyone else.
If, on the other hand, you're selling something specialized that Wal-Mart doesn't have the time or
energy to be an expert in, such as selling antique
watches or refrigerator magnets, you have the
potential to prosper.

"Another pitfall new online merchants run into
is they create a poorly designed Web site. Our
design tools will automatically save you from making
the worst design mistakes, but we also have a long
list of professional Web site designers who we can
refer individuals to if they need help designing their
site.

"The next big pitfall is that people create fabu-
lous sites, but then generate zero traffic to their site.
This is a result of poor marketing and promotion.
You've got to make sure people can *find* your site.

Unofficially...
Yahoo! Store was
the first e-com-
merce solution
offered to busi-
nesses on the
Web. It was
launched in the
summer of 1995.

Since most people begin their Web-surfing experiences from a search engine or information portal, it's an absolute must that your online business be registered with all of the major search engines. When someone becomes a Yahoo! Store merchant, this is a free service we automatically provide.

"The final major pitfall I've seen many companies run into is that they offer bad customer service and lose tremendous amounts of business as a result. Having fabulously good customer service will help ensure repeat business from customers and help generate word-of-mouth business. Without exception, the most successful online merchants all offer a highly personalized level of customer service."

Bright Idea
E-mail your customer immediately after he has placed an online order, and be sure to notify him if there will be any delay in processing and shipping it. Advertising will generate traffic to a Web site, but positive word-of-mouth from your customers will generate business.

Rich: "What are some of the things an online merchant can do to enhance his customer service?"

Graham: "As soon as an online order is received, the merchant should send his customer an e-mail message of thanks for the order. When the order is actually shipped, a second e-mail should be sent indicating when the customer can expect to receive that order and include a tracking number. These e-mail messages should be personalized.

"Any e-mailed questions or inquiries you receive from potential customers should be addressed immediately, not ignored for a week. If an item ordered is out of stock, the customer should be informed immediately so he can make alternate arrangements if the purchase is time-sensitive and needed for a birthday gift, for example."

Rich: "Does the design of a Web site affect how it gets listed on a search engine, such as Yahoo!?"

Graham: "Yes. This is something that most people, including some of our biggest competitors, don't realize. If your Web pages are dynamically generated, they won't be included in certain search engines. 'Dynamically generated' means the Web pages are created on the fly from a database and are customized to a visitor's preferences. Search engine crawlers, used to compile a search engine's database of Web sites, will ignore dynamically created Web sites. It's much easier, from an engineering point of view, to create Web site design software that creates dynamically created Web pages as opposed to static HTML pages. Web sites created using our tools end up as static HTML pages, ensuring they'll get listed with the major search engines.

"This is something that happens behind the scenes, without the online merchant actually realizing it. It results in more traffic getting referred to a site and is something that shouldn't be taken for granted. The easiest way to determine if your Web site uses dynamically created Web pages is to use a Web browser to access the site online and see if a question mark ('?') appears within in the URL. That's the test many of the search engine crawlers use."

Rich: "Should people expect a lot of traffic to their site once it's launched?"

Graham: "Growth can be slow in the beginning, so expectations should be realistic. The great thing about e-commerce is that as word gets out about your site, traffic increases. Also, unlike traditional retail businesses, the growth potential of an online business never stops. In a retail store, people drive by it, and within three or four months, you'll know what level of business you can expect. With an online store, the potential customer base is huge and will continue to grow, because it's not limited by geographic boundaries or limitations."

Rich: "Can you describe the technical support services offered by Yahoo! Store to its merchants?"

Graham: "We offer online and telephone support. On our Web site, we have online FAQs and tutorials containing virtually everything someone will need to know to successfully design, launch, and manage an online business. While we're not set up to walk someone through every step of the process directly through our telephone technical support department, we are available to answer questions and help solve problems. We can also refer people to professional Web designers who, for an additional fee, will walk someone through every step of the process. Our Web site (www.store.yahoo.com—click on the 'Selling Online' link) offers a vast online resource of information created for people exploring the various online business development and implementation options. You don't have to use our services to visit this Web site and read the information, which is based on our experience working successfully with thousands of online businesses."

Rich: "What else does someone need to know in order to operate a successful online business?"

Graham: "You absolutely need to understand the fundamentals of operating any type of business. You have to know how to manage inventory, process orders, and maintain financial records, for example. It's also important to understand what a good Web site is. Thus, I suggest that a prospective online merchant spend a considerable amount of time first becoming an online shopper. Place orders with at least ten different online stores, and experience what it's like as a customer. This will help someone determine what works and what doesn't when it comes to creating her own site."

Rich: "Aside from the flat monthly costs to become a Yahoo! Store merchant, what other costs are associated with getting an online business operational?"

Graham: "You have to register your domain name with InterNIC and obtain a merchant account in order to accept credit cards. If you choose to hire a Web site designer, that's another fee you'll need to pay. There are also costs associated with advertising and promoting your online business."

Tim Brady: "When someone opens a Yahoo! Store, his store is promoted in the shopping area of Yahoo! This is a free service. There are also other advertising and merchandising opportunities through Yahoo! that are available only to our merchants. As a company, Yahoo! does extensive marketing to Web surfers educating them about the benefits of shopping online. Yahoo! is traditionally where Web surfers turn to find whatever it is they're looking for on the Web. We're using our resources to help drive customers, directly and indirectly, to the sites of our merchants."

Rich: "Tracking Web traffic to a site is important. What tracking and reporting services does Yahoo! Store offer?"

Graham: "As an online merchant, we offer tools to help people track their visitors. We can tell you where your visitors are coming from. If they link from a search engine, for example, we can tell you what search phrase or keyword they used to find you. We can also tell you what keywords generate the most sales per capita. When you're doing advertising, this is valuable information that's provided free of charge to our merchants.

Timesaver
Good reporting services can save you money and time in the long run by giving you specific information with which you can plan future changes. For example, getting a report of click trails will show you exactly how the visitor clicked through your path—this can suggest ways to reorganize or simplify your site.

"We also provide real-time traffic reports by Web page, so you know exactly where people are going within your site. We can also tell you what people searched for within your site, which can be used as an indication if something is missing or difficult to find. By providing click trails, you can see the exact path someone followed as they explored your site. We believe that unless you have the proper feedback, it's very difficult to improve your site."

Rich: "Yahoo! Store offers users the ability to implement affiliate programs. How can an online merchant take advantage of this?"

Graham: "Any number of affiliates can link to your site, and you can determine what type of financial arrangements to make with them for the referrals. We can help you track everything. Adding an affiliate is as easy as clicking on a button. We provide all of the tracking and reporting necessary for a merchant to create an affiliate program; this can be a powerful marketing tool for generating traffic to your site."

Rich: "One online business model discussed in this book involves the sale of downloadable goods. Does Yahoo! Store support this type of online business?"

Graham: "One of our most successful merchants, PilotGear, sells software for the 3Com PalmPilot PDAs. Customers can download software as soon as their credit card information is processed. Setting up this type of business is very easy."

Rich: "One of the issues facing online merchants is security. Does Yahoo! Store provide the security and data encryption necessary to process secure transactions?"

Graham: "Individual merchants need their own merchant account, but our software and servers deal with all of the security issues. This is something that happens behind the scenes and isn't something a merchant designing their site with Yahoo! Store has to deal with."

Rich: "Internet technology is advancing quickly. What are some of the technological innovations online business operators using Yahoo! Store should be aware of?"

Graham: "We currently offer the ability to incorporate audio and video into a Web site; however, even with Web surfers accessing a site at 56K, this still isn't viable for most business applications. One technological advancement Yahoo is working on is fraud screening."

Brady: "Fraud screening helps detect people using fake or stolen credit cards to make online purchases. We're writing software that will automatically warn merchants if an order is about to be processed that looks suspicious. [Given] the fact that we have thousands of online stores working off our servers, we can follow patterns and more readily detect fraud. Aside from how fraud is detected and dealt with, I don't foresee any major technological advancements that will impact how online stores operate, at least for a few years."

Just the facts

- By advertising on the same sites as other well-known and established businesses, you will elevate your company's image in the eyes of your customers.

- Developing a successful online business takes a lot of hard work and time. If you put in the effort and make the necessary financial commitment, there could be a huge reward and payback.

- It's important to carefully define your needs before you begin gathering and using the tools, software, and services you'll need to develop your site and go online.

- People spend a lot of time and money developing their site and getting it online, but they don't realize that once all of this work is done, their job is just starting. Once your business is online, you have to attract people to your site and generate traffic.

- Starting at $100 per month, with no start-up costs, no software to purchase, and no long-term commitments, anyone can design, create, launch, and maintain an online business using the turnkey solutions offered by Yahoo! Store.

Successful E-Commerce Entrepreneurs Speak Out

Chapter 16

Throughout this book, you've read about the many steps involved in coming up with an idea for an e-commerce Web site, designing your site, and launching an advertising and marketing campaign. We've also looked at what's involved in managing the day-to-day operations of your online business venture.

By this point, hopefully, you realize that while there are incredible opportunities for success in cyberspace, striking it rich by launching an online business isn't something that will happen quickly. It's going to take a great business idea, hard work, careful planning, and a significant investment of time and money.

Even if you've already gathered together all of the resources necessary to create and launch your business, there are still potential pitfalls, many of which have already been discussed in this book.

Before you proceed further in establishing your online-based business, take a look at several entrepreneurs who have already achieved success in cyberspace.

By reading these interviews, you'll get a firsthand perspective of what it takes to achieve success, as well as what dangers to watch out for. You'll also get a taste of what the e-commerce industry is really like. The entrepreneurs interviewed within this chapter are:

Bright Idea
If you know people already involved in e-commerce, consider asking them about their own experiences. They might have tips you can apply to your own business.

> Cara France
> Founder and president, ArtisanGifts.com
>
> Mark Giordani
> Founder and president, LefKey International
>
> Chris Gwynn
> Founder and president, Fridgedoor.com
>
> Ken Young
> Director of public relations, 1-800-Flowers

The online business opportunities available to entrepreneurs are extremely diverse. While the advice offered by the people interviewed in this chapter worked for them, not everything discussed here may be applicable to your situation. Remember to keep in mind the special circumstances you face—the type of business you plan to launch, how you plan to promote it, and how you will manage operations.

In addition, there are no definitive right or wrong ways of doing things when it comes to operating an online business. Thus, you may not agree with everything the people interviewed here have to say, and that's fine. The purpose of this chapter is simply to give you an idea of the types of businesses that can be successful in cyberspace and to explain how these people were able to make their online business ventures successful.

Cara France—ArtisanGifts.com

Cara France is the founder and president of ArtisanGifts.com (www.artisangifts.com), a company created to help consumers without a lot of time to select, wrap, and send unusual gifts. The company's products are handcrafted and sent to the recipient in elegant giftwrap. The company has reviewed the work of over 1,500 artisans from around the world, selected the most distinctive and affordable items, and made them available for sale exclusively on its Web site.

The ArtisanGifts.com site offers over 200 distinctive items, priced between $30 and $160. ArtisanGifts.com uses the Yahoo! Store service. All purchases are processed on Yahoo!'s secure server. All products sold by ArtisanGifts.com can be refunded or exchanged within 30 days with receipt, eliminating a customer's potential fear of making a purchase online and not being pleased with an item.

To make navigating around the ArtisanGifts.com online store easier, the products are divided into categories, including:

Gifts for the home

Gifts for him

Gifts for her

Gifts for the office

Gifts for the kids

Jewelry

Wedding gifts

Gifts under $50

Bright Idea
By dividing your product line into convenient categories, such as type of product or price level, you make it easier for your potential customer to locate what she wants quickly.

ArtisanGifts.com
is a fast-growing
online-based
business.

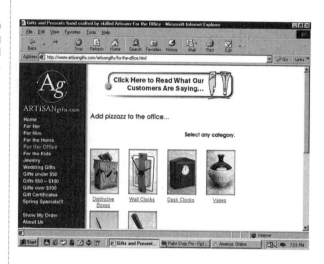

Gifts $50–$100

Gifts over $100

Cara France has discovered that operating a business in cyberspace can lead to financial success and emotional rewards. Launching ArtisanGifts.com has allowed France to bring her professional talents, personal interests, and passions together. She has a graduate degree in business, and currently lives and works in Palo Alto, Calif.

While traveling through southeast Asia in early 1998, France got the idea to launch a business that would allow artisans from across America and throughout the world to sell their handcrafted items to customers worldwide.

Jason Rich: "What got you interested in establishing an online business as opposed to a traditional retail store or catalog-based mail-order business?"

Cara France: "I always thought being involved in a really artistic type of store environment would be fun and interesting. But the idea of being chained down to a retail store and having to invest in leases, payroll, and inventory, for example, was completely unappealing to me. To get a traditional mail-order business up and running, the initial financial investment is huge, and it usually takes several years before you can even hope to break even on that investment. I wasn't willing to take that risk. What was appealing about an online business is you could reach a broad audience, located virtually anywhere in the world. Also, the type of business I wanted to establish couldn't really be done as a mail-order business using a traditional printed catalog, because all of the items I offer are handmade in small quantities. If I had a printed catalog, it would be outdated almost the moment it was shipped to potential customers. Using an online business model, when I run out of inventory on an item, I can update the Web site in minutes."

Timesaver
One advantage of online catalogs is that you can quickly revise your product list, prices, and so forth. Traditional catalogs have to be printed, then distributed (usually by mail).

Rich: "Financially, what did it take for you to get ArtisanGifts.com online?"

France: "It takes a much bigger financial investment than most people think to launch an online business and do it well, but it is still a much smaller investment than opening a retail store or establishing a traditional mail-order business. Initially, I made a five-figure financial investment to establish ArtisanGifts.com."

Rich: "In a nutshell, what does it take to be successful managing an online business?"

France: "The companies that will be successful in cyberspace will be the ones operated by people who truly understand the business basics. It's important to deliver a great product, offer a good value, and give customers more than they expect. In addition to understanding business, it's important to have a strong creative side."

Rich: "Once you had a business idea in mind, what steps did you take to actually create and establish ArtisanGifts.com in cyberspace?"

France: "I came up with the concept in July 1998 and spent the next month writing a detailed business plan and thinking through the various issues. I identified what my business strategy and competitive advantages were, and determined who my potential customers would be and what I'd deliver to them. Then I determined what it would take to make this business concept thrive. Part of creating a business plan meant establishing a well-thought-out financial strategy.

"By late August, I had established a basic game plan for getting started. I really wanted to create a business that allowed people to purchase truly unique and distinctive gifts that didn't look like items available at every mall across America. Given that objective, it became very important to create a unique presentation for the gifts. By offering unique packaging for the gifts, in the form of satin bags and handwoven fabric boxes, I knew this would help to brand the company and set it apart. The next big challenge was finding inventory and making contact with dozens upon dozens of artists. I also had to get the store up and running, which meant actually creating the Web site and establishing procedures and strategies for order processing and fulfillment."

> **"**
> The absolute most important component in establishing a successful online business, at least from my perspective, is the marketing strategy.
> —Cara France
> **"**

Rich: "Since your company's initial marketing strategy was clearly important, what did it entail?"

France: "The goal was obviously to generate as much traffic as possible to the site once it was established. For me, this meant putting a lot of time and effort into establishing partnership deals and launching an aggressive public relations campaign. Creating an overall corporate identity was also very important. The company name, logo, the overall look and feel of the Web site, and how we branded ourselves were all important considerations."

Rich: "Early on, how much research did you do, and what type of research did you conduct?"

France: "My professional background included working in the high-tech field for several Internet companies, so I was already familiar with what was involved in getting Web sites designed, built, and put online. My background gave me a definite advantage over people who might first be starting an online business with no previous experience with e-commerce or creating Web sites. In terms of Web site creation issues, I spent a considerable amount of time doing online research to learn what technologies were out there that I could utilize to get my business up and running. After much work, I narrowed my options down to using the turnkey solutions offered by Yahoo! Store or I-Cat. After reading several articles, I determined that for me, Yahoo! Store offered several advantages, such as the ability to easily establish an affiliate program and get listed in Yahoo! Store's online shopping area. Now that ArtisanGifts.com is up and running using Yahoo! Store, I am extremely pleased with my decision to use this service."

Rich: "What were some of the features of Yahoo! Store that were particularly appealing to you?"

France: "First, when choosing a service to host your online business, don't rely on the marketing materials supplied by the service itself. It's important to also read articles that compare the various services and do your own research to determine if a specific service offers the features you need to make your particular business successful. If I relied solely on the marketing materials provided by the various services, I might have used the I-Cat service. However, by reading articles in magazines that compared I-Cat, Yahoo! Store, and other services, I saw that Yahoo! Store offered several clear advantages.

"Being able to upload information about a huge number of inventory items in a batch using the Yahoo! Store service, for example, is a feature I really rely upon. Also, being able to batch upload photographs is important to me. Yahoo! Store has technology that allows thumbnail photos to download very quickly to someone's browser and be enlarged on command. Since the sale of my products evolve around photos, fast download of photos is very important. If you plan to have an online store with several hundred items, these features are particularly useful.

"I was also very impressed with Yahoo! Store's easy-to-use affiliate program features. I have a tremendous amount of control over the affiliate programs and partnership deals I pursue. These deals have played a critical role in my company's success. One feature I'd like to see made available (that none of the services yet offer) is real-time inventory management and tracking."

Rich: "For the computer novice, what is the learning curve for using Yahoo! Store?"

France: "There's definitely a learning curve involved, whether you use Yahoo! Store, another service, or off-the-shelf Web design software. How much of a learning curve will depend a lot on how far you want to go with your site. Many pretty basic stores that use the Yahoo! Store service were clearly

Watch Out!
Pay close attention to the technology you'll need for your particular business. For example, if you'll rely on a large number of photos to display your products, it's imperative to use a host that can easily handle photo downloading.

created quickly by someone with little or no experience developing Web sites. I wanted my site to give the impression that it was a real, well-established business right from the start, so I was willing to invest a lot of time in the actual development of my site."

Rich: "As you were designing your site, what were some of the pitfalls you ran into?"

France: "I struggled with how to handle inventory management and tracking issues. I also had issues with how Yahoo! Store's templates allowed for order entry and the way customer information was gathered, so I had to do some customization. As I was learning how to use the Yahoo! Store service, there were certainly issues I ran into that required me to learn how to do certain tasks, but I was ultimately able to get my site up and running after about three weeks of full-time work."

Rich: "Now that your business is operational, how do you spend your time?"

France: "Most of my time is spent on order fulfillment. It takes time to keep the site up-to-date, but actually fulfilling the orders is what's time-consuming. If a holiday is coming up and I need to create a special area on the site to promote holiday gifts, or if we add several new artists to the site at once, I have to dedicate some extra time actually working on the Web site."

Rich: "What are some of the things you've done to promote ArtisanGifts.com since launching the business?"

France: "I participate in the LinkExchange service, which is one way to generate traffic to the site. We also invested in an online and traditional public relations effort. The online efforts worked really

Bright Idea
Be aware of the difference between online advertising and more traditional ads. If someone sees your URL in a newspaper ad, for example, she'll have to log onto the Internet and type your address to access your site. If, however, you have an ad on an Internet site, a visitor can just click on the ad and be connected to your site.

well. The site was featured in places like MSNBC Online, and that directly generated traffic to the site. Online PR is great, because the person reading the article can simply click on a link and visit your site. Offline, traditional PR is good, but for very different reasons. This type of PR is good for establishing a company's credibility, which is useful for creating partnership deals.

"Traditional PR doesn't generate a tremendous level of traffic to the site. If you're trying to generate traffic, I have found your best bet is to obtain online coverage for your business. Initially, I spent thousands of dollars and hired an independent PR firm to help generate publicity for the company. Developing partnership deals and obtaining exposure on other Web sites has been one of the key things that has lead to our success. Developing partnership deals requires using gorilla marketing techniques and a considerable effort, especially when you're a start-up company. When trying to create partnerships, it's important to focus on what makes your business unique and to sell the partnership concept based on why the potential partner would want to work with you. Actually creating the affiliate program from a technical standpoint is very easy using Yahoo! Store. The trick is actually obtaining the affiliate partners."

Rich: "Have you used traditional online advertising or paid banner ads to promote your business?"

France: "No, and I won't. To do online advertising that works, you have to be prepared to spend a lot of money …. The results companies are getting as a result of online advertising tend to be pretty dismal. I have found that for small start-up companies, using gorilla marketing is far more beneficial than paying for banner advertising. LinkExchange, for example, is useful. For no money, you can experiment with various banner ad promotions. I have also found using the auction sites is a great way to sell and promote product."

Rich: "In terms of your initial expectations for how successful ArtisanGifts.com was going to be, have you reached those expectations?"

France: "It is very, very hard to establish realistic expectations for an online business. I am very excited because the company is doing well, but based on my experience, there are very few overnight successes when it comes to selling anything online. It takes time to build an online-based business. On a monthly basis, ArtisanGifts.com was profitable within one year of going online; however, a substantial financial investment was made initially, and that investment is still being paid back after almost one year of operation."

Rich: "How important is providing good customer service?"

France: "It's crucial. Every customer needs to be treated like gold. Orders need to be filled immediately. Inquiries need to be responded to as soon as they're received, and if a problem arises with a customer, it needs to be dealt with promptly and professionally. Customers who are treated well and who have a good online shopping experience will come back, and tell their friends about your business. Whatever I put in front of customers needs to be professional and exceed their expectations. As a business operator, you will receive orders that require special attention, and it's important to deal with problem situations carefully, promptly, and professionally. Dealing with problems can be time-consuming, but it's time that needs to be spent. The online businesses that have been successful, like Amazon.com, all share this philosophy."

Rich: "What advice do you have for someone first starting his own online business?"

France: "Using a service like Yahoo! Store puts a lot of powerful e-commerce technology at your disposal, but it's just a set of tools. You're going to need to learn how to market your site and drive traffic to it in order to be successful, and there's no one answer for how to best do this. A marketing strategy should be comprised of many different components. Operating an online business has the same headaches and pitfalls as any other type of business. You're going to invest a lot of time and money, and you're not doing to get rich overnight. Just as with any type of business, to make your online business grow and prosper, it needs to be nurtured. This requires time, energy, and effort. The payoff for your efforts may take several months to be realized.

"As a potential online business operator, you should watch out for scams. I saw an infomercial recently where a company was offering everything needed to quickly establish an online business and make tons of money. The product cost only $49.95 and was hyped as offering the ultimate e-commerce solutions for everyone. I spent the entire 30 minutes of this infomercial laughing, because it was such garbage.

"Even Yahoo! Store promotes that anyone can get started for only $100 per month. This is [technically] true, but to do it right takes a much larger financial investment."

Rich: "What is the biggest benefit of operating an online-based business?"

> **"**
> It wasn't the miners who made money during the gold rush. It was the people who sold them the shovels. A lot of people are now looking to strike it rich in cyberspace, and there are a lot of people selling shovels. They're the ones getting rich by misleading potential online business operators.
> —Cara France
> **"**

France: "There are several. The flexibility in your schedule is certainly very appealing. It's also a lot of fun operating this type of business."

Mark Giordani—LefKey

Mark Giordani is the founder and president of LefKey International (www.lefkey.com; 888-69-LEFKEY). Based in Wareham, Mass., Mark Giordani is also the president of The Portfolio Group, Inc. For a decade he worked as a self-employed computer consultant in the Boston area. Initially, most of his time was spent on site at his various clients' offices, installing and maintaining computer networks.

Giordani recently sold his computer consulting business after choosing to work full-time expanding his online-based business. LefKey International is a home-based company that markets and sells specially designed computer keyboards for left-handed computer users. LefKey is primarily a mail-order business that does business on the Internet using a custom-designed e-commerce site created with Symantec's Visual Page software. The site is hosted using a New England-area ISP capable of processing secure Web transactions.

The LefKey keyboard offers the appropriate left-hand orientation of directional arrow keys and the dual-purpose directional and numeric keypad.

From his home office, Giordani shared his thoughts on operating an online business.

Rich: "What made you want to work for yourself?"

Mark Giordani: "My father is a successful business owner. While I was given the opportunity to work for him, and did so for a few years after graduating from college, I was excited by the challenge of establishing

Lefkey International is a home-based online business that sells computer keyboards designed specifically for left-handed PC users.

my own company and being my own boss, especially after pursuing entrepreneurial studies in college. I was interested in exploring my own ideas and creativity."

Rich: "Why did you choose to work from a home office?"

Giordani: "I didn't want to be tied to a desk or be tucked away in an office day after day. The concept of working from home was an appealing one, and something I chose to pursue early on. In addition to the luxury of working from home, I'm able to save a fortune each month not having to pay rent or the expenses involved in maintaining a traditional office. This is money that goes right to the bottom line."

Rich: "How did you get started?"

Giordani: "I was always fascinated by computers and technology. When I was a teenager, I was given my first personal computer, and I taught myself how to use it. Computers were my hobby growing up, and something that I really enjoyed. Over the years, I continued enhancing my computer skills, and in college, supplemented my self-taught knowledge with formal computer training."

Rich: "What's the biggest benefit of working from a home office?"

Giordani: "I'd have to say it's the convenience of being able to roll out of bed and be on the job, literally. Not being married or having children, I have total freedom to make my own hours. If I choose, I can take a day off, I can work late into the night, or at anytime, take a break to make myself a snack. If I choose to work at night, I have all my business documents and resources right there, and don't have to travel back and forth to an office. I personally do my best work in a casual environment, when I'm surrounded by windows, natural light, and fresh air."

Rich: "What's the biggest drawback?"

Giordani: "It's sometimes very hard to be at home in the evening trying to relax, knowing that just a few feet away, I have paperwork to do, bills to pay, letters to write, and financial records that need to be kept up-to-date. Since I don't maintain any type of normal business hours or the same daily routine each day, I am sometimes drawn to my desk to get work done at very odd hours."

Rich: "What is your most useful business tool?"

Giordani: "My desktop computer is by far my most useful business tool. From my PC, I create all of my correspondence, maintain my company's Web site, manage my company's finances, handle virtually all of the details associated with my mail order business [using a program called Mail Order Manager from Dydacomp Development Corporation, www. dydacomp.com/mainmom.asp], process my client's

Bright Idea
While you don't need much specialized skill to start your own online business, any experience you have can give you a competitive advantage. For example, computer and design skills can help you design your site, and marketing skills can help you understand how to establish your brand effectively.

credit card payments, maintain my daily schedule, and keep a database of all my business-related contacts using a powerful program from Symantec called Act! I also have separate telephone lines and a fax machine for my business, and I use a pager and cellular phone so I can be reached in an emergency. These days, computers and home office automation technology is extremely powerful and makes operating a home-based business much easier."

Rich: "What advice can you offer to someone interested in working from a home office?"

Giordani: "Don't get involved in anything without doing the proper research first. Also, make sure you get involved in a business or profession that you really enjoy and have an interest in. I started LefKey International because I started to get burned out running around Boston catering to the needs of my clients as a computer consultant, and I needed a change in my daily routine. Starting a mail-order business requires a lot of planning and having the financial resources available to you to do things properly. Maintaining inventory, for example, can be a costly endeavor, even if you're able to cut costs using a grassroots marketing approach.

"Be prepared to work hard, but take the time to enjoy the fruits of your labors. To launch a successful mail-order business, you need a product or idea that's unique, fills a definite need, and is relatively easy to market and promote. You also need to have a product with enough of a profit margin so you can earn a profit even after covering all of your business expenses."

Rich: "How did the idea to sell computer keyboards designed for left-handed computer users come about?"

Giordani: "I was looking for a unique product that could be marketed online to a niche audience. I came across a company that manufactured these keyboards outside of the U.S., and after several months of negotiations, managed to obtain the exclusive North American marketing and distribution rights for the product. At the same time, I negotiated wholesale pricing that would allow me to earn a profit, even after covering my marketing and Web site creation and maintenance costs.

"One of my biggest challenges early on was raising enough capital to buy and import the quantity of inventory necessary to meet the requirements stipulated by the manufacturer for exclusivity in North America. My initial investment in inventory was over $30,000."

Rich: "After obtaining the rights to market and distribute left-handed keyboards in the U.S., what was the next step in establishing your online business?"

Giordani: "There were two major steps. First, I had to create a brand for my product, so I coined the name LefKey as the name of the keyboard and designed a product and company logo. The actual Web site also had to be created. I decided to use an off-the-shelf Web site creation program, called Visual Page, because a friend recommended it highly. I then had to find and begin working with an ISP.

"The infrastructure of the business needed to be created before the site actually went online. Through my previous business as a computer consultant, I already had a merchant account, so I was able to accept credit cards. I had to work with my ISP, however, to ensure that secure order processing

Watch Out!
Having a great idea isn't enough to be successful. You have to be realistic about all aspects of your online business, including how much capital you need to produce your product or deliver your service.

from my site was possible. Instead of having credit card orders automatically processed, I use an off-the-shelf program to process credit card orders. The actual paperwork for the orders is processed and managed using a program called Mail Order Manager. The financial aspects of my business are managed using the latest version of Intuit Software's QuickBooks Pro software [www.quickbooks.com]."

Rich: "Once your business began to take shape, what steps did you take to promote the launch of the business and the Web site?"

Giordani: "The very first thing I did was have a short press release written that announced the formation of the company and described the LefKey product. [A copy of the press release appears at the conclusion of this interview.] This press release was distributed electronically, via e-mail, to several hundred newspaper, magazine, and TV reporters. This generated a decent amount of coverage for the company, both online and in major publications, such as *The New York Times* and *Computer Shopper.* I also began registering my site with all of the major Internet search engines. This, too, generated a decent amount of traffic to the site.

"To date, we continue to focus our efforts on grassroots marketing and PR as opposed to using traditional paid advertising to promote the company."

Rich: "What were some of the obstacles you encountered when establishing your business?"

Giordani: "The design of the Web site went through several iterations as we attempted to create a site that was informative, visually appealing, intuitive, and professional-looking. I continue to fine-tune the site based on feedback I receive from customers.

The biggest challenge was creating a process for fulfilling the orders after they're received.

"Ideally, I wanted potential customers to visit the Web site and place their orders online using a credit card, so there would be no direct telephone, in-person, or e-mail contact. This, however, I quickly learned wasn't going to be the case. No matter how easy and informative your Web site is to use, people always want to call your toll-free number, send an e-mail message, or send a fax in order to ask a question or place their order offline. Thus, I wind up spending a considerable amount of time on the phone with customers, dealers, and others interested in learning more about the LefKey product. The majority of my time is spent dealing with order fulfillment and customer service issues."

Bright Idea
No matter how easy it is for your potential customers to order your product or service online, many will still choose to place orders by phone or mail. So you'll need to offer good customer service in these more traditional areas as well.

Rich: "What surprised you about your business's success?"

Giordani: "Like so many other people, I figured that as soon as I put my Web site online, people would flock to it and start placing orders in droves. I hoped to earn a quick fortune. This isn't how it's happened, however. While orders started to trickle in immediately, it took months before the company could be considered established in terms of receiving a steady flow of orders. The level of traffic to the site is directly proportional to the amount of time I spend doing PR or special marketing. Knowing my niche audience is left-handed computer users and finding ways to reach these people has been an ongoing challenge."

Rich: "What advice do you have for others looking to start their own online business venture?"

Giordani: "Spend time doing research and carefully planning your business venture before you move

Timesaver
See Chapter 10 for tips on how to compose an effective press release for your own business.

forward. People who surf the Web still have definite concerns about placing orders online, so it's important to clearly display a toll-free phone number, fax number, and e-mail address people can use to contact you with their questions or to place orders [offline].

"Also, watch how you spend your money. It's very easy to spend a fortune creating a flashy Web site, paying for expensive marketing and advertising campaigns, stocking up on inventory, and so forth. Focus on finding ways to save money using grass-roots marketing and PR, for example. Also, if you're not familiar with Web site creation techniques, seek out help from a professional Web designer or even a friend who has experience designing and programming Web sites. I am someone who heavily researches all of my options in advance and then does detailed planning. I believe these traits have helped me save money throughout the life of my business."

Chris Gwynn—niche marketing

Fridgedoor.com (www.fridgedoor.com) is one of the Web's many e-commerce success stories. When company founder Chris Gwynn began searching for an online business opportunity, he wanted a product to sell that would be of interest to a niche market, fun to work with, easy to ship, and one that customers could decide to purchase easily based on seeing a picture. After considering various products and doing research on various industries, Gwynn decided to sell refrigerator magnets on the Web. After all, he thought, everyone has a refrigerator, and many people enjoy decorating their kitchen's largest appliance with cute magnets. Fridgedoor. com also caters to a growing collector's market.

The following press release was issued by LefKey International when the company was originally formed and the LefKey product was made available via the company's Web site:

LefKey International Introduces a Computer Keyboard Designed Specifically for <u>Left-Handed</u> Users

(Recently Featured in the New York Times)

<u>For Immediate Release</u>

<u>Contact</u>: Ellen Bromfield

LefKey International

(888) 69-LEFKEY/(508)291-8000

Wareham, Mass.—LefKey International has begun shipping its flagship product—the world's finest computer keyboard designed exclusively for *Left-Handed* users. Priced at just $129.00 (which includes shipping and handling), the LefKey keyboard offers the appropriate left-hand orientation of both the directional arrow keys and the dual-purpose directional and numeric keypad. Thus, left-handed users no longer need to conform to the awkward and uncomfortable keyboards created for right-handed people.

The LefKey is an ergonomic, 101-Key "Active-Response" Enhanced Keyboard that offers a full 3-year warranty and 30-day money-back guarantee. This top-quality, full-travel, tactile mechanical keyboard is sure to satisfy even the left-handed "power" user for years to come.

LefKey Keyboards are 100 percent compatible with all IBM and compatible computers running Windows (all versions), DOS (all versions), IBM OS/2, Linux, Unix, etc. The keyboard does <u>not</u> require any software drivers. It is fully Plug-and-Play compatible with all IBM and/or compatible systems.

"We're offering this product to left-handed computer users because there simply isn't another product like it on the market," stated Mark Giordani, president and founder of LefKey International.

"Why should left-handed people be forced to conform to the design of a right-handed keyboard, and have to deal with the discomfort and inconvenience of having the numeric keypad on the wrong side? Any left-handed computer user who uses their PC for any type of financial or numeric calculations, spreadsheet management, Web surfing, or even to play games will quickly discover the advantages our keyboard offers," added Giordani.

The LefKey keyboards can be ordered online directly from LefKey's secure Web site (www.lefkey.com) or by calling toll-free (888)69-LEFKEY. All major credit cards are accepted. LefKey International is a division of The Portfolio Group, Inc.

#   #   #

Fridgedoor.com is
a niche-oriented
online business
that sells only
refrigerator
magnets.

The concept for Fridgedoor.com first began taking shape in May 1997. Gwynn had spent over a decade working for large companies in the online business industry. During his career, he experienced five massive layoffs (several of which he survived) within the companies he was working for, and he wanted to find a career opportunity that offered greater stability and control. He decided to launch an online business, at first as a project in his spare time to supplement his income.

These days, Fridgedoor.com is Gwynn's full-time job. He currently has two part-time employees who assist with online marketing and order fulfillment. Based on the growing success of his company, he has begun expanding into other collectible markets by launching spin-off businesses, including Actionfigureauctions.com (www.actionfigureauctions.com).

Rich: "After you came up with the idea to sell refrigerator magnets online, what steps did you take to make your business idea a reality?"

Chris Gwynn: "One of my previous employers was AT&T. I was a product manager for a service they were developing designed to help small businesses build their own Web site. While working on that project, I learned about all of the services out there, and chose Yahoo! Store to develop my e-commerce site with. I believe Yahoo! Store offers the greatest ease of use and the most power. Their service is also competitively priced. I had taken some HTML programming courses, but I don't consider myself a programmer or Web site designer.

"I took advantage of Yahoo! Store's introductory offer, and for $100, created a mini-store selling twenty different magnets. I wanted to see if this was a viable business before making a large investment of time and finances. The research I did beforehand on the magnet industry showed that it could be viable. Nobody was selling magnets on the Web. I created the online mini-store in May 1997. After I discovered this type of business had potential, I spent most of my spare time that summer actually creating a complete e-commerce site/online store for Fridgedoor.com. I had to contact many different manufacturers of magnets to acquire inventory, create the Web site, and develop a marketing plan.

"It was in September 1997 that I actually launched Fridgedoor.com as a full-scale online business with over 500 items. Currently, I offer over 1,500 different magnet items, all of which I keep in inventory."

Rich: "When you first decided to sell refrigerator magnets online, did you do a lot of research about the magnet industry?"

Gwynn: "I had seen a chain of retail stores that sold nothing but refrigerator magnets. The stores are

Timesaver
Remember: When you're targeting a niche market, you don't need a market that's large in absolute numbers. You just need one that's potentially large enough for you to turn a profit.

located primarily in high-rent tourist areas, and they seemed to be earning money. I realized that if a chain of retail stores could survive selling nothing but magnets, an online-based store could be successful as well. I did my own research to determine the size of the market and learned about the major manufacturers and distributors of refrigerator magnets. I determined that the overall magnet market is pretty small, but it was big enough for me to create an online store and be successful at it."

Rich: "Where is your business based?"

Gwynn: "Fridgedoor.com is based in my home in Quincy, Mass. My basement is my warehouse, and several spare rooms in my house are used as offices."

Rich: "What type of initial financial investment was made in the company?"

Gwynn: "I invested my own money. I'd rather not give an exact figure in terms of my investment, but it was over $20,000. Getting a Web site actually created and online is only a small part of the time and financial investment necessary to operate a successful online business. The costs of inventory, computer equipment, and marketing are all substantial. I had to purchase a rather sophisticated mail order management software package, called Mail Order Manager from Dydacomp Development Corporation, which represented an over $2,000 investment in software alone. This software is used to automate almost every aspect of the business's operation, from order fulfillment to inventory management. The software isn't 100 percent ideal, but it's the best software I could find to meet the needs of my business."

Rich: "What is one of the most important lessons you've learned since starting Fridgedoor.com?"

Gwynn: "I discovered it's critical to control the entire order fulfillment process. This means having your inventory on hand, instead of having products drop-shipped. When an order comes in, you need to immediately send the customer an e-mail acknowledging the order. That order then needs to be processed promptly, with the merchant being in total control of the package's look and content. When the order is sent, a second e-mail needs to be sent to the customer providing the shipment's tracking number, if applicable. I buy my inventory from over 50 different suppliers, so having products drop-shipped, while it might look like an attractive business option on paper, really isn't viable for my business."

Rich: "You mentioned making a substantial investment in the marketing of your company. What exactly did this entail?"

Gwynn: "A lot of the advertising and marketing we tried early on was expensive and didn't work. I tried using paid banner ads, and wound up wasting a lot of money. Our average order is about $20, so finding paid advertising opportunities that would pay for themselves was very difficult.

"I have since focused exclusively on gorilla marketing techniques to promote the business. I created an affiliate program that has worked extremely well. Fridgedoor.com is always looking for related sites to place a link back to us. In return we will pay these sites 15 percent of all sales that are generated from their site's traffic. Payments are made quarterly by check, and are accompanied by a detailed traffic/revenue report. In addition, affiliates are provided with a URL to view the daily updates to their traffic/revenue report. This report is generated by an independent third party, our hosting provider, not us.

"For people who are interested in magnets or the characters featured on the magnets, such as Jeff Gordon or NASCAR magnets, one of the best ways to reach them is to develop relationships with the many small Jeff Gordon or NASCAR fan-operated Web sites, for example. I have someone working part-time doing nothing but contacting various fan Web sites about joining our affiliate program. We have over 400 affiliates, and that generates a good portion of our daily traffic.

"I also continue to spend a considerable amount of time keeping our site optimized for all of the Internet search engines. We've also had a lot of success in creating traffic for our site using online and offline public relations efforts…Since we're part of Yahoo! Store, we benefit from traffic that Yahoo! generates for us, but we can't rely on this traffic to support our entire business."

Rich: "How is marketing an online business different from marketing a traditional business?"

66
Having good customer service has generated a lot of repeat and word-of-mouth business. If anyone ever has a problem with our products, we promptly refund their money with no questions asked.
—Chris Gwynn, FridgeDoor.com
99

Gwynn: "Based on my experience, a traditional business will typically spend about two to twenty percent of its gross revenue on marketing and advertising. To successfully promote an online business and generate enough traffic to the site to make it viable, it's necessary to spend upwards of sixty percent of gross revenue. Thus, if you don't have enough money set aside in your budget to market your online business properly, you should seriously reconsider launching it."

Rich: "What are some of the lessons you've learned based on your experiences dealing with customers online?"

Gwynn: "It's important to respond to people immediately, whether it's to fill an order or answer a question. Never fight with a customer. Give them what they want to make them happy. I try to provide our customers with as much information as possible about us as a company, our products, our shipping procedures, and whether or not our products are on back-order. People really appreciate receiving e-mail that keeps them up-to-date on the status of their orders."

Rich: "How do you deal with people who are afraid or hesitant to place credit card orders online?"

Gwynn: "On our Web site, we list our phone number and a fax number for placing orders. We don't, however, offer a toll-free number. I have found that some people feel more comfortable faxing their credit card information when placing an order than they do placing it directly on the Web site. About eighty percent of our orders are placed online. The rest are either faxed in or placed by phone.

"On our site, we explain the online security we use; if someone is afraid to place an order online, however, there is nothing we can say to convince them it's safe. These people prefer actually speaking with a person. Being a small company, people don't necessarily know who we are, so I think it's more of a trust issue than an issue of online security. On our Web site, we have an 'Info' area that describes our company and contains a picture of us, so people can see the human beings behind the company."

Rich: "How do you spend your time dealing with the day-to-day operations of your business?"

Gwynn: "This is now a full-time job for me. I start working every weekday around 8:30 a.m. and keep working until around 6:00 p.m. If necessary, I'll also spend time working in the evenings and on weekends. About fifty percent of the man-hours spent operating the business are spent filling orders. A lot of my time is also spent on marketing."

Rich: "Now that Fridgedoor.com is successful, how are you expanding the business?"

Gwynn: "We've created an umbrella company, called collectiblemarkets.com, and recently launched a company called actionfigureauctions.com. This uses a very different business model than fridgedoor. com. Eventually, I plan to create a whole series of businesses that target the niche collectibles market. This company is a business-to-consumer auction site, which is different from services like eBay.com, which offer consumer-to-consumer auctions. We sell collectible action figures via auction using specialized software from OpenSite Technologies [www. opensite.com]. The site is hosted by an ISP in Utah. To promote this business, we have successfully used some paid banner advertising, but continue to focus on other marketing and promotional efforts to generate traffic to the site."

Rich: "Why did you decide to take an online auction approach to selling collectibles?"

Gwynn: "I was looking for something that would differentiate us from other collectible action figure dealers. This is a much more competitive business than magnets. I thought the auctions would make the shopping experience more enjoyable for the customer. I think people enjoy the whole auction process and the possibility of getting a really good deal on an item. All of the products we sell are brand new. We set a reserve price on everything, which is our cost. As long as someone meets our

Unofficially...
OpenSite Auction, an online Web auction service from OpenSite Technologies (http:// www.opensite. com), offers businesses auction features with minimal set-up time and management. For free tips on how to create your own online action Web site, point your Web browser to: www. opensite.com/ gettingstarted/ index.html.

reserve price, we're not losing money. I think services like eBay, Yahoo! Auction, and Amazon.com Auction have created a huge demand for this type of online business. I didn't create actionfigureauctions.com to compete head-on with these companies. I'm taking a different approach and focusing on very niche markets."

Rich: "What has been one of the biggest challenges in operating an online business?"

Gwynn: "I think one of the most important lessons someone operating this type of business needs to learn is how to transform a visitor to your Web site into a paying customer who actually places an order. A huge part of this involves making people feel comfortable and welcome when they visit your site.

"I have learned that having a well-structured site is also important. People need to be able to find the items they're looking for as quickly as possible. I believe having a Web site design that's as clean and basic as possible is important. We use simple graphics and a basic layout, which makes it easier for a customer to navigate through our site."

Rich: "What steps do you take to generate repeat business and build customer loyalty?"

Gwynn: "In addition to offering top-notch customer service, we are constantly adding new items to the Fridgedoor.com site. We also change the featured item each week, and every month have some type of special offer. One of the most successful special offers we've run is to include free first class mail shipping on all orders over $25. On our home page, we also invite people to subscribe to our free monthly e-mail-based newsletter. Each month, we send out this newsletter which describes new items and mentions our special promotions. This newsletter has been a very successful tool for generating repeat business."

Ken Young—1-800-Flowers

Ken Young is director of public relations for 1-800-Flowers (www.1800flowers.com). This company provides fresh flowers, gift baskets, and floral-related items to customers around the world. The company has been at the forefront of several marketing trends, including the use of toll-free technology and Web marketing.

Currently in its fifth version (a redesign occurs about every eight months), www.1800flowers.com offers users detailed product information, including photography, contests, home decorating/how-to tips and floral trends, gift-giving suggestions, information about special events and offers, and a secure place to shop online. The entire 1-800-Flowers product line is available via the site, including fresh-cut floral arrangements, plants, balloons, gift baskets, gourmet products, and decorative keepsakes.

In this interview, company spokesperson Ken Young discussed how 1-800-Flowers went from being a traditional retailer and mail-order business to also becoming a pioneer in e-commerce.

Rich: "What was the thinking behind creating an online presence for your company back in 1992, before the Internet even existed in its current form?"

Ken Young: "We already had a successful chain of retail stores and had created a virtual buying experience for our customers via our toll-free phone number. We had a comfort for embracing new technologies, and in the early 1990s, we began exploring the possibility of selling our products in cyberspace because we saw the potential of this interactive medium."

Rich: "Currently, what percentage of your business is done online as opposed to through the retail stores or the toll-free phone number?"

Ken Young: "As a private company, we don't typically release sales figures; however, I can say that well in excess of ten percent of our business is done online, and that figure is growing quickly."

Rich: "Is the growth in your Internet business a result of heavy marketing on 1-800-Flowers' part, or due to the change in the general buying habits of consumers as a whole?"

Young: "I think it's both. On the one hand, you have a lot of people who want to experiment with shopping online and who are looking for well-known, brand-name merchants to do business with. I give a lot of credit for our online sales success to the brand we've established offline. I believe online shoppers want to experience a strong comfort level, and placing orders with online merchants they already know and have done business with in the past certainly boosts that comfort level. As a company, we aggressively market our online store."

Rich: "In terms of 1-800-Flowers' online presence, what are the benefits to the company?"

Young: "These days, any company that wants to be taken seriously by its customers must have an online presence. Having an online presence gives our overall company credibility. The Web also offers us several major advantages. We've spent a lot of money, time, and energy training people to answer the phone. As good as we are at order-taking via

> 66
> Originally, we simply displayed our URL within all print and TV ads for the company. Now, our ads, TV commercials, and all our direct mail pieces emphasize that customers should visit the Web site.
> —Ken Young, 1-800-FLOWERS
> 99

telephone, however, during the various holiday periods, our phone lines get swamped and a customer can have one of several thousand different shopping experiences based on which of our telephone order takers answers the phone.

"When someone shops online, we can offer one consistent brand experience and showcase a full assortment of our over 2,000 products. Customers can actually see pictures of our products online [a feature not available to people who place orders via telephone].

"We also now offer online customer service in real time via chat, so customers can get their questions answered instantly. This keeps our customers from going elsewhere to make their purchases if they run into a question or have a problem with our service. We believe offering real-time customer service removes some barriers to making sales, improves the overall service we offer, and helps build customer loyalty.

"In the near future, we'll see Web sites offering the ability to click an icon on a site that will allow customers to speak with a company [representative] directly while online. This will probably lead to online video conferencing between the company and the consumer sometime in the not-so-distant future. Online customers are becoming increasingly more demanding, and they want the same level of service—or better service—than they'd typically receive shopping at a retail store or calling a toll-free phone number to place an order."

Rich: "Do you believe your company's online presence will eventually replace your toll-free number?"

Young: "Not at all. Companies that were created as virtual companies are now discovering a need to incorporate some type of toll-free order-taking and customer service to complement their online services. We started with a very successful telephone order-taking and customer service department and then went online, which is to the advantage of our customers and our relationship with them. We currently see a growing percentage of our customers migrating back and forth between placing orders online and using our toll-free telephone service."

Rich: "Does 1-800-Flowers offer services or features online that aren't available to customers who place their orders via telephone?"

Young: "We offer a reduced service charge to people who place their orders online. In terms of products, customers can actually see what they're ordering when they shop online. We also provide a large amount of information about flower and plant care for flower and gardening enthusiasts that's only available online. In addition, we periodically run online-based contests or special live chats that are only available to online customers. From our standpoint, having an online presence allows us to do e-mail marketing to our existing customers. This is a much cheaper and more effective marketing tool than direct mail."

Rich: "How significant has 1-800-Flowers' financial investment been in establishing its online presence?"

Young: "Originally, we made a reasonably small investment; over time, however, the financial investment we've made has become extremely significant. Operating a cutting-edge e-commerce site is getting more expensive, because the bar keeps getting raised; this means new technologies need to be developed and implemented into our site. For us,

Moneysaver
Once you've established an online presence and a list of existing customers, you'll be able to market to them much more cheaply and effectively than you could with traditional tools. E-mail marketing is faster and cheaper than its print-mail counterpart.

having a very basic and simple Web site wouldn't work."

Rich: "What are some of the technical problems or obstacles you've had to overcome in order for 1-800-Flowers to become a leader in the e-commerce industry?"

Young: "I think the biggest challenge continues to be predicting the volume of traffic we'll receive to the site and being able to manage that volume. Obviously, during holiday periods, like Mother's Day or Valentine's Day, the traffic to our site increases dramatically. How much traffic a site receives has a lot to do with the marketing efforts used to promote the site."

Rich: "Has it been necessary for 1-800-Flowers to try to change your customers' buying habits to get them to shop online?"

Young: "I think it's always a challenge to attempt to change people's buying habits. We've definitely benefited from having the early Internet adopters gravitate to us. Having a strong offline brand has helped us dramatically, giving people a strong comfort level when they initially visit our site. Much of our online success has been a result of our offline marketing and advertising efforts."

Rich: "With cutting-edge Internet technologies changing so quickly, how does 1-800-Flowers decide which of these technologies to incorporate into its site?"

Young: "That's an ongoing challenge we face. Our people attend all sorts of conferences, read Internet-related magazines, and track various trends. They then analyze each new potential technology to determine what, if anything, it will add to our site. We also spend a lot of time exploring the

Web sites of other companies, in other industries, and we see what's working for them. Operating a successful online-based business means constantly trying new things. It's an ongoing learning experience."

Rich: "How has 1-800-Flowers dealt with the security concerns of customers who are hesitant to shop online?"

Young: "The 1-800-Flowers Web site uses all of the state-of-the-art security measures available on the Internet. There are messages describing these security features throughout the site. Also, when someone calls our toll-free number, we describe our security features via a recorded message when they're on hold. As a company with an established brand, it's much easier to alleviate a customer's concerns."

Rich: "The 1-800-Flowers Web site is graphic-oriented, yet the download times for each page are quick. How was this accomplished?"

Young: "We're using proprietary technology to do this; however, one of our biggest concerns in regards to the operation of the Web site is to keep all of our pages' download times as short as possible. It's important to remember that a huge percentage of Web surfers still use 28.8K or 56K dial-up connections, so it's important to design a Web site to accommodate these people. We're always very careful about how graphics are used on our site."

Rich: "In terms of marketing and promoting the 1-800-Flowers Web site, what has worked particularly well for your company?"

Young: "We have established partnerships with AOL, MSN, and Excite. We pay for this presence on these prominent sites, but it broadens our overall

Watch Out!
As mentioned repeatedly in this book, always keep in mind the technology your customers have. For example, although faster technologies exist, many Web surfers have 28.8K or 56K connections. You need to design your Web site so that it's convenient for them.

reach and exposure. We have also created an affiliate program, and have signed up over 2,500 affiliate partners. Our affiliate program is operated by LinkShare [www.linkshare.com]. This traffic generation program represents a very small initial financial outlay, since the affiliates get paid a commission on all sales that occur as a result of them linking a customer to our site. Whether it's the big relationship with companies like AOL, or the small relationships with individual Web site operators, alliances are very important for generating traffic to a site in the online world.

"In addition, we develop promotional relationships whenever possible to promote our Web site. For example, we did a promotion with the movie *You've Got Mail* which was very successful. We've also developed a free gift reminder program that our customers can take advantage of, and we use e-mail marketing to reach existing customers to inform them of specials, sales, or upcoming events."

Rich: "What additional advice can you offer to established companies looking to create an Internet presence?"

Young: "Keep in mind that you can't just put up a Web site and ignore it. Think of it as a living creature that needs to be nurtured and updated on an ongoing basis. Every eight months or so, we do a complete overhaul and redesign of our site, but all along the way, we're constantly making changes to our site, so each time a customer returns, there is something new for them to see."

Just the facts

- While there are incredible opportunities for success in cyberspace, striking it rich by launching an online business isn't something that will happen quickly.

- It takes a much bigger financial investment than most people think to launch an online business and do it well, but it is still a smaller investment than opening a retail store or establishing a traditional mail-order business.

- When choosing a service to host your online business, don't rely on the marketing materials supplied by the service itself. It's important to do your own research to compare various services.

- It's critical to control the entire order fulfillment process. This means having your inventory on hand, instead of having products dropshipped.

Glossary

The following are definitions for a few terms you'll need to know when investigating online advertising opportunities. These definitions were taken from Yahoo!'s Ad Sales Glossary. For a more comprehensive listing of online advertising-related terms, visit Yahoo!'s Ad Sales Glossary site at https://sales.yahoo.com/public/research/information/glossary.html. Additional online advertising-related glossaries are available from AOL.Com at http://mediaspace.aol.com/glossary.html and MSN at http://msnsales.com/glossary2.asp.

Ad Click   The user's action of clicking on an advertising-related file. A click does not guarantee that the user actually arrives at the requested (target) URL. Ad clicks are nearly always greater than ad clickthroughs. (Contrast to ad transfer.)

Ad Transfer (Also ad clickthrough)   The successful arrival of a user at an advertiser's Web site, resulting from the user's click on an ad banner. (In some cases, because of technical difficulties, an ad click may not result in an ad transfer.)

Ad View   The view of an advertisement that results when an ad is downloaded (and presumably seen) by a user. (Equivalent to Ad Impression.)

Animated Ad   An ad that automatically changes in appearance. These ads are most frequently created using the GIF89a graphical file format, but also created using Shockwave, Javascript or Java.

CPM   Cost per *mille* (French for *thousand*). CPM refers to the total cost of 1,000 visitor requests to view an ad. The CPM describes the advertiser's cost for making 1,000 impressions with their ad.

GIF   Acronym for Graphic Interchange Format. A standard format used to encode graphic images across different types of computers or computer software. For stylized images such as icons or logos, the GIF format is usually more compact than alternative encodings of the same image.

GIF89a   a GIF format that contains several separate GIF images that are presented sequentially by a Web browser; the sequence of images is usually used to create a visual animation.

Hit   A request for a document or other Web asset received by a Web server from a user's Web browser. Note that a hit is generated for each distinct file included in a Web document: a Web page containing a graphical navigation bar, an ad banner and a company logo image would generate four hits to a Web server (the document plus the three images). Hits typically inflate the count of actual page requests by about 5 to 10 times; page requests inflate the number of unique users by about 4 times.

Impressions   The number of times an ad banner is requested by a site visitors' browsers and hopefully actually seen by the Web surfer. In an advertising contract, the number of 'Guaranteed Impressions' refers to the minimum times an ad banner has the opportunity to be seen by visitors.

Traffic A measure of the volume of electronic files distributed to the volume of individual visitors to a Web site. Traffic has been measured in terms of hits, page views, sessions, or unique users.

Unique users The number of different individuals who visit a Web site within a specified period of time. The implicit redundancy (there is no such thing as a "non-unique user") arises from Web sites' past difficulty with (or indifference to) counting traffic or impressions as hits rather than as individual users. Currently, Web site registration and/or user cookies are the standard methods for identifying unique users.

Resource Guide

The following are the Web site addresses mentioned in this book (listed alphabetically).

Organization	Web site address
!Register-It!	www.registerit.com
1-800-Flowers	www.1800flowers.com
24/7 Media, Inc.	www.247media.com
A+ Domain Name Registration Center	www.aplus-domain.com
Acer	www.acer.com
Adauction.com	www.adauction.com
Ad-Guide	www.ad-guide.com/ Media_Buying_and_Selling
Adobe	www.adobe.com
Adobe Illustrator	www.adobe.com/prodindex/ illustrator/main.html
Adobe PhotoShop 5.0	www.adobe.com/prodindex/ photoshop/main.html
Advertising Age	www.adage.com
Advertising Law Internet Site	www.webcom.com/~lewrose/
AdWeek	www.adweek.com
Ad-Xchange	www.ad-xchange.com
Aid4 Writing A Press Release	y4i.com/pressreleasewriting.html

Organization	Web site address
Airborne Express	www.airborne.com
AltaVista	www.altavista.com
America Online	www.aol.com
America's Business Funding Directory	www.businessfinance.com
American Express	www.americanexpress.com
AOL.Com	www.aol.com
Applets.com	www.applets.com
ArtisanGifts.com	www.artisangifts.com
Ask Jeeves	www.askjeeves.com
AT&T WorldNet	www.att.net
Bacon's Media Directories	ww.baconsinfo.com
Banner 123	www.123banners.com
BannerSwap	www.bannerswap.com
Basic Facts About Registering a Trademark	www.uspto.gov./web/offices/ tac/doc/basic
Bell Atlantic Internet Solutions	www.bellatlantic.net
BigInfo.net	www.biginfo.net/pages/ OnlineTools
BizPlanBuilder Interactive	www.jianusa.com
Bonzi.Com Software	www.bonzi.com
Broadcast Interview Source	www.yearbooknews.com
Buildashop Standard 6.0	ignite.rocketfuel.com/home
Burrelle's Media Directories	www.burrelles.com
Business HeadStart	www.planet-corp.com
Business Plan Pro 3.0	www.pasware.com
C/Net Builder.Com	www.builder.com
ChannelSeven	www.channelseven.com
Chris Cobb's Obligatory Java Applets Page	www.ccobb.org/javalinks.asp
Click Z	www.clickz.com
Clip-Art.Com	www.clip-art.com
Commercial Photograph Library	www.photodisc.com/am /default.asp
Compaq	www.compaq.com
CompuServe	www.compuserve.com

Organization	Web site address
Copyright Office	www.loc.gov/copyright
Corel Draw 8	www.corel.com
Corel Xara! 2.0	www.corel.com
CyberReps	www.cybereps.com
Day-Timer	www.daytimer.com
Dell	www.dell.com
Direct Line Domain Name Registration	www.siteleader.com/ domain-registration
DirectPC	www.directpc.com
Domain Agency	www.domainagency.com
Domain Bank	www.domainbank.net
Domain Name Registration.Com	www.domainnameregistration. com
Domain Name Registry	www.domainnameregistry.com
Dydacomp Development Corporation	www.dydacomp.com
EarthLink	www.earthlink.net/
Ebay	www.ebay.com
Editor & Publisher	www.mediainfo.com
eGroups.com	www.egrpoups.com
Entrepreneur	www.entrepreneurmag.com/visa/ visa_smartbiz.hts
ET Applets	www.entanke.se
Exchange-It	www.exchange-it.com
Excite	www.excite.com
Expressive Systems Group	www.eons.com/216color.htm
FatPipe	www.fatpipeinc.com
Federal Trade Commission	www.ftc.gov/
FedEx	www.fedex.com
Find-A-Host.Com	www.findahost.com
Forrester Research	www.forrester.com
Free Stuff Center	www.freestuffcenter.com/ graphics.html
Freeware Java.Com	www.freewarejava.com
Fridgedoor.com	www.fridgedoor.com
Galaxy Internet Services	www.gis.net
Gateway	www.gateway.com

Organization	Web site address
Gebbie Gebbie Press	pertinent.com/pertinfo/business/gebbiePress1.html
GifWizard	www.gifwizard.com
Global Internet News Agency	www.gina.com
GoTo	www.goto.com
GTE	www.gte.net
Hello Direct	www.hellodirect.com
Home Office Computing	www.smalloffice.com
Home Office Direct	www.homeofficedirect.com
Home Office Furniture System	www.hofs.com
Host Index	www.hostindex.com
HostReview.Com	hostreview.com
HostSearch.Com	www.hostsearch.com
Hotbot	www.hotbot.com
I-ADVERTISING	www.internetadvertising.org
IBM Internet Connection Services	www.ibm.net
IBM	www.ibm.com
IBM Net.Commerce	www.software.ibm.com/commerce/net.commerce
IBM's E-Business Solution	www.ibm.com/e-business
iCat Professional Electronic Commerce Suite	carbo.icat.com/icat/business/register.icl
iGoldRush.com	www.igoldrush.com
Infoscavenger	www.infoscavenger.com
Infoseek	www.infoseek.com
Instant Domain Registration Center	www.instant-domain.com
Inter@ctive Week	www.interactiveweek.com
Internet Advertising Resource Guide	www.admedia.org
Internet Domain Bureau	www.idbnet.com/idb-home.shtml
Internet Fraud Watch	www.fraud.org
InternetList.Com	webhostlist.internetlist.com
InterNIC	www.internic.net
ISP Internet Yellow Pages	wwww.index.org
I-Stores Banner Exchange	www.i-stores.com/bannerx

Organization	Web site address
Jamison/Gold Interactive Agency	www.jamisongold.com
Java Boutique	javaboutique.internet.com
Java.Sun.Com	java.sun.com/applets/index.html
JenniCAM	www.jennicam.org
JustAddCommerce	www.richmediatech.com/jacmain.html
LefKey International	www.lefkey.com
Levenger	www.levenger.com
LinkExchange	www.linkexchange.com
ListBot	www.listbot.com
Listz's Usnet Newsgroups Directory	www.liszt.com/news
LookSmart	www.looksmart.com
Lycos	www.lycos.com
Macromedia Fireworks	www.macromedia.com/software/fireworks
Magellan	magellan.excite.com
Mastercard SET	www.mastercard.com/shoponline/set
MCI/Worldcom	www.internetmci.com
Media Information	www.mediainfo.com
Media Metrix, Inc.	www.mediametrix.com
Media One	www.mediaone.net
Media Online Yellow Pages	www.webcom.com
Meta Medic	northernwebs.com/set/setsimjr.html
Micron	www.micron.com
Microsoft Front Page '98 / FrontPage 2000	www.microsoft.com/frontpage
Microsoft Network	www.msn.com
Microsoft Site Server Commerce	www.microsoft.com/siteserver/commerce
Millard Brown Interactive	www.mbinteractive.com
Mindspring Internet Services	www.mindspring.net
MS-Links Exchange	ms-links.com
MSN	www.msn.com
MultiActive's ecBuilder Pro	www.multiactive.com

Organization	Web site address
Name.Space	name.space.xs2.net/
NameWave	httpds.dmans.com/namewave
Netcom	www.netcom.com
NetCount	www.netcount.com
NetFind	www.netfind.com
NetMechanic	www.netmechanic.com
Netscape	www.netscape.com
NetSnap	www.netsnap.com
Network Solutions	www.networksolutions.com
Newsbytes News Network	www.nbnn.com
Northern Light	www.northernlight.com
Northern Webs	northernwebs.com/set/set02.html
One For One Banner X-Change	www.1for1.com
Online Merchant	www.alphasoftware.com
Packard Bell	www.packardbell.com
Paint Shop Pro 5	www.jasc.com
PaletteMan	www.paletteman.com
PC Magazine's Top 100 Web Sites	www.zdnet.com/pcmag/special/web100/index.html
Pitney Bowes	www.pitneybowes.com
PLANMaker	www.planmaker.com
PlanWrite	www.brs-inc.com
PR Newswire	www.prnewswire.com
PressFlash	www.pressflash.com
Prodigy Internet	www.prodigy.com
Publishing Perfection Catalog	www.publishingperfection.com
QuickBooks Pro '99 (Intuit Software)	www.intuit.com/quickbooks
QuickTime 4.0	www.apple.com/quicktime
RealAudio	www.real.com
SCORE	www.score.org
Search Engine Secrets	www.simple123.com/secrets01.htm
Search.Com	www.search.com
Shockwave	www.macromedia.com/shockwave
ShopSite Manager 3.3	www.openmarket.com

Organization	Web site address
SideNet	www.sidenet.com/faq.html#java
SkyTel	www.skytel.com
Small Biz Assocation Software	www.sba.gov/shareware/ starfile.html
Smart Business Plan	www.smartonline.com
National Fraud Information Center	www.fraud.org
Snap	www.snap.com
Sony	www.sony.com
Sprint PCS	www.sprintpcs.com
SRDS Online	www.srds.com
SSL Secure Socket Layer (SSL)	developer.netscape.com/docs/ manuals/security/sslin/index.htm
Submit It	www.submitit.com
Sun Microsystems	java.sun.com/openstudio/ guide.html
Symantec	www.symantec.com
The FontSite	www.fontsite.com
The Go Network	www.go.com
The Industry Standard	www.thestandard.com
The Internet Advertising Bureau	www.iab.net
The Internet Alliance	www.internetalliance.org
The List: The Definitive ISP Buyer's Guide	thelist.internet.com
The NameStormers	www.namestormers.com
The National Press Club	npc.press.org
The Unofficial Cookie FAQ	www.cookiecentral.com/faq
United States Postal Service	www.usps.gov
UPS	www.ups.com
USPTO's Trademark Database	www.uspto.gov/tmdb/index.html
Virtual Spin Internet Store	www.virtualspin.com
Visa	www.visa.com
Web Commerce Today	www.wilsonweb.com/wct
Web Safe Color Palette	www.visibone.com/colorlab

Organization	Web site address
Web Site Garage Web Site Garage	www.websitegarage.com/ 0=register/turbocharge/metatag/ index.html
WebBusiness Builder	www.imsisoft.com
WebCam Now	webcamnow.com
WebCrawler	www.webcrawler.com
Webpedia Animation Archive	www.webpedia.com/animations
WebPromote	www.webpromote.com
Whatis.com	www.whatis.com
WorldNIC	www.worldnic.com
WorldSubmit	www.worldsubmit.com
Yahoo!	www.yahoo.com
Yahoo! Auctions	auctions.yahoo.com
Yahoo! Store	store.yahoo.com

Recommended Reading List

Bayne, Kim M. *The Internet Marketing Plan*. Wiley Computer Publishing.

Cataudella, Joe, Ben Sawyer, and Dave Greely. *Creating Stores on the Web*. Peachpit Press.

Davis, Jack, and Susan Merritt. *The Web Design Wow! Book*. Peachpit Press.

Donovan, John J. *The Second Industrial Revolution: Reinventing Your Business on the Web*. Prentice Hall PTR.

Gielgun, Ron E. *121 Internet Businesses You Can Start from Home*. Actium Publishing.

Mead, Hayden, and Brad Hill, comps. *The On-Line/E-Mail Dictionary*. Berkley Publishing.

Sellers, Don. *Getting Hits: The Definitive Guide to Promoting Your Website*. Peachpit Press.

Shafran, Andy. *Creating Paint Shop Pro Web Graphics: Second Edition*. Muska and Lipman Publishing.

Yesil, Magdalena. *Creating the Virtual Store*. Wiley Computer Publishing.

Zeff, Robbin, and Brad Aronson. *Advertising on the Internet*. Wiley Computer Publishing.

Important Documents

Respecting copyrights and trademarks you don't own

As you begin planning and creating your Web site, you may be tempted to "borrow" artwork, text, graphics, audio clips, video clips, animation sequences, or other materials that you don't own. On the Web, hundreds of sites offer royalty-free, public domain Web page content you're free to download and use on your page. If any type of content you want to use is copyrighted or trademarked by another individual or organization, however, you should obtain permission to use that content before adding it to your site. Unless the content you want to use specifically states that it's available royalty-free and copyright free, assume the content is copyrighted.

Information about copyrights

According to the Library of Congress Copyright Office, "Copyright" is a form of protection provided by the laws of the United States Title 17 to the authors of "original works of authorship," including literary, dramatic, musical, artistic, and certain other intellectual works. This protection is available to both published and unpublished works. Title 17 of the 1976 Copyright Act generally gives the owner of copyright the exclusive right to do and to authorize others to do the following:

- To reproduce the copyrighted work in copies or phonorecords;

- To prepare derivative works based upon the copyrighted work;

- To distribute copies or phonorecords of the copyrighted work to the public by sale or other transfer of ownership, or by rental, lease, or lending;

- To perform the copyrighted work publicly, in the case of literary, musical, dramatic, and choreographic works, pantomimes, and motion pictures and other audiovisual works;

- To display the copyrighted work publicly, in the case of literary, musical, dramatic, and choreographic works, pantomimes, and pictorial, graphic, or sculptural works, including the individual images of a motion picture or other audiovisual work; and

- In the case of sound recordings, to perform the work publicly by means of a digital audio transmission.

It is illegal for anyone to violate any of the rights provided by the copyright code to the owner of copyright. These rights, however, are not unlimited in scope. Title17/1-107 through Title17/1-120 of the 1976 Copyright Act establish limitations on these rights. In some cases, these limitations are specified exemptions from copyright liability. One major limitation is the doctrine of "fair use," which is given a statutory basis in title17/1-107 of the 1976 Copyright Act. In other instances, the limitation takes the form of a "compulsory license" under which certain limited uses of copyrighted works are permitted upon payment of specified royalties and compliance with statutory conditions. For further information about the limitations of any of these rights, consult the copyright code or write to the Copyright Office.

Copyright protects "original works of authorship" that are fixed in a tangible form of expression. The fixation need not be directly perceptible so long as it may be communicated with the aid of a machine or device. Copyrightable works include the following categories:

1. literary works;

2. musical works, including any accompanying words

3. dramatic works, including any accompanying music

4. pantomimes and choreographic works

5. pictorial, graphic, and sculptural works

6. motion pictures and other audiovisual works

7. sound recordings

8. architectural works

These categories should be viewed broadly. For example, computer programs and most "compilations" may be registered as "literary works"; maps and architectural plans may be registered as "pictorial, graphic, and sculptural works."

Several categories of material are generally not eligible for Federal copyright protection. These include among others:

Works that have *not* been fixed in a tangible form of expression.

Titles, names, short phrases, and slogans; familiar symbols or designs; mere variations of typographic ornamentation, lettering, or coloring; mere listings of ingredients or contents.

Ideas, procedures, methods, systems, processes, concepts, principles, discoveries, or devices, as distinguished from a description, explanation, or illustration.

Works consisting entirely of information that is common property and containing no original authorship (for example: standard calendars, height and weight charts, tape measures and rulers, and lists or tables taken from public documents or other common sources).

The use of a copyright notice is no longer required under U.S. law, although it is often beneficial. Because prior law did contain such a requirement, however, the use of notice is still relevant to the copyright status of older works.

Notice was required under the 1976 Copyright Act. This requirement was eliminated when the United States adhered to the Berne Convention, effective March 1, 1989. Although works published without notice before that date could have entered the public domain in the United States, the Uruguay Round Agreements Act (URAA) restores copyright in certain foreign works originally published without notice.

The Copyright Office does not take a position on whether copies of works first published with notice before March 1, 1989, which are distributed on or after March 1, 1989, must bear the copyright notice.

Use of the notice may be important because it informs the public that the work is protected by copyright, identifies the copyright owner, and shows the year of first publication. Furthermore, in the event that a work is infringed, if a proper notice of copyright appears on the published copy or copies to which a defendant in a copyright infringement suit had access, then no weight shall be given to such a defendant's interposition of a defense based on innocent infringement in mitigation of actual or statutory damages, except as provided in title17/5-504 of the copyright code. Innocent infringement occurs when the infringer did not realize that the work was protected.

The use of the copyright notice is the responsibility of the copyright owner and does not require advance permission from, or registration with, the Copyright Office.

The notice for visually perceptible copies should contain all of the following three elements:

1. The symbol © (the letter in a circle), or the word "Copyright" or the abbreviation "Copr."; and

2. The year of first publication of the work. In the case of compilations or derivative works incorporating previously published material, the year date of first publication of the compilation or derivative work is sufficient. The year date may be omitted where a pictorial, graphic, or sculptural work, with accompanying textual matter, if

any, is reproduced in or on greeting cards, post-cards, stationery, jewelry, dolls, toys, or any useful article; and

3. The name of the owner of copyright. The name of the owner of copyright in the work, or an abbreviation by which the name can be recognized, or a generally known alternative designation of the owner. Example: © 1998 John Doe

In general, copyright registration is a legal formality intended to make a public record of the basic facts of a particular copyright. However, registration is not a condition of copyright protection. Even though registration is not a requirement for protection, the copyright law provides several inducements or advantages to encourage copyright owners to make registration. Among these advantages are the following:

- Registration establishes a public record of the copyright claim.

- Before an infringement suit may be filed in court, registration is necessary for works of U.S. origin and for foreign works not originating in a Berne Union country.

- If made before or within 5 years of publication, registration will establish prima facie evidence in court of the validity of the copyright and of the facts stated in the certificate.

- If registration is made within 3 months after publication of the work or prior to an infringement of the work, statutory damages and attorney's fees will be available to the copyright owner in court actions. Otherwise, only an award of actual damages and profits is available to the copyright owner.

- Registration allows the owner of the copyright to record the registration with the U.S. Customs Service for protection against the importation of infringing copies. For additional information, request Publication No. 563 from: http://www.customs.ustreas.gov/index.htm, ATTN: IPR Branch, Franklin Court, Suite 4000, U.S. Customs Service, 1301 Constitution Avenue, N.W., Washington, D.C. 20229.

- Registration may be made at any time within the life of the copyright. Unlike the law before 1978, when a work has been registered in unpublished form, it is not necessary to make another registration when the work becomes published, although the copyright owner may register the published edition, if desired.

To register a work, send the following three elements in the same envelope or package to:

Library of Congress
Copyright Office
Register of Copyrights
101 Independence Avenue, S.E.
Washington, D.C. 20559-6000

- A properly completed application form;

- A nonrefundable filing fee of $20 for each application.

- A non-returnable deposit of the work being registered. The deposit requirements vary in particular situations.

All copyright application forms may be downloaded from the Internet and printed for use in registering a claim to copyright. The forms may be accessed and downloaded by connecting to the

Copyright Office homepage on the World Wide Web. The address is: http://www.loc.gov/copyright.

You must have Adobe Acrobat installed on your computer to view and print the forms. Adobe Acrobat Reader may be downloaded free from Adobe Systems Incorporated through links from the same Internet site from which the forms are available ("http://www.adobe.com/prodindex/acrobat/readstep.html").

Print forms head to head (top of page 2 is directly behind the top of page 1) on a single piece of good quality, $8^1/_2"\times 11"$ white paper. To achieve the best quality copies of the application forms, use a laser printer.

Trademark information

A trademark is either a word, phrase, symbol or design, or combination of words, phrases, symbols or designs, which identifies and distinguishes the source of the goods or services of one party from those of others. A service mark is the same as a trademark except that it identifies and distinguishes the source of a service rather than a product. The terms "trademark" and "mark" are used to refer to both trademarks and service marks whether they are word marks or other types of marks. Normally, a mark for goods appears on the product or on its packaging, while a service mark appears in advertising for the services.

A trademark is different from a copyright or a patent. A copyright protects an original artistic or literary work; a patent protects an invention. For copyright information call the Library of Congress at 202-707-3000.

What is a trademark? A trademark includes any word, name, symbol, or device, or any combination, used, or intended to be used, in commerce to identify and distinguish the goods of one manufacturer or seller from goods manufactured or sold by others, and to indicate the source of the goods. In short, a trademark is a brand name.

A service mark is any word, name, symbol, device, or any combination, used, or intended to be used, in commerce, to identify and distinguish the services of one provider from services provided by others, and to indicate the source of the services.

Trademark rights arise from either (1) actual use of the mark, or (2) the filing of a proper application to register a mark in the Patent and Trademark Office (PTO) stating that the applicant has a bona fide intention to use the mark in commerce regulated by the U.S. Congress. Federal registration is not required to establish rights in a mark, nor is it required to begin use of a mark. However, federal registration can secure benefits beyond the rights acquired by merely using a mark. For example, the owner of a federal registration is presumed to be the owner of the mark for the goods and services specified in the registration, and to be entitled to use the mark nationwide.

There are two related but distinct types of rights in a mark: the right to register and the right to use. Generally, the first party who either uses a mark in commerce or files an application in the PTO has the ultimate right to register that mark. The PTO's authority is limited to determining the right to register. The right to use a mark can be more complicated to determine. This is particularly true when two parties have begun use of the same or similar marks without knowledge of one another and neither has a federal registration. Only a court can render a decision about the right to use, such as issuing an injunction or awarding damages for infringement. It should be noted that a federal registration can provide significant advantages to a party involved in a court proceeding. The PTO cannot provide advice concerning rights in a mark. Only a private attorney can provide such advice.

Unlike copyrights or patents, trademark rights can last indefinitely if the owner continues to use the mark to identify its goods or services. The term of a federal trademark registration is 10 years, with 10-year renewal terms. However, between the fifth and sixth year after the date of initial registration, the registrant must file an affidavit setting forth certain information to keep the registration alive. If no affidavit is filed, the registration is canceled.

Anyone who claims rights in a mark may use the ™ (trademark) or service mark designation with the mark to alert the public to the claim. It is not necessary to have a registration, or even a pending application, to use these designations. The claim may or may not be valid. The registration symbol, ®, may only be used when the mark is registered in the PTO. It is improper to use this symbol at any point before the registration issues. Please omit all symbols from the mark in the drawing you submit with your application; the symbols are not considered part of the mark.

To learn more about trademarks and trademark law, contact a lawyer or visit United States Patent and Trademark Office's Web site at http://www. uspto.gov. You can Search the USPTO's Trademark Database Online at http://www.uspto.gov./tmdb/index.html.

If you need answers to specific trademark questions or want to know more about trademarks in general, contact the Trademark Assistance Center at 1-800-786-9199. If you live in Northern Virginia, the number is 703-308-9000.

Important Statistics

Media Metrix, Inc. (www.mediametrix.com) provides leading advertising agencies, new and traditional media companies, e-commerce marketers, financial institutions, and technology companies with comprehensive coverage of all digital media (including more than 15,000 Web sites and online properties). Media Metrix tracks and measures 40,000 people in U.S. homes and businesses, yielding monthly, weekly, and real-time data collection and reporting.

The top 20 busiest Web sites in February 1999, according to Media Metrix, are listed in the chart below. As you can see, the majority of these sites are search engines.

TOP 10 WEB SITES IN THE HOME AND OFFICE

Top 10 Web sites at home

1.	aol.com	24,947
2.	yahoo.com	24,198
3.	msn.com	16,223
4.	geocities.com	15,305
5.	go.com	14,061
6.	netscape.com	13,269
7.	excite.com	11,915
8.	microsoft.com	10,990
9.	lycos.com	10,846
10.	bluemountainarts.com	9,964

Top 10 Web sites at work

1.	yahoo.com	11,365
2.	aol.com	8,209
3.	netscape.com	8,150
4.	msn.com	7,466
5.	go.com	7,317
6.	microsoft.com	5,860
7.	geocities.com	5,701
8.	excite.com	5,553
9.	lycos.com	5,095
10.	Altavista Search Services	3,740

Numbers reflect unique visitors, in thousands
Measurement period 2/1/99–2/28/99

(Source: Media Matrix)

How to Contact InterNIC

To contact InterNIC for technical support, to get domain name registration-related questions answered, or to solve billing issues, Network Solutions can be reached by telephone, fax, e-mail, or via U.S. Mail. The company accepts checks and major credit cards for domain name registration payments.

Contacting InterNIC/Network Solutions via telephone

Telephone support is available Monday through Friday, between 7 a.m. and 9 p.m. (EST) by calling the Registration Help Desk at 703-742-4777. Be prepared to be kept on hold for a while before you'll be able to speak with an actual living, breathing person. The best time to speak with a Help Desk representative, according to Network Solutions, is between 7 a.m. and 9 a.m., or 7 p.m. and 9 p.m. (EST).

If you have questions, but don't need to speak directly with a Help Desk representative, you can take advantage of the company's Fax Back service or automated voice response system, both of which can be accessed by calling the main Help Desk phone number.

To use the company's automated voice response system for credit card payments relating to domain name registrations and annual fees, call toll-free 888-771-3000 or 402-496-9798 (long distance charges apply). For information about the Domain Name Dispute Policy, call 703-742-4882.

Contacting InterNIC/Network Solutions via e-mail

To reach Network Solutions via email, point your Web browser to: http://www.internic.net/contact. html to reach the "Contact the InterNIC" page. From here, you'll be asked what your email correspondence is regarding. Your options include: Domain Name Registration or Modification, Billing or Payment, InterNIC's Web or FTP Sites, or the Domain Name Dispute Policy. Upon choosing one of these options, you'll be prompted to enter your email address, and then have the option to type a message to the appropriate department at InterNIC/Network Solutions.

Contacting InterNIC/Network Solutions via fax

To fax your questions to InterNIC/Network Solutions, choose the appropriate fax number based upon the topic of your correspondence.

Type of Question	Fax Number
Questions regarding domain name registration	703-742-9552
Questions regarding billing or payment	703-318-9125
Questions regarding the domain name dispute policy	703-742-8706
All other questions	703-742-9552

Contacting InterNIC/Network Solutions via U.S. Mail

To send check or money order payments for domain name registrations or annual fees, send your check along with the Invoice Payment Stub provided by InterNIC/Network Solutions to:

Network Solutions, Inc.
P.O. Box 17305
Baltimore, MD 21297-0525

If you're sending a check or money order payment, but don't have a copy of the Invoice Payment Stub provided by InterNIC/Network Solutions, use the following address:

Network Solutions, Inc.
P.O. Box 17304
Baltimore, MD 21297-0524

To send your check or money order payment via an overnight express courier, such as FedEx, use the following address:

Network Solutions, Inc.
ATTN: InterNIC Billing
505 Huntmar Park Drive
Herndon, VA 20170
703-742-4777

All general correspondence relating to domain name registration that's being sent via U.S. Mail should be addressed to:

Network Solutions, Inc.
ATTN: InterNIC Registration Services
505 Huntmar Park Drive
Herndon, VA 20170

The *Unofficial Guide*™ Reader Questionnaire

If you would like to express your opinion about starting a business online or this guide, please complete this questionnaire and mail it to:

The *Unofficial Guide*™ Reader Questionnaire
Macmillan Lifestyle Group
1633 Broadway, floor 7
New York, NY 10019-6785

Gender: ___ M ___ F

Age: ___ Under 30 ___ 31–40 ___ 41–50
___ Over 50

Education: ___ High school ___ College
___ Graduate/Professional

What is your occupation?

_____

How did you hear about this guide?
___ Friend or relative
___ Newspaper, magazine, or Internet
___ Radio or TV
___ Recommended at bookstore
___ Recommended by librarian
___ Picked it up on my own
___ Familiar with the *Unofficial Guide*™ travel series

Did you go to the bookstore specifically for a book on starting a business online? Yes ___ No ___

Have you used any other Unofficial Guides™?
Yes ___ No ___

If Yes, which ones?

_____
_____
_____

What other book(s) on starting a business online have you purchased? _____

_____

_____

Was this book:
___ more helpful than other(s)
___ less helpful than other(s)

Do you think this book was worth its price?
Yes ___ No ___

Did this book cover all topics related to starting a business online adequately?
Yes ___ No ___

Please explain your answer:

_____

_____

_____

Were there any specific sections in this book that were of particular help to you? Yes ___ No ___

Please explain your answer:

_____

_____

_____

On a scale of 1 to 10, with 10 being the best rating, how would you rate this guide? ___

What other titles would you like to see published in the *Unofficial Guide*™ series?

_____

_____

Are Unofficial Guides™ **readily available in your area?** Yes ___ No ___

Other comments:

_____

_____

_____

_____

Get the inside scoop...with the *Unofficial Guides*™!

Health and Fitness

The Unofficial Guide to Alternative Medicine
ISBN: 0-02-862526-9 Price: $15.95

The Unofficial Guide to Conquering Impotence
ISBN: 0-02-862870-5 Price: $15.95

The Unofficial Guide to Coping with Menopause
ISBN: 0-02-862694-x Price: $15.95

The Unofficial Guide to Cosmetic Surgery
ISBN: 0-02-862522-6 Price: $15.95

The Unofficial Guide to Dieting Safely
ISBN: 0-02-862521-8 Price: $15.95

The Unofficial Guide to Having a Baby
ISBN: 0-02-862695-8 Price: $15.95

The Unofficial Guide to Living with Diabetes
ISBN: 0-02-862919-1 Price: $15.95

The Unofficial Guide to Overcoming Arthritis
ISBN: 0-02-862714-8 Price: $15.95

The Unofficial Guide to Overcoming Infertility
ISBN: 0-02-862916-7 Price: $15.95

Career Planning

The Unofficial Guide to Acing the Interview
ISBN: 0-02-862924-8 Price: $15.95

The Unofficial Guide to Earning What You Deserve
ISBN: 0-02-862523-4 Price: $15.95

The Unofficial Guide to Hiring and Firing People
ISBN: 0-02-862523-4 Price: $15.95

Business and Personal Finance

The Unofficial Guide to Investing
ISBN: 0-02-862458-0 Price: $15.95

The Unofficial Guide to Investing in Mutual Funds
ISBN: 0-02-862920-5 Price: $15.95

The Unofficial Guide to Managing Your Personal Finances
ISBN: 0-02-862921-3 Price: $15.95

The Unofficial Guide to Starting a Small Business
ISBN: 0-02-862525-0 Price: $15.95

Home and Automotive

The Unofficial Guide to Buying a Home
ISBN: 0-02-862461-0 Price: $15.95

The Unofficial Guide to Buying or Leasing a Car
ISBN: 0-02-862524-2 Price: $15.95

The Unofficial Guide to Hiring Contractors
ISBN: 0-02-862460-2 Price: $15.95

Family and Relationships

The Unofficial Guide to Childcare
ISBN: 0-02-862457-2 Price: $15.95

The Unofficial Guide to Dating Again
ISBN: 0-02-862454-8 Price: $15.95

The Unofficial Guide to Divorce
ISBN: 0-02-862455-6 Price: $15.95

The Unofficial Guide to Eldercare
ISBN: 0-02-862456-4 Price: $15.95

The Unofficial Guide to Planning Your Wedding
ISBN: 0-02-862459-9 Price: $15.95

Hobbies and Recreation

The Unofficial Guide to Finding Rare Antiques
ISBN: 0-02-862922-1 Price: $15.95

The Unofficial Guide to Casino Gambling
ISBN: 0-02-862917-5 Price: $15.95

All books in the *Unofficial Guide* series are available at your local bookseller, or by calling 1-800-428-5331.